BILLY GRAHAM
IN QUOTES

BILLY GRAHAM
IN QUOTES

Franklin Graham

with Donna Lee Toney

THOMAS NELSON
Since 1798

NASHVILLE   DALLAS   MEXICO CITY   RIO DE JANEIRO

Published in Nashville, Tennessee, by Thomas Nelson. Thomas Nelson is a registered trademark of Thomas Nelson, Inc.

Thomas Nelson, Inc. titles may be purchased in bulk for educational, business, fund-raising, or sales promotional use. For information, please e-mail SpecialMarkets@ThomasNelson.com.

Unless otherwise noted, Scripture quotations are taken from *Holy Bible*, New Living Translation. © 1996, 2004, 2007. Used by permission of Tyndale House Publishers, Inc., Wheaton, Illinois 60189. All rights reserved.

Scripture quotations marked AMP are from the Amplified® Bible, © 1954, 1958, 1962, 1964, 1965, 1987 by The Lockman Foundation. Used by permission. (www.Lockman.org)

Scripture quotations marked NIV are from the Holy Bible, New International Version®. © 1973, 1978, 1984 by Biblica, Inc.™ Used by permission of Zondervan. All rights reserved worldwide. www.zondervan.com.

Scripture quotations marked NKJV are from the New King James Version®. © 1982 by Thomas Nelson, Inc. Used by permission. All rights reserved.

Scripture quotations marked KJV are from the King James Version of the Bible.

Scripture quotations marked NASB are from the New American Standard Bible®, © The Lockman Foundation 1960, 1962, 1963, 1968, 1971, 1972, 1973, 1975, 1977, 1995. Used by permission.

Scripture quotations marked TLB are from *The Living Bible*. © 1971. Used by permission of Tyndale House Publishers, Inc., Wheaton, Illinois 60189. All rights reserved.

Scripture quotations marked ASV are from the Authorized Standard Version of the Bible.

Scripture quotations markedd ESV are from the English Standard Version. © 2001 by Crossway Bibles, a division of Good News Publishers.

Scripture quotations marked MSG are from *The Message* by Eugene H. Peterson. © 1993, 1994, 1995, 1996, 2000. Used by permission of NavPress Publishing Group. All rights reserved.

ISBN: 978-0-8499-4833-6 (hardcover)

Library of Congress Cataloging-in-Publication Data

Graham, Billy, 1918–
  [Selections. 2011]
  Billy Graham in quotes / [edited by] Franklin Graham with Donna Lee Toney.
     p. cm.
  Includes bibliographical references (p. 389–432).
  ISBN 978-0-8499-4649-3 (pbk.)
  1. Graham, Billy, 1918—Quotations. I. Graham, Franklin, 1952– II. Toney, Donna Lee. III. Title. IV. Title: In quotes.
  BV3785.G69A25 2011
  230'.6—dc22   2011003592

Printed in the United States of America

11 12 13 14 15 QGF 5 4 3 2 1

Contents

Foreword by Franklin Graham   xi

Introduction   xiii

Billy Graham on Abortion   1

Billy Graham on Addiction   3

Billy Graham on Age   9

Billy Graham on America   11

Billy Graham on Angels   17

Billy Graham on Anger   19

Billy Graham on Anxiety   22

Billy Graham on the Bible   24

Billy Graham on the Blood   36

Billy Graham on Character   38

Billy Graham on Children   40

Billy Graham on Choice   44

Billy Graham on Christianity   47

Billy Graham on Church   59

Billy Graham on Comfort   68

Billy Graham on Commitment   70

Billy Graham on Compromise   73

Billy Graham on Conforming   76

Billy Graham on Conscience   79

Billy Graham on Conversion   83

Billy Graham on Convictions   85

CONTENTS

Billy Graham on Creation   87

Billy Graham on the Cross   90

Billy Graham on Death   95

Billy Graham on Deception   101

Billy Graham on Decision   103

Billy Graham on the Devil/Satan   106

Billy Graham on Disappointment   113

Billy Graham on Discipleship and Discipline   116

Billy Graham on Encouragement   119

Billy Graham on End Times   121

Billy Graham on Eternity   125

Billy Graham on Evangelism   127

Billy Graham on Evil   130

Billy Graham on Faith   133

Billy Graham on Family   137

Billy Graham on Followers   140

Billy Graham on Forgiveness   143

Billy Graham on Glorifying God   145

Billy Graham on God   147

Billy Graham on God's Will   154

Billy Graham on the Gospel   156

Billy Graham on Grace   159

Billy Graham on Greed   161

Billy Graham on Grief   163

Billy Graham on Happiness   165

Billy Graham on the Heart   168

Billy Graham on Heaven   170

Billy Graham on Hell   174

Billy Graham on Holiness   177

Billy Graham on the Holy Spirit   179

Billy Graham on Home   183

Contents

Billy Graham on Hope   188

Billy Graham on Human Nature   190

Billy Graham on Imagination, Entertainment, and Fun   193

Billy Graham on Influence   195

Billy Graham on Integrity   197

Billy Graham on Jesus   200

Billy Graham on Joy   203

Billy Graham on Judgment   205

Billy Graham on Knowledge   208

Billy Graham on Life   210

Billy Graham on Living the Christian Life   220

Billy Graham on Loneliness   224

Billy Graham on Love   226

Billy Graham on Lust   230

Billy Graham on Marriage   233

Billy Graham on Money   239

Billy Graham on Morals   243

Billy Graham on Parents   246

Billy Graham on Patience   249

Billy Graham on Peace   251

Billy Graham on People   255

Billy Graham on Persecution   260

Billy Graham on Pleasure   263

Billy Graham on Prayer   265

Billy Graham on Preaching   278

Billy Graham on Pride   282

Billy Graham on Race   284

Billy Graham on Religion   287

Billy Graham on Repentance   295

Billy Graham on the Resurrection   298

Billy Graham on Right and Wrong   300

CONTENTS

Billy Graham on Salvation 303

Billy Graham on Service 306

Billy Graham on Sin 309

Billy Graham on Society 317

Billy Graham on the Soul 320

Billy Graham on Speech 325

Billy Graham on Strength 328

Billy Graham on Success 330

Billy Graham on Suffering 333

Billy Graham on Surrender 338

Billy Graham on Temptation 340

Billy Graham on Testimony 344

Billy Graham on Thankfulness 346

Billy Graham on Time 348

Billy Graham on Truth 351

Billy Graham on War 354

Billy Graham on Witnessing 356

Billy Graham on the Word of God 359

Billy Graham on Work 364

Billy Graham on the World 367

Billy Graham on World Evangelism 376

Billy Graham on Worry 379

Billy Graham on Worship 381

Billy Graham on Young People 383

Notes 389

About the Authors 433

If anyone speaks, he should do it
as one speaking the very words of God.

—1 PETER 4:11 NIV

When the Gospel of Jesus Christ is presented with
authority—quoting from the very Word of God—
He takes that message and drives it
supernaturally into the human heart.

—BILLY GRAHAM

FOREWORD

Do not worry about how or what you should speak.
For it will be given to you in that hour what you should speak;
for it is not you who speak, but the Spirit of your Father who speaks in you.

—MATTHEW 10:19–20 NKJV

MY FATHER, BILLY GRAHAM, IS KNOWN FOR SPEAKING OUT about the one and only thing that matters in this world: the Gospel of the Lord Jesus Christ. He remembers the call of God more than seventy years ago to preach the Word of God to all those who would listen about salvation that comes only through Christ. He took this high calling with seriousness and boldness in obedience to the God of all creation. He once said, "I will travel anywhere in the world to preach if there are no strings on what I am to say."

Billy Graham has been quoted and misquoted countless times, which led him to clarify words from his own lips: "I am constantly concerned about being quoted in the press and perhaps saying the wrong thing or having what I say misinterpreted and bringing reproach to the name of Christ. People do not come to hear what Billy Graham has to say; they want to hear what God has to say. Jesus tells us not to be misled by the voices of strangers. There are so many strange voices being heard in the religious world of our day. We must compare what they say with the Word of God."

This book contains hundreds of quotes from my father, whose voice is not strange or silent. He says, "God speaks from heaven through the Bible, His written word. This is why I use the phrase 'the Bible says.' I would not have the authority to say what I do in sermons unless it was based upon the Word of God."

My father's sermons are anchored to the Scriptures. I have often heard him say, "Man will surrender to the impact of the Word of God."

"When we preach or teach the Scriptures," he wrote, "we open the door for the Holy Spirit to do His work. God has *not* promised to bless oratory or clever preaching. He has promised to bless His Word." My father prayed that his words would reflect God's standard of truth as the basis to claim, "I have given them Your word" (John 17:14 NKJV).

The quotes contained in this book are taken predominantly from my father's writings from 1947 to 2010 (spanning seven decades). I trust that the message will penetrate your heart and encourage you in life.

—FRANKLIN GRAHAM

INTRODUCTION

Let the words of my mouth . . . be acceptable in Your sight, O LORD.

—PSALM 19:14 NKJV

I AM HUMBLED AND ENORMOUSLY GRATEFUL FOR WHAT HAS been compiled in this book; quotes taken from my literary works through the years. Most of all, I am pleased that these quotes have their foundation in the Word of God. Each topic has been selected based upon Bible verses that address these same issues. It has been exciting to focus this project on what God directed His prophets, apostles, and disciples to write down through the inspiration of His Holy Spirit as the very Word of God.

As you peruse these quotes, refer often to the anchor verse of each subject and let God's Word challenge you, convict you, encourage you, and help you discover His abiding love to all who faithfully follow Him. The Bible speaks of God's Word in many different ways. When you see words in Scripture such as *promises, truths, doctrines,* and *laws,* these are insights into the mind and heart of God.

Because my eyesight dims more each year, I am grateful for the many Scripture passages I was able to commit to memory through my years of study, and I draw strength from them day by day. I can still enjoy listening to the Bible through many forms of technology devices. Regardless of the format, the very words of God are living and powerful (Hebrews 4:12 NKJV), and the teaching of His Word gives light so that even the simple can understand (Psalm 119:130 NKJV). Jesus told His followers, "Human effort accomplishes nothing. And the very words I have spoken to you are spirit and life" (John 6:63).

The Bible says, "The Lord gives the word, and a great army brings the good news" (Psalm 68:11). What privilege has been mine to be among a swelling army of those whom God has raised up to preach this Good News—the Gospel message of the Lord Jesus Christ—to wandering souls. My hope is that those who do not know Him as their personal Savior will be moved by the message found in these pages and be drawn by the Holy Spirit to the foot of the cross, where forgiveness is found and salvation through grace is granted.

—BILLY GRAHAM
Montreat, North Carolina
November 2010

BILLY GRAHAM ON
ABORTION

You saw me before I was born and scheduled each day of my life
before I began to breathe. Every day was recorded in your book!

—PSALM 139:16 TLB

———

The widespread acceptance of abortion is a symbol or sign of something
deeper within our society that should also concern us greatly.
This is the tendency today to decide moral
issues or questions only on the basis of
whether or not they are convenient or bring pleasure to a person.[1]

———

I do not feel the church as an organization should
become involved in political matters . . .
However, when political issues also have
moral and spiritual dimensions . . .
we have a responsibility to speak for the truth.
I believe things like abortion are morally wrong . . .
we have a responsibility to take a stand.[2]

———

Abortion has divided our nation like no other issue in recent times . . .
The Bible places the highest value on human life. It is sacred and
of inestimable worth to God, who created it "in His own image."
The Bible recognizes the unborn as being fully human.[3]

I

As Christians we have an obligation to show others what God says
about living self-controlled lives and being responsible for our moral
actions, as God defines them. We must never think that we can
solve one moral crisis by condoning another, especially the crime
of murder, for unrestrained abortion is nothing less than that.[4]

How ironic this maudlin defense of immorality sounds in the light of
its devastating legacy to the nation: millions of illegitimate births,
shattered personalities, divorce, abortions, and rampant
sexual diseases—some of which are incurable.
God expressly forbids irresponsible sexual behavior,
in order to spare us the disastrous consequences.[5]

[Abortion] would destroy [a] precious life within [a woman], which would
be wrong in God's eyes since that little life bears the image of God . . .
Every day I get letters from those who have
had an abortion and now are riddled
with guilt and depression over what they have done.[6]

The issue [of] abortion is not whether you have a
right to terminate the life of a child . . .
The real issue is whether or not you will insist on running
your own life according to your own standards,
or whether you will instead let God run your life.[7]

BILLY GRAHAM ON
ADDICTION

Wine is a mocker, strong drink is a brawler,
and whoever is led astray by it is not wise.

—PROVERBS 20:1 NKJV

———

Some of the most heart-breaking letters I receive
are from people who tell how alcohol or drugs have
ravaged their lives and destroyed their families.[1]

———

Each generation becomes more addicted to the sedatives of life,
to dull the pain of living.[2]

———

The Bible condemns the use of any substance which alters
or distorts our thinking (including alcohol,
which was the most common drug in ancient times).[3]

———

When the headlines get black and foreboding,
the sale of alcohol and barbiturates rises in the country,
as millions try to escape from the grim realities of [such] dangers.[4]

3

Many people turn to alcohol to try to drown the [cries]
and longings of the soul.
Others attempt to quiet the longings of their souls in other ways.
Nothing but God ever completely satisfies,
because the soul is made for God.[5]

Some years ago I was invited to be on a television talk show
with one of the most famous personalities in America.
Afterward she took me aside and told of the emptiness in her life.
"My beauty is gone," she said, "I am getting old,
I'm living on alcohol, and I have nothing to live for."[6]

One of the most conspicuous modes of escape is alcoholism,
which is now a national catastrophe.[7]

This self-confident generation has produced more alcoholics,
more drug addicts, more criminals, more wars, more broken homes,
more assaults, more embezzlements, more murders, and more suicides . . .
it is time all of us . . . begin to take stock of our
failures, blunders, and costly mistakes.
It is about time that we place less confidence in ourselves
and more trust and faith in God.[8]

Escapism seems to be the order of the day . . .
Escape with drugs or alcohol, and the bitterness
of living will be blurred . . .
We can't escape from God.[9]

———•———

Researchers have found that peer pressure exerted within a clique
has caused every one of its members to experiment with drugs,
to engage in murderous gang fights, to steal autos,
and to violate the seventh commandment.[10]

———•———

Liquor is not necessary either for health or
for so-called gracious living . . .
It is the cause of untold sorrow, suffering, and material loss,
not to mention the spiritual implications of drinking.[11]

———•———

Drunkenness. This Greek word means overindulgence in alcohol.
Alcohol may be used for medicine,
but it can also become a terrible drug.
The way it is used in our world is probably
one of the great evils of our day.
It is a self-inflicted impediment that springs from "a man taking a drink,
a drink taking a drink, and drink taking the man."
Distilled liquors as we have them today were unknown in Bible times.[12]

———•———

In Houston, Texas, a man was born again in one of our meetings.
He owned a liquor store.
The next morning he had a sign on the front of his door saying,
"Out of business."[13]

———•———

Drinking has become one of the most serious social problems.
It is basically the result of an attempt to escape
from the responsibilities and realities of life.[14]

A senator once confided to me that the greatest need
in Washington was the elimination of the cocktail party.
He said: "It consumes so much of our time
that we don't have time for matters of state."[15]

Volumes could be written on the problem of [drug] addiction.
Millions of barbiturates are swallowed every
night to help the nation sleep.
Millions of tranquilizers keep us calm during the day.
Millions of pep pills wake us up in the morning.
The Bible warns that these flights from reality
bring no lasting satisfaction.[16]

The Greek word used in the New Testament to designate a sorcerer
or a person who practiced occult magic is "pharmakeus,"
or one who mixed drugs and used them to induce spells . . .
Such practices are included in the list of "acts of the sinful nature"
in Galatians 5:19–21 that God will judge.[17]

Many people are trying to steady themselves by taking tranquilizers.
Jesus is the greatest tranquilizer of all.
He can straighten out your life and put you back on center.[18]

One of the characteristics of some drugs (such as cocaine)
is that they make a person feel strong and alert—
when in fact the opposite is the case.
Don't allow yourself to be deceived.[19]

—◆—

Among young people . . . drinking is for getting drunk.
And many go on to become alcoholics.[20]

—◆—

Drunkenness is not a new vice.
Its ravages have always been a scourge on the human race . . .
Alcohol is a killer, a murderer.[21]

—◆—

Thousands are killed and injured every year by teenagers driving
too fast or under the influence of drugs and drink . . .
others are killing [themselves] with alcohol or heroin overdoses.[22]

—◆—

In Christ alone there is deliverance from man's tortured thoughts and
freedom from the sordid habits which are destroying so many people.
Why does the Bible so clearly denounce drunkenness?
Because it is an enemy of human life.
Anything that is against a person's welfare, God is against.[23]

—◆—

Do not seek solace in alcohol. Alcohol obscures good
judgment and leaves you unable to think clearly or
understand what God is trying to say to you.[24]

—◆—

What began as an apparently harmless pastime has ended up
as a frightening, overpowering addiction or obsession.[25]

—◆—

Some [young people] are taking pills called "heaven or hell" drugs,
because you're liable to experience either one.[26]

Drinking and other forms of body-wrecking pleasures are
signs of weakness rather than manliness. It takes a better man
to live a clean life—free from the stimulants, depressants,
and drugs—than to be artificially [stimulated].[27]

The cult of self has become an addiction—
feeding off the ego of self-glorification.
The word *cult* encompasses many movements and ideas,
but simply put, it describes a culture of
alternative beliefs, fads, and trends,
and tampers with just enough truth to knock many off balance.[28]

There is hope for the alcoholic:
God is able to deliver from this as well as any other addiction.[29]

BILLY GRAHAM ON
AGE

Listen to Me . . . Even to your old age,
I am He, and even to gray hairs I will carry you!

—ISAIAH 46:3–4 NKJV

———◆———

Old age has its compensations. More than ever
I see each day as a gift from God. It is also a time to reflect back
on God's goodness over the years and an opportunity to assure others
that God truly is faithful to His promises.[1]

———◆———

Many people plan financially for retirement—
but not spiritually and emotionally.[2]

———◆———

Old age is Satan's last chance to blow us off course.[3]

———◆———

God isn't finished with you when you retire!
When we know Christ, we never retire from His service.[4]

God wants us to work (whether at home or on the job),
but that doesn't mean it's wrong to retire.
The Levites (who assisted in Israel's worship)
were required to retire at fifty.[5]

Ask [God] to help you reflect Christ as you grow older,
instead of turning sour or grumpy.[6]

Life can grow sweeter and more rewarding as we grow older if we
possess the presence of Christ. Sunsets are always glorious.
It is Christ who adds colors, glory, and beauty to man's sunsets.[7]

Life has its share of joys and laughter—but we also know
life's road is often very rough. Temptations assail us;
people disappoint us; illness and age weaken us;
tragedies and sorrows ambush us; evil and injustice overpower us.
Life is hard—but God is good, and *heaven is real!*[8]

BILLY GRAHAM ON
AMERICA

Come here and listen, O nations of the earth.
Let the world and everything in it hear my words.

—ISAIAH 34:1

———◆———

America has probably been the most successful experiment in history.
The American Dream was a glorious attempt.
It was built on a religious foundation.
Its earliest concepts came from Holy Scripture.[1]

———◆———

Just as America has grown and prospered within the
framework of our Constitution,
so Christianity has flourished and spread according to the laws
set forth in the Bible.[2]

———◆———

We have so many battles going on in America today
that we should be a people of prayer.
Our government needs prayer. Our leaders need prayer.
Our schools need prayer. Our youth need our prayers.
Our families need our prayers.[3]

You can put a public school and university in the middle
of every block of every city in America—
but you will never keep America from rotting morally
by mere intellectual education.[4]

I believe America has gone a long way down the wrong road.
If we ever needed God's help, it is now.[5]

God honored and blessed America as few nations in history.
However, in recent years the nation has been moving away
from its religious heritage.[6]

America's Declaration of Independence speaks
of "the pursuit of happiness,"
but nowhere in the Bible are we told to pursue this.
Happiness is elusive, and we don't find it by seeking it.[7]

America is said to have the highest per capita
boredom of any spot on earth!
We know that because we have the greatest variety and greatest
number of artificial amusements of any country.
People have become so empty that they
can't even entertain themselves.[8]

A terrifying spiritual and moral tide of evil has already loosed us
from our spiritual moorings.
Monstrous new ideas that could easily destroy our freedoms
are rushing into the vacuum.[9]

Nations rise, they flourish for a time, and then they decline.
Eventually every empire comes to an end;
not even the greatest can last forever.[10]

There is no doubt that nations come to an end
when they have ceased to fulfill the function that God meant for them.[11]

The secret strength of a nation is found in the faith
that abides in the hearts and homes of the country.[12]

We talk out of both corners of our mouth at once.
We say we are a Christian nation, but much of our literature,
our social practices, our deep interests are not Christian at all.
They are totally secular.[13]

Spiritually, we have wandered far from the faith of our fathers . . .
no nation which relegates the Bible to the background,
which disregards the love of God and flouts the claims
of the Man of Galilee, can long survive.[14]

No form of government has been able to establish righteousness, justice,
and peace, the three elements without which we can never
have continued national prosperity or international peace.[15]

Our government is certainly going to fall like a rope of sand
if unsupported by the moral fabric of God's Word.
The moral structure in our country grew from Judeo-Christian roots.
When those values are applied, they produce moral fruits.
But if that structure disappears,
the moral sentiment that shapes our nation's
goals will disappear with it.[16]

The Pilgrims . . . put their ideals ahead of all material considerations.
It is not surprising that the Pilgrims had little and succeeded,
while we have much and are in danger of failing.
No civilization can make progress unless some great principle
is generously mixed into the mortar of its foundations in life.[17]

The Pilgrims had vision and hope
because they lived in the dimension of eternity.
Their strength of spirit was forged by a personal faith in God,
by tough discipline, and by regular habits of devotion.[18]

Our nation grew strong in an era when moral standards
were emphasized, and it will grow weak when we
condone that which we once condemned.[19]

The nation's image has become more like a chameleon—accepting
whatever trend marketers concoct. Gone are the days of reverencing
a holy God in the church or within ourselves. Yet the Bible tells us,
"Happy is the man who is always reverent" (Proverbs 28:14 NKJV).[20]

What I find disturbing in America is the consuming desire
for leisure, convenience, and fun. It seems we, as a nation,
have traded God for gadgets. We have traded eternal truth
for momentary self-gratification—worshipping false gods of
materialism and humanism instead of the Creator of all things.[21]

As long as we are on this earth, we possess dual citizenship.
On one hand we owe allegiance to our nation
and are called to be good citizens. But we are also citizens
of the kingdom of God. Our supreme loyalty is to Him.[22]

All the nations that make up the world are burdened down with
riches or poverty, obesity or malnutrition, success or failure.[23]

At the bitter end of an era of liberation—
women's lib, kids' lib, animal lib, and everything-but-ethics lib—
America has apparently been liberated from its moral foundations.
But for too many, the good life has become a living hell.[24]

The great flaw in the American economic
system has finally been revealed:
an unrealistic faith in the power of prosperity
rather than in the ultimate power and benevolence of God.[25]

The American Dream became America's god;
wealth and abundance have become the measure of America's success.
But—as recent events have shown—we have been living an illusion.[26]

No matter how hard we try, words simply cannot
express the horror, the shock, and the revulsion we all
feel over what took place in this nation on 9/11.
My prayer today is that we will feel the loving arms of God
wrapped around us, and will know in our hearts
that He will never forsake us as we trust in Him.[27]

The blood of Christ "purchased men for God from
every tribe and language and people and nation" (Revelation 5:9 NIV).[28]

BILLY GRAHAM ON
ANGELS

Bless the LORD, you His angels, who excel in strength, who do His word.
—PSALM 103:20 NKJV

I believe in angels because the Bible says there are angels;
and I believe the Bible to be the true Word of God.[1]

We face dangers every day of which we are not even aware.
Often God intervenes on our behalf through the use of His angels.[2]

Some people seem to put the devil on a par with God.
Actually, Satan is a fallen angel.[3]

[Angels] guide, comfort, and provide for the people of God
in the midst of suffering and persecution.[4]

The empire of angels is as vast as God's creation.
If you believe the Bible, you will believe in their ministry.[5]

Whether or not we sense and feel the presence of the
Holy Spirit or one of the holy angels, by faith we are
certain God will never leave us or forsake us.[6]

[Angels] crisscross the Old and New Testaments,
being mentioned directly or indirectly nearly 300 times.[7]

Just as millions of angels participated in the dazzling show
when the morning stars sang together at creation,
so will the innumerable hosts of heaven help bring to pass God's
prophetic declarations throughout time and into eternity.[8]

BILLY GRAHAM ON
ANGER

He brought us forth by the word of truth . . . everyone must be
quick to hear, slow to speak and slow to anger.

—JAMES 1:18–19 NASB

———

Anger and bitterness—whatever the cause—only end up hurting us.
Turn that anger over to Christ.[1]

———

Never underestimate anger's destructive power.[2]

———

[God] wants to help you overcome the bitterness and anger that you feel,
and He wants to encourage you . . . He knows that anger and depression
will never help you deal with your problems—
they only make them worse.[3]

———

When someone hurts us, our natural instinct is to strike back—
but when we do, we not only destroy any possibility of reconciliation,
but we also allow anger and hate to control us.[4]

We must face honestly the toll that anger and bitterness take on our lives. They are our enemies! The Bible says, "An angry person stirs up dissension, and a hot-tempered one commits many sins."[5]

Don't let hatred control you, no matter what others do that causes [anger]. You would only become guilty of the same sin that afflicts them, and nothing would be solved.[6]

[God] alone is perfect. Even His anger is righteous, because it is directed solely against evil.[7]

Every destructive emotion bears its own harvest, but anger's fruit is the most bitter of all.[8]

Can we overcome our anger, instead of constantly being overcome by it? Yes—with God's help. Peter's anger was channeled into boldness for Christ. Paul's anger against Christians was replaced with a burning passion to spread the Gospel. Is this your goal?[9]

Anger flees when the Spirit's fruit fills our hearts.[10]

On the cross Christ took upon Himself every sin we've ever committed— including anger.[11]

If you have been harboring anger or bitterness or
jealousy in your heart toward someone—a parent,
an ex-spouse, a boss—hand it over to Christ,
and ask Him to help you let it go.[12]

There are many irritations in life. They become prime
opportunities for Satan to lead us into evil passion.
Keep anger clear of bitterness, spite, or hatred.[13]

Anger makes us lash out at others,
destroying relationships and revealing our true nature.
The history of the human race is largely the history of its anger.[14]

Bitterness is anger gone sour, an attitude of deep discontent
that poisons our souls and destroys our peace.[15]

We get angry when others hurt us, both by what they say and
what they do. We get angry when we don't get our own way or our
plans and dreams are frustrated. Anger may arise in an instant,
erupting like a volcano and raining destruction on everyone in
sight. Often, anger simmers just below the surface, sometimes for a
lifetime. Like a corrosive acid, this kind of anger eats away at our
bodies and souls, yet we may not even be aware of its presence.[16]

Don't let the acids of bitterness eat away inside.
Learn the secret of trusting Christ in every circumstance.[17]

BILLY GRAHAM ON
ANXIETY

Anxiety in the heart of a man causes depression,
but a good word makes it glad.

—PROVERBS 12:25 NKJV

———

Though we have less to worry about than previous generations,
we have more worry.
Though we have it easier than our forefathers, we have more uneasiness.
Though we have less real cause for anxiety than our predecessors,
we are inwardly more anxious.[1]

———

Historians will probably call our era "the age of anxiety."
Anxiety is the natural result when our hopes are centered
in anything short of God and His will for us.[2]

———

Hypochondriacs who have a fanciful anxiety about their health
will never be well regardless of their physical condition.[3]

———

Is it any wonder that fear and anxiety have
become the hallmarks of our age?[4]

Anxiety and fear are like baby tigers:
The more you feed them, the stronger they grow.[5]

God's star promised peace to the whole world . . .
too often man's synthetic stars bring fear and anxiety.
Our gadget-filled paradise, suspended in a hell of international
insecurity, certainly does not offer us the happiness of which
the last century dreamed. But there is still a star in the sky.[6]

No situation is beyond God's control.
Over my wife's desk are these words:
"Fear not the future; God is already there."[7]

Men and women who give [Christ] first place find that there is
no need for anxiety about this world's goods.[8]

BILLY GRAHAM ON
THE BIBLE

The Scriptures say, "People do not live by bread alone,
but by every word that comes from the mouth of God."

—MATTHEW 4:4

People reading the Bible for the first time are often surprised to discover
how much human drama it contains. Almost every conceivable
human dilemma and conflict is reflected in its pages.[1]

The Bible is the only Book in the world that predicts the future.
The Bible is more modern than tomorrow morning's newspaper.[2]

The Bible is God's book of promises, and, unlike the books of men,
it does not change or get out of date.[3]

Let the study of the Bible become central in your life—
not just so you will know it, but that you will obey it.[4]

The sword of the Spirit—the Bible—is the weapon God has provided
for us to use in this battle between truth and deception.
Make it a priority to wield that sword skillfully.[5]

[The Bible] has survived attack of every kind.
Neither barbaric vandalism nor civilized scholarship has touched it.
Neither the burning of fire nor the laughter of skepticism has
accomplished its annihilation. Through the many dark ages of man,
its glorious promises have survived unchanged.[6]

I learned the importance of the Bible and came to believe
with all my heart in its full inspiration.
It became a sword in my hand to break open the hearts of men,
to direct them to the Lord Jesus Christ.[7]

It is man and not the Bible that needs correcting.
Greater and more careful scholarship has shown that
apparent contradictions were caused by incorrect
translations, rather than divine inconsistencies.[8]

Today there are more people who know the
words to a television commercial
than know the words in the Bible.[9]

Every graveyard and every cemetery testify that the Bible is true.[10]

———•———

Make the Bible part of your daily life,
and ask God to engrave its truths on your soul.[11]

———•———

The very practice of reading [the Bible] will have
a purifying effect upon your mind and heart. Let
nothing take the place of this daily exercise.[12]

———•———

Discover the Bible for yourself.[13]

———•———

If I stick to the Bible and preach the principles and the teachings
of the Bible, and quote the Bible, it has an impact of its own.[14]

———•———

We can trust the Bible because it points us
to the most important events in human history:
the life, death, and resurrection of Jesus Christ.[15]

———•———

From one end of the Bible to the other,
God assures us that He will never go back on His promises.[16]

———•———

Come back to the Bible. Begin to read it.
Study it and God will speak to you and change you—
and through you perhaps history can be changed.[17]

———•———

The Bible is actually a library of books—some long, some short—
written over hundreds of years by many authors.
Behind each one, however, was [the] Author: the Spirit of God.[18]

Some of the strongest warnings about judgment in the Bible
come from the lips of Jesus.[19]

When we approach the Bible as history and biography,
we approach the Bible in the wrong spirit.
We must read the Bible, not primarily as historians seeking information,
but as men and women seeking God.[20]

People from all walks of life are searching for answers to life's problems.
I believe the Bible has the answer to man's deepest needs.[21]

The main "food" God has given to strengthen us is the Bible,
the Word of God.[22]

Each of us has our reference point and as a Christian the reference point
by which I measure my life and thought is the Bible.[23]

I don't think people can live without hope.
What oxygen is to the lungs, hope is to our survival in this world.
And the Bible is filled with hope.[24]

The Bible is not an option; it is a necessity.
You cannot grow spiritually strong without it.[25]

The Bible is the constant fountain for faith, conduct,
and inspiration from which we drink daily.[26]

God gave the Bible to us because He wants
us to know Him and love Him
and serve Him. Most of all, He gave it to us
so we can become more like Christ.[27]

In the Bible God speaks to us; in prayer we speak to God.
Both are essential.[28]

Man is precisely what the Bible says he is.
Human nature is behaving exactly as the Bible said it would.
The course of human events is flowing just as Christ predicted.[29]

The Bible teaches that man's chief problem is spiritual.[30]

In the textbook of revelation, the Bible, God has spoken verbally;
and this spoken word has survived every scratch of the human pen.[31]

The Bible . . . is the only Book that offers man a redemption
and points the way out of his dilemmas.
It is our one sure guide in an unsure world.[32]

We have become a nation of biblical illiterates.[33]

The Bible is to be our basis of authority.
We must "by faith" accept [Jesus] as the Son of the living God.
This sounds narrow and intolerant, and in a sense it is![34]

The Bible is the textbook of revelation.
In God's great classroom there are three textbooks—
one called nature, one called conscience, and one named Scripture.
In the written textbook of revelation—
the Bible—God speaks through words.[35]

Without the Bible,
this world would indeed be a dark and frightening place,
without signpost or beacon.[36]

Those who read the Scriptures as magnificent literature,
breath-taking poetry, or history and overlook the story of salvation
miss the Bible's real meaning and message.[37]

As we cast our frightened eyes around for something that is
real and true and enduring,
we are turning once more to this ancient Book [the Bible] that has given
consolation, comfort, and salvation to millions in the centuries past.[38]

God never leads us to do anything that is contrary to the Bible.[39]

The Bible stands as the supreme Constitution for all mankind,
its laws applying equally to all who live under its domain,
without exception or special interpretation.[40]

The Bible can stand the onslaught of any enemy.[41]

I have yet to discover a source of information, practical advice,
and hope that compares to the wisdom found in the Bible.[42]

As the Constitution is the highest law of the land [in America],
so the Bible is the highest law of God.
For it is in the Bible that God sets forth His spiritual laws.
It is in the Bible that God makes His enduring promises.
It is in the Bible that God reveals the plan of
redemption for the human race.[43]

Become grounded in the Bible.
As Christians, we have only one authority, one compass:
the Word of God.[44]

The words of this Book have a way of filling in the missing pieces,
of bridging the gaps, of turning the tarnished colors of our life to
jewel-like brilliance. Learn to take your every problem to the Bible.
Within its pages you will find the correct answer.[45]

Before you "re-think" your faith, it may be wise to
examine the critics of the Bible.
In the end your faith will be even stronger.[46]

Make use of this tool of communication by which God speaks
to us—namely, the Bible! Read it, study it, memorize it.
It will change your entire life. It is not like any other book.
It is a "living" book that works its way into your heart, mind, and soul.[47]

I find something new in the Bible every time I read it . . .
that can be the experience of everyone who comes to it
wanting to discover more of God's truth.[48]

When you are told that science has disproved the Bible,
ask specifically where such is the case.
True science and a true understanding of
the Bible are never at variance.[49]

The Bible is a living Book and can be trusted
for its advice and direction and knowledge of God.[50]

[God] speaks from heaven through the Bible, His written Word.
This is why I use the phrase "the Bible says."
I would not have the authority to say what I do
in sermons unless it was based upon the Word of God.[51]

We should read the Bible expectantly, systematically, and obediently . . .
The Bible can change our lives as we read it
and obey its teachings every day.[52]

God has spoken to us through a Book: the Bible.[53]

No book ever takes the place of the Bible.
It is its own best commentary.[54]

Most of us do not understand nuclear fission, but we accept it . . .
Why is it so easy to accept manmade miracles
and so difficult to accept the miracles of the Bible?[55]

The Bible is God's gift to us.
It came from God, and it points us to God.[56]

The Bible is a guidebook, leading men [and women] to God in a
personal faith. Like a map or guidebook, it will show you the way,
but you must take it one step at a time.[57]

The Bible is to your soul what bread is to your body. You need it daily.
One good meal does not suffice for a lifetime.[58]

I'm afraid most Bibles remain unopened and unread.
Don't let this be true of yours![59]

The vitality [of] the Bible [is] exhibited in every generation . . .
Its power to transform lives is its best apologetic.[60]

There is nothing which indicates the inspiration of the Scriptures
more than the factual and faithful record of men and their failures . . .
These records are for our warning and instruction.
They show us how sinful man needs God.[61]

Just as the Bible is God's written Word, so Jesus is God's living Word.[62]

One can approach the Bible with a cold, rationalistic attitude,
or one can do so with reverence and the desire to hear God speak.[63]

I do not understand why reading the Bible in public
should make others feel uncomfortable . . . it may be such an example
that serves to remind them of the Book they have neglected.[64]

The [Bible's] message is concerned with earth dwellers, their origin,
the reason for their existence, the cause of their misery,
and the plan of redemption for a fallen race.[65]

We are not free to pick and choose the parts of the
Bible we want to believe or obey. God has given us all of it,
and we should be obedient to all of it.[66]

Psalms teaches us how to relate to God,
and Proverbs teaches us how to relate to others.[67]

The Bible is our authority in everything it touches. This means the
Bible is our guide to show us how to live . . . it is our instructor.[68]

The Bible has stood the test of time because it is
divinely inspired by Almighty God, written in ink
that cannot be erased by any man, religion,
or belief system.[69]

The Word does not change.
The Dead Sea scrolls, archeology, modern science—
they do not change the Bible; they confirm it.[70]

Man has not changed. Man still rejects the testimony of the Scripture.[71]

Don't take your Bible for granted! For centuries ordinary believers had
no access to the Bible; Bibles had to be painstakingly copied by hand
and were very expensive. The only access most people had to the Bible
was by hearing it read in church. The invention of the printing press
changed all that, however, and today the Bible is readily available in
multiple translations and hundreds of languages around the world.[72]

Every generation has found [the Bible's] message
indispensable, and its influence on individuals and
society over the centuries has been enormous.[73]

God's laws for the spiritual world are found in the Bible. Whatever else
there may be that tells us of God, it is more clearly told in the Bible.[74]

The Bible will always be the center of controversy.[75]

The only place we can find a clear, unmistakable message
is in the Word of God [the Bible].[76]

We should begin the day with the Bible, and as it comes to
a close let the Word speak its wisdom to our souls.
Let it be the Staff of Life upon which our spirit is nourished.
Let it be the Sword of the Spirit which cuts away the evil of
our lives and fashions us in His image and likeness.[77]

The central theme of the Bible is salvation,
and the central personality of the Bible is Christ.[78]

The whole world ought to know the story of the Bible.[79]

The Bible is God's love letter to us.[80]

The Bible opens with a tragedy and ends in a triumph.[81]

BILLY GRAHAM ON
THE BLOOD

This is the message which we have heard from Him . . .
the blood of Jesus Christ His Son cleanses us from all sin.

—1 JOHN 1:5, 7 NKJV

—•◆•—

Have you ever seen a person who was receiving a blood transfusion?
The blood was precious, life-giving, and certainly not repulsive.
The blood of Christ may seem to be a grim and repulsive subject . . .
[but] the blood of Christ is precious.[1]

—•◆•—

Blood is the symbol of the life sacrificed for sin.[2]

—•◆•—

Once for all God made complete and perfect provision
for the cure of man's sins;
without the blood of Christ, it is indeed a fatal disease.[3]

—•◆•—

We are called to obey Christ. He is the Master of
our lives and has washed us in His blood, which
cleanses our souls, our minds, and our mouths.
The world is watching. What do they see and hear?[4]

To many people, the mention of the blood of Christ is distasteful.
However, on [a] visit to Mayo Clinic I noticed that
at each reception desk there were pamphlets entitled
A *Gift of Life,* urging people to donate blood.
Anyone who has gone through surgery and looked up to see
the bag of blood dripping slowly into his veins,
realizes with gratitude the life-giving property of blood.[5]

Blood is mentioned 460 times in the Bible.
Fourteen times in the New Testament Jesus spoke of His own blood.
Why? Because by the shedding of His blood,
He accomplished the possibility of our salvation.[6]

The distinctive feature of Christianity is blood atonement.
Without it we cannot be saved.
Blood is actually a symbol of the death of Christ.[7]

[Today] there is less emphasis on redemption by the blood of Christ.[8]

Today the idea of the shed blood of Christ is becoming
old-fashioned and out of date in a lot of preaching.
It is in the Bible. It is the very heart of Christianity.[9]

Peter preached about [the blood].
Paul wrote about it, and the redeemed in heaven sing about it.
In a sense, the New Testament is the Book of the Blood.[10]

BILLY GRAHAM ON
CHARACTER

When God desired to show . . . the unchangeable character
of his purpose, he guaranteed it with an oath.

—HEBREWS 6:17 ESV

God never directs in a way contrary to His character.
When the Scriptures tell us that He will direct our paths,
we can be assured that when He is in control,
no matter how thorny the path, He will not tell us to jump off a cliff.[1]

True greatness is not measured by the headlines a person commands
or the wealth he or she accumulates. The inner character of a person—
the undergirding moral and spiritual values and commitments—
is the true measure of lasting greatness.[2]

A chain is only as strong as its weakest link, and so is our character.[3]

A godlikeness of character
is the Christian's proper heritage in this earthly walk.[4]

—❖—

Trials and difficulties may assail the life of a believer,
but they also have the ability to remold his character and banish from
his life those impurities which might impair growth and service.[5]

—❖—

Consistency, constancy, and undeviating diligence
to maintain Christian character
are a must if the older generation is to command respect,
or even a hearing, from the young.[6]

—❖—

A few years ago, honesty was the hallmark of a man of good character.
But it's been set aside for an
"It's all right if you don't get caught" philosophy.[7]

—❖—

It is unfair to attribute virtues beyond a person's true character.[8]

—❖—

In character-building and in living the Christian
life, concentration is important.
The [person] who has a general interest in everything
usually isn't too good at anything.[9]

—❖—

One of the real tests of Christian character is to be found
in the lives we live from day to day.[10]

BILLY GRAHAM ON
CHILDREN

Assemble the people before me to hear my words
so that they may . . . teach them to their children.

—DEUTERONOMY 4:10 NIV

———◆———

It may shock some parents to learn that we don't own our children.
God has given them to us in trust . . . however,
God may transfer our children to His home at any time.[1]

———◆———

I missed the joy of seeing our children grow and change.
I thank God for watching over them during those years.[2]

———◆———

Our lives speak loudly to those around us,
especially the children in our home.[3]

———◆———

One of life's mysteries is why two children growing up in the same home
sometimes take radically different paths—
one following Christ, the other rebellious and scornful. Yet it happens.[4]

———◆———

God gave us our children so we could prepare them to become adults.[5]

Ruth once wrote, "Dear Journal, Never let a single day pass
without saying an encouraging word to each child . . .
'More people fail for lack of encouragement,' someone wrote,
'than for any other reason.'"[6]

Children will learn far more by watching than by just listening.[7]

One of the worst things we can do is allow our children
to grow up thinking they don't need to keep any rules.
A spoiled child becomes a spoiled adult.[8]

Love your children—and let them know you love them.
Children who experience love find it far
easier to believe God loves them.[9]

If a child is to survive, he or she must know the rules of safety.
If he is to be healthy, he must know the rules of health.
If he is to drive a car, he must know the rules of the road.
If he is to become a ball player, he must learn the rules of the game.
And, contrary to popular thinking, children appreciate rules.[10]

There is always the exceptional child,
but the average tells us that the child is largely
what the home has made him.[11]

Children respect discipline. They want to be guided.
It gives them a sense of belonging, a sense of security.[12]

If our children grow up with no understanding of right and wrong . . .
no desire to live with integrity . . . no faith in God . . .
their souls will be impoverished and they will miss life's highest good.[13]

Children do need the guidance of their parents,
and we guide them more by the example we set than by any other way.
We need to be firm and sane and fair and consistent—and, above all,
we need to discipline in a spirit of love.[14]

Many children today are growing up without discipline.
As they become adults and the discipline of job or family demands
are placed upon them, they do not know how to cope . . .
children need discipline to be useful members of society.
Likewise, God's children need discipline to be
useful members of His family.[15]

Children, pray for the salvation of your parents.[16]

Parents need much wisdom in relating to their grown children—
and much prayer. Children likewise have much to learn
about relating to their parents as the years pass.[17]

The television, iPod, and Internet have trespassed upon the innocence
of America's children, while preoccupied mothers and dispassionate
fathers stare aghast wondering what went wrong. They don't stop
to think of their own contributions to the persuasions influencing
their children. After all, where do kids as young as elementary
age get money to rent rock videos and the latest rap DVDs?[18]

The Bible warns [parents] against extremes
in dealing with our adult children.
It tells us to avoid trying to control [them] once they become adults.
When children become independent, a major transition takes place:
They are no longer under our authority.[19]

To injure, ignore, disrespect, and violate the innocence of a child
are among the greatest evils known to man.[20]

Truth is easier for a child to handle than evasiveness.[21]

Before the seventeenth century, a child passed directly
into the adult world between the ages of five and
seven . . . then came the industrial revolution . . .
so the child-centered home was born.[22]

By the 1960s the United States had a new ruling class—the teenager![23]

Children must be taught obedience just as much as they need
to be taught to read and write.[24]

Someday your children will leave;
you can't hold on to them or control them forever, nor should you.[25]

BILLY GRAHAM ON
CHOICE

Who is the man who fears the LORD*?*
Him will he instruct in the way that he should choose.

Some people resist the idea of a choice of any sort.
They don't want to be called "narrow."
But Jesus taught that there are two roads,
and you have to choose which road you will take.[1]

There are two masters,
and you have to choose which master you are going to serve.[2]

There is not a day that we do not have a chance to choose
between the devil's clever promises and God's sure Word.[3]

From the beginning of time until the present moment,
man's ungodly quest for power,
his determination to use his gift of free choice for his own selfish ends,
has brought him to the brink of doom.[4]

Our families cannot choose Christ for us. Our friends cannot do it.
God is a great God, but even God can't make the decision for us . . .
we have to make our own choice.[5]

[God] created us free to choose how we would live . . .
but leaves us free to pursue our own ends
with tragic, natural consequences.[6]

The Bible clearly teaches that when we turn our backs on God
and choose to disregard His moral laws
there are inevitable consequences.
Furthermore it is not God who is to blame for the consequences,
but the person who has broken His law.[7]

The Antichrist . . . will be the embodiment of evil,
and will have great power to deceive those who choose to follow him.[8]

[Our] problems boil down to one of moral choices.
God wanted a world based on moral values,
thus He created mankind with the ability to respond to moral choices.
Faced with the moral option of living selfishly or unselfishly,
people can and do make wrong decisions.
We are free to choose, but we reap the
consequences of bad moral decisions.[9]

Ultimately, every human being must face this question:
What do you think of Christ? Whose Son is He?
We must answer this question with belief and action.
We must not only believe something about Jesus,
but we must do something about Him.
We must accept Him or reject Him.[10]

The destiny of your own soul is in your own
hands by the choice you make.[11]

BILLY GRAHAM ON
CHRISTIANITY

The word of God continued to spread,
and there were many new believers . . .
(It was at Antioch that the believers were first called Christians.)

——◆——

If it is Christian, it will be Bible-centered.[1]

——◆——

Christianity has no shrines to visit, no dusty remains to venerate,
no tombs at which to worship.[2]

——◆——

I believe there is an obedience to the Gospel,
there is a self-denial and a bearing of the cross,
if you are to be a follower of Christ.
Being a Christian is a serious business.[3]

——◆——

Only the Christian faith claims that its Leader
died and rose again and is alive at this moment.
Many gravestones carry the inscription, "Here lies . . . ,"
but on Christ's tomb are emblazoned the words, "He is not here."[4]

Christians should be a foreign influence,
a minority group in a pagan world.[5]

The secret of the power of Christianity is not in its ethics.
It is not in Christian ideas or philosophy . . .
the secret of Christianity is found . . . in the Lord Jesus Christ.[6]

If we have our eyes upon ourselves, our problems, and our pain,
we cannot lift our eyes upward.
A child looks up when he's walking with his father,
and the same should be true for the Christian.[7]

What makes us Christians shrug our shoulders when
we ought to be flexing our muscles? What makes us
apathetic in a day when there are loads to lift,
a world to be won, and captives to be set free?
Why are so many bored, when the times demand action? Christ told
us that in the last days there would be an insipid attitude toward life.[8]

To a sinner, a righteous person is an oddity and an abnormality.
A Christian's goodness is a rebuke to the wicked; his being right-side up
is a reflection upon the worldling's inverted position.[9]

Ninety-five percent of the difficulties you will experience as a Christian
can be traced to a lack of Bible study and reading.[10]

——◆——

God says it is our duty as Christians to take care of widows and orphans
and to help the poor within the Christian society . . .
And Jesus said, "Inasmuch as ye have done it unto one of the least of
these my brethren, ye have done it unto me" [Matthew 25:40 KJV].[11]

——◆——

We must have a virile, dynamic, aggressive Christian who lives Christ
seven days a week, who is ready to die, if necessary, for his faith.[12]

——◆——

We can never live this [Christian] life on the highest plane
unless we are continually growing and moving forward.
You should be closer to God today in heart, soul, and body
than at any other time so far in your life.[13]

——◆——

A great problem in America is that we have an anemic
and watered-down Christianity that has produced an
anemic, watered-down, and spineless Christian who is not
willing to stand up and be counted on every issue.[14]

——◆——

Christianity is not primarily a matter of externals,
nevertheless it does find expression in conversation, habits,
recreation, emphasis, and ambitions to be noted in our daily life.[15]

——◆——

The Christian is to take his place in society with moral courage
to stand up for that which is right, just, and honorable.[16]

——◆——

Christianity has become so respectable and so conventional
that it is now insipid. The salt has lost its flavor.[17]

The Christian's journey through life isn't a sprint but a marathon.[18]

Tragic as it is when a child fails to develop physically or mentally, even more tragic is a Christian who fails to develop spiritually.[19]

Christianity is not an insurance policy against life's ills and troubles.[20]

Christians, pray for an outpouring of God's Spirit upon a willful, evil, unrepentant world.[21]

We aren't only called to *become* Christians; we are also called to *be* Christians.[22]

As Christians we are constantly bombarded with attitudes and values which are contrary to biblical teaching.[23]

The faithful Christian steward acknowledges that God owns all he has, and it is his responsibility to manage and dispose of his possessions in a way that is acceptable to the Lord.[24]

I fear that so often we Christians give the idea that the truth is fiction by the way we live and by the lack of dedication to the teachings of our Lord.[25]

Don't be a half-Christian. There are too many of such in the world.
The world has a profound respect for people
who are sincere in their faith.[26]

Too many so-called Christians are like the little chameleon
which adapts its coloration to that of its surroundings.
Even a critical world is quick to recognize a real Christian
and just as quick to detect a counterfeit.[27]

Would Christ feel comfortable in an environment where men
and women are consuming alcoholic beverages, gambling away
their money, and engaging in conversation that is often filled
with the baser things of life? It is a relevant question.
As a Christian, Christ lives in you and you carry Him wherever you go.
The Bible tells us to "come out from them and
be separate" [2 Corinthians 6:17 NIV].[28]

For the Christian, all is not hopeless
unless his affections are centered on the things of this world.[29]

There are too many professed Christians
who never get "wrought up" about anything;
they never get indignant with injustice, with corruption in high places,
or with the godless traffics which barter away
the souls and bodies of people.[30]

The Christian is not to be disturbed by the
chaos, violence, strife, bloodshed,
and threat of war that fill the pages of our daily newspapers.
We know that these things are the consequences of man's sin and greed.
Every day as I read my newspaper I say: "The Bible is true."[31]

Christianity is a Gospel of crisis.
It proclaims unmistakably that this world's days are numbered.[32]

It is a tragic fact that the vast majority of Christians today
are living a sub-normal Christian life.[33]

The greatest need in the world today is for fully committed Christians.[34]

It's tough to be a Christian in our world.
We need to be willing to take on Jesus' unpopularity
and the scorn that is often heaped on Him.[35]

There are Christians who have never really learned the
biblical truth of separation:
separation from unclean thoughts and unclean habits.[36]

Millions of professing Christians are only just that—"professing."
They have never possessed Christ.
They live lives characterized by the flesh.[37]

Christianity is not an accretion, it is not something added.
It is a new total outlook which is satisfied with nothing less
than penetration to the furthest corners of
the mind and the understanding.[38]

We have made Christianity too easy.[39]

Our generation has become well versed in Christian terminology
but is remiss in the actual practice of Christ's principles and teachings.
Hence, our greatest need today is not more Christianity
but more true Christians.[40]

All of Christianity is based on a person—Jesus Christ.
Christ Himself is the embodiment of the Gospel.[41]

Christianity cannot expect the world to live the truths of the Gospel
until it has the life that the Gospel provides in Christ.
We Christians ought to be light and salt in
the society in which we live.[42]

Christianity increases the scope and area of our lives.[43]

Christianity is not a spectator sport,
it's something in which we become totally involved.[44]

Affliction may be for our edification and Christian development.[45]

In some churches and religious television programs,
we see an effort to make Christianity popular and always positive.
This may be a comfortable cushion for those who find
the hard facts too difficult.[46]

Christianity has its roots in the deep, firm soil of history.
Jesus' incarnation—God invading human history with His presence
in the form of man—is on the record.
Every time you write the date, you attest to the fact
that God entered human history.[47]

Every Christian should become an ambassador of Christ . . .
every Christian should be so intoxicated with
Christ and so filled with holy fervor
that nothing could ever quench his [passion] . . .
Let us capture some of the magnificent obsession
that [the] early Christians had![48]

Christians, saints of God,
pray that the dew of heaven may fall on earth's dry thirsty ground,
and that righteousness may cover the earth as the waters cover the sea.[49]

If you are a true Christian . . .
you will reveal through your daily life the fruit of the Spirit . . .
and all the other Christian virtues which
round out a Christlike personality.[50]

A born-again Christian should no more think
of going back to the old life than an adult to his childhood.[51]

Many Christians who profess Christ
do not live as though they possess Him.[52]

Within the New Testament, there is no indication that Christians
should expect to be healthy, wealthy, and successful in this present age.[53]

Many people ask about Christianity the same [way] they
ask about everything else today: "What's in it for me?"
In our selfishness, we think of God as we think of everyone else.
What can He contribute to us, personally?[54]

Just because a person claims to be a Christian
does not necessarily mean that he is one.[55]

The Christian has a great obligation to be
ethical and honest in all things,
even sometimes at personal hazard.
It is in the difficult situation that the qualities of a Christian are seen.[56]

The difference between the non-Christian and the Christian
is that the non-Christian makes sin a practice;
the true Christian does not.[57]

A baby isn't meant to stay a baby forever,
and neither is a new Christian.[58]

The goal of a child's life is maturity—
and the goal of a Christian's life is spiritual maturity.[59]

Today our churches are filled,
but how many are actually practicing Christianity in daily life?[60]

My wife has said that a bitter, sour Christian
is one of Satan's greatest trophies—and she's right.[61]

Christians are becoming disengaged in following the Scripture
that tells us not to conform to the world's system.[62]

Christians are expected to carry the marks of the Lord Jesus,
not adapt to the fashionable counterculture driven by marketing traps.[63]

I like the bumper sticker that reads, "Christians
aren't perfect, just forgiven."
But that does not give us license to live below God's standard.[64]

When confronted with the world's problems, we Christians say
automatically: "Christianity is the answer." But this is not true!
It is the application of Christianity that is the answer.[65]

We cannot inherit Christianity . . . God has no grandchildren.[66]

A contentious, belligerent Christian isn't living according to
the Spirit but according to the flesh. When we stubbornly
insist on our own way and are insensitive to others,
peace is not our goal.[67]

What makes Christians different from everyone else is
that God Himself lives within them by His Holy Spirit.
When we come to Christ and give our lives to Him,
God actually takes up residence within us.[68]

Some people think that going to church on Sunday and
owning a dust-covered Bible makes a person a Christian.
That is not true. A Christian is one in whom Christ dwells,
and the person's life will give evidence of this.[69]

When Rome was at the height of her glory and power, there
appeared a disturbing sect called Christians. Because of a fire that
burned within them, these people dared to be different . . . they
refused to be defiled by the sensual practices of a disintegrating
civilization. In a period when human life was cheap, they put a
high value upon human beings, their souls, and their destiny.
These Christians refused to be absorbed into the godless society
of Rome. They had not heard of the rule that we hear today,
"When in Rome, do as the Romans do."[70]

The feet of the Christian need to tread the
narrow path that the Savior trod,
keeping in step with Him.[71]

True Christianity finds all of its doctrines in the Bible;
true Christianity does not deny any part of the Bible;
true Christianity does not add anything to the Bible.
For many centuries the Bible has been the most available book on
the earth. It has no hidden purpose. It cannot be destroyed.[72]

Christians are not powerless. We have the mighty power of God
available through God the Holy Spirit, even in this world.[73]

Becoming a Christian is the work of a moment;
being a Christian is the work of a lifetime.[74]

BILLY GRAHAM ON
CHURCH

God blesses the one who reads the words of this prophecy to the church.

—REVELATION 1:3

———◆◆———

Pentecost was the day of power of the Holy Spirit.
It was the day the Christian church was born.[1]

———◆◆———

The word *church* as applied to the Christian
society was first used by Jesus Himself
when He told Peter, "Upon this rock I will
build my church" [Matthew 16:18].
He is the foundation of all Christian experience.[2]

———◆◆———

The blood of the martyrs is the seed of the church.[3]

———◆◆———

The blood of Christ purchased the church.[4]

If we in the church want a cause to fight, let's fight sin.
Let's reveal its hideousness.
Let's show that Jeremiah was correct when he said:
"The heart is deceitful above all things,
and desperately wicked" [Jeremiah 17:9 NKJV].[5]

I am convinced if the church went back to the main task of
proclaiming the Gospel it would see people being converted to Christ,
and it would have a far greater impact on the social, moral,
and psychological needs of people than
anything else it could possibly do.[6]

In some churches today and on some religious television programs,
we see the attempt to make Christianity popular and pleasant.
We have taken the cross away and substituted cushions.[7]

Statistics indicate that the church is rapidly
losing in the population explosion.
There are fewer Christians per capita every day.[8]

Thousands of people have entered churches
without discovering a vital experience with Jesus Christ.
The substitutes have been handed them in the guise of religious rituals,
good works, community effort, or social reform . . .
none of which can gain a person a right relationship with God.[9]

———◆———

Sometimes it is difficult to differentiate the
Christian from the man of the world.
In America, for example, churchgoing has become popular,
but churchgoing may not necessarily be accompanied
by genuine depth in prayer and Bible study or a change in lifestyle.[10]

———◆———

In thousands of churches [people] are led astray theologically.
Thus spiritually and morally they are drifting aimlessly,
without compass or guide.[11]

———◆———

The church in America has been deeply infiltrated by the "world,"
and in the process it is beginning to copy and resemble the world
in many of its activities.[12]

———◆———

Preaching the whole council of God
involves man's environment and physical being as well as his soul.
There is no doubt that the church is in danger of
getting off the main track and getting lost.[13]

———◆———

God did not ordain that the church should drift aimlessly
in the seas of uncertainty without compass, captain, or crew.[14]

———◆———

The church should be setting the pace.
The church should be taking its proper place
of leadership in the nation . . .
God help the church to wake up![15]

The church holds the key to revival. It is within our grasp.[16]

America and Western Europe are on a moneymaking,
pleasure-mad spree unparalleled in the history of the world.
God is generally ignored or ridiculed.
Church members in many cases are only halfhearted Christians.
Judgment is coming.[17]

We have been trying to solve every ill of society as though society
were made up of regenerate men to whom we had an obligation
to speak with Christian advice.[18]

God's church is a Bible-centered church,
and it grows strong under persecution.[19]

Before three thousand people were brought
into the church on the day of Pentecost,
the disciples had spent fifty days in prayer, fasting, and spiritual travail.[20]

The Bible nowhere teaches that the church will
ultimately convert the whole world to Jesus Christ.
There has never been a generation in history,
nor will there ever be a generation, in which the majority of the people
will believe in Christ.[21]

I am afraid the church is trying to speak out on too many issues
that really do not concern the church.
There are certain issues we know to be wrong—
racial injustice, crime, gambling, dishonesty, pornography.
On these matters we must thunder forth as the prophets of God.[22]

There will come a time when people hungering for the truth will seek
it where it is supposedly disseminated, such as books and churches,
but they will not hear the Word of the Lord.
Instead of receiving a message to satisfy their spiritual longings,
they will hear a sermon on some current political or social problem,
or a sermonette on art and literature.
And so they wander from one place to another,
going from hope to despair,
and eventually giving up.[23]

Unless the church quickly recovers the authoritative biblical message,
we may witness the spectacle of millions of Christians going outside
the institutional church to find spiritual food.[24]

What right does any church have even
attempting to approve of lifestyles
or certain acts for which God prescribed the death penalty
in the Old Testament?[25]

There are many who sit in some churches week after
week, year after year, without hearing the whole Gospel
and knowing what it is to be born again.
They hear a gospel which is incomplete,
and consequently not good news at all.[26]

[Satan] invades the Sunday school, the Bible class, and even the pulpit.
He even invades the church under cover of an orthodox vocabulary,
emptying sacred terms of their biblical sense.[27]

The church has lost its ability to discipline members who live openly
in sin. Consequently, we have lost our witness in the community.[28]

The church is a storehouse of spiritual food
whereby the inner man is fed, nourished,
and developed into maturity.
If it fails, it is not fulfilling its purpose as a church.[29]

It could be said that going to church will not make one a Christian.
But . . . refusing to fellowship with believers
will not make you one either.[30]

I hope the day will never come when the church abandons
the "class meeting" and the prayer service . . .
The old-fashioned "testimony" meeting should be revived,
for through this medium we can share with others
our faith and triumphs as well as our needs and mistakes.[31]

———

Down through the centuries the church has contributed more than
any other single agency in lifting social standards to new heights.[32]

———

The church isn't just a particular building or congregation
but the spiritual fellowship of all who belong to Jesus Christ.
If we belong to Christ, we also belong to each other.[33]

———

Many churches have molded their programs around the community—
not the Word of God.[34]

———

The Lord did not design the church to cater to people's needs—
the Lord breathed life into the church to proclaim His truths.[35]

———

The church does not prey on the lost; it prays for the perishing.[36]

———

If the church is acceptable to this present age
and is not suffering reproach,
then it is not the true church that our Lord founded.[37]

———

The church should not reflect pop culture but portray godly attributes.
The church should not seek pleasures but seek after God.[38]

———

The church is blending into the community
by embracing what the world enjoys
and, in turn, bringing inside the church
the world's ideas and interests.[39]

Christ's church is a place to grow people up in the Lord,
not to enhance our leisure time.[40]

Church is not for pretenders and performers. Church
is a place for pastors to preach principles of the
faith in order to prepare believers to face
the storms of life on the stage of an unbelieving world.[41]

The church is in turmoil today.
The church is not to reflect the world but
to be a portrait of Jesus Christ.[42]

No church is perfect, but don't let that discourage you.
Someone has said that if you ever find one that is,
it will stop being perfect the minute you join![43]

The church should not be pampered but rather prepare for,
and expect, persecution—
for it is Christ's body on earth.[44]

We have become so tolerant and accepting of the world's ways
that it is hard for many in the church to notice
the sin much less answer how it crept in.
The church is to be in the world,
but worldliness is not to infiltrate the church.[45]

When the church begins to entertain the flock
and respond to the cult of self—
it is diminished to a mere community center.[46]

The fiercest storm is taking place in some of our churches—
the unbelief and disobedience of God's Word.[47]

In our desire to make Christ known and to
increase the influence of the church,
we are many times prone to think that Christians and the church
can be made popular with the unbelieving world.
This is a grave mistake on the part of the church.[48]

It is vitally important for local church leaders to keep in touch with
the spiritual state of their members, to discuss their level of biblical
knowledge, and to teach them how to study God's Word and pray.[49]

The church is far greater than [a building or denomination].
It includes the whole family of God—that vast unseen fellowship
of men and women throughout the ages who
belong to Christ. Paul wrote of
"God's household, which is the church of the
living God" [1 Timothy 3:15 NIV].[50]

BILLY GRAHAM ON
COMFORT

I can take comfort in this . . . I have not denied the words of the Holy One.

—JOB 6:10

It is a comfort to hear the words of God in times of stress.[1]

God doesn't comfort us to make us comfortable,
but to make us comforters.[2]

Comfort and prosperity have never enriched the world
as much as adversity has done.[3]

We should go to no place that we would not go in His Presence.
But He is not with us just to judge or condemn us;
He is near to comfort, protect, guide, encourage,
strengthen, cleanse, and help.[4]

There are countless opportunities to comfort others,
not only in the loss of a loved one,
but also in the daily distress that so often creeps into our lives.[5]

———⊰•⊱———

Because tragedy happened to you, it gives you a greater sense of
oneness with others who experience tragedy.
Because we have been comforted through the Word of God,
we in turn may be able to comfort others.[6]

———⊰•⊱———

When we are a comfort and encouragement to others,
we are sometimes surprised at how it comes back to us many times over.[7]

———⊰•⊱———

Humanity wants comfort in its sorrow, light in its darkness,
peace in its turmoil, rest in its weariness,
and healing in its sickness and diseases:
The Gospel gives all of this to us.[8]

BILLY GRAHAM ON
COMMITMENT

So commit yourselves wholeheartedly to these words of mine.

—DEUTERONOMY 11:18

———◆———

We must understand what this word "believe" implies.
It means "commit" and "surrender."
Believing is your response to God's offer of mercy, love, and forgiveness.[1]

———◆———

Christ can give you power to overcome every sin and habit in your life.
He can break the ropes, fetters, and chains of sin;
but you must repent, confess, commit, and
surrender yourself to Him first.
Right now, it can be settled, and you can know
the peace, joy, and fellowship of Christ.[2]

———◆———

True repentance is a turning from sin—
a conscious, deliberate decision to leave sin behind—
and a conscious turning to God with a commitment
to follow His will for our lives.
It is a change of direction, an alteration of attitudes,
and a yielding of the will.[3]

———◆———

Jesus didn't use subtlety or gimmicks to gain followers.
Rather, He honestly laid before them the
tough demands of discipleship—
total commitment and total involvement.[4]

———◆———

Commitment means burning all bridges behind you.[5]

———◆———

There is a high price of commitment. Jesus never offered a bargain.
Some of your friends won't want a person
around them who lives a clean life
and talks about God and reads the Bible and prays.[6]

———◆———

Satan doesn't need for us to fall into gross sin in order to defeat us;
a large dose of laziness will do the trick just as well.
Put Christ first in your life, and then commit
every hour of the day to Him.[7]

———◆———

Saving faith involves an act of commitment and trust,
in which I commit my life to Jesus Christ
and trust Him alone as my personal Savior and Lord.[8]

Saving faith is a *commitment* to Jesus as Savior and Lord.
It is a personal and individual decision. It is more than assent
to historical or theological truth given to us in God's Word.
It is faith in the promises of God as the
believer's only hope for eternal life
(John 5:24; 1 John 5:10–11).[9]

BILLY GRAHAM ON
COMPROMISE

Follow the instructions of the LORD.... Do not compromise with evil.
—PSALM 119:1, 3

———◆———

From compromise to deceit is a small step.[1]

———◆———

If we are at peace with this world,
it may be because we have sold out to it and compromised with it.[2]

———◆———

Daniel and his companions were tempted to forsake
their godly heritage but they refused.
They even faced a fiery furnace rather than compromise.[3]

———◆———

We are to renounce the evil influence of the
world, the flesh, and the devil.
There can be no parleying, bargaining, compromise, or hesitation.
Christ demands total loyalty.[4]

Too many Christian TV and radio programs have been geared
to please, entertain, and gain the favor of the world.
The temptation is to compromise,
to make the gospel more appealing and attractive.[5]

Thousands of Christians compromise their faith
in Jesus Christ by denying Him.
Even some clergymen neglect or deliberately refuse to close
a public prayer in the name of Jesus for fear of offending an unbeliever.
They cannot endure the persecution that may follow
an acknowledgment of Jesus Christ.[6]

Christ needs people today who are made of martyr stuff!
Dare to take a strong, uncompromised stand for Him.[7]

The devil has successfully fooled many churches,
convincing them to follow the world.
Biblical standards have been compromised
by convenient social theories.[8]

The Scripture teaches that popularity with the world means death.
Satan's most effective tool is conformity and compromise.
He is aware that one man standing in the midst of a pagan people
can move more people in the direction of God
than thousands of insipid professors of religion.[9]

Compromising and conforming to the world's
standard is against God's Word.[10]

Satan is the sower of compromise—weaving a bit of God's truth
into the dirty rags of sin. Satan is the commander in deceit.
Satan is the ringleader in rebellion against the faithful.
Satan is the sly serpent of temptation.
Satan is the false hope of security.
Satan is the great pretender.
Satan is the great spoiler of everything good.
And Satan wants to destroy you.[11]

Instead of clinging to the only Lifeboat that can save,
we have tossed overboard biblical truths in the name of
[compromise], living on the edge of life, like the man who rides
the parameter of a hurricane, daring it to sweep him away.[12]

Be attractive and winsome,
but do not compromise your convictions for the sake of popularity.[13]

BILLY GRAHAM ON
CONFORMING

As obedient children, do not be conformed to the former lusts . . .
because it is written, "YOU SHALL BE HOLY, FOR I AM HOLY."

—1 PETER 1:14, 16 NASB

———

There are those today that say we must do as others do,
that we must conform to the world [to win it],
that we must swim with the tide,
that we must move with the crowd. But the believer should say, "No."[1]

———

The prophets who spoke to their generations for God
did not please and conform; they irritated and opposed.[2]

———

One of our most deep-seated fears is that
we might be called an "outsider."
This fear has led us down the road to conformity,
has put the imprint of "the organization man" on our souls,
and has robbed us of originality of thought, individuality of personality,
and constructive action.[3]

Peer pressure accounts for much of the promiscuous sex
in high schools and colleges. "Conform or get lost."
Since no one enjoys losing friends or being cast out of his own circle,
peer pressure—especially during the years of adolescence—
is an almost irresistible force.[4]

It is a tragedy that many of God's people
have conformed themselves to the world and its thinking,
rather than being transformed by the renewing of their minds.[5]

Don't conform to those who have been overwhelmed
by the tide of immorality sweeping our country![6]

The pagan world is still trying to put its stamp of conformity
on every follower of Jesus Christ.
Every possible pressure is being brought to bear upon Christians
to make them conform to the standards of the present world . . .
be a committed follower of Jesus Christ.[7]

The apostle Paul said, "Be not conformed to this world."
These words cut like a sharp sword across our way of life.
They have the tone of the battle call in them.
They separate the weak from the strong.
But they are words of inspiration, and we need to hear them today.[8]

It is often asked, "How could the early disciples
turn the world upside down
when·millions of Christians can't even keep it right side up today?"
The answer is they didn't conform their faith to match the world.
They had the truth, and they refused to water it down.
They had a faith that would not compromise.[9]

The apostle Paul urges Christians everywhere
in all ages to be nonconformists
as far as the world system is concerned.
We are not to conform.
A true Christian, living an obedient life,
is a constant rebuke to those who accept the
moral standards of this world.[10]

God's purpose for us is that we ought to be
conformed to the image of His Son.
The world may exert its pressure to deform us,
but we are told to "be transformed" [Romans 12:2 NIV].[11]

Pure hearts will be Christlike.
It is God's desire that we be conformed to the image of His Son.[12]

BILLY GRAHAM ON
CONSCIENCE

God's law is written in their hearts, for their own conscience and
thoughts either accuse them or tell them they are doing right.

—ROMANS 2:15

God speaks to us through our conscience.
This may be a "still small voice" that will not let us go
until we do what we know is right . . .
we must never silence that inner voice—
[but] check what we think it is saying against the Scriptures.[1]

Conscience is the detective that watches the direction of our steps
and decries every conscious transgression.[2]

Conscience is a vigilant eye before which
each imagination, thought, and act
is held up for either censure or approval . . .
There is no greater proof of the existence of a moral
law and Lawgiver in the universe than this little light
of the soul. It is God's voice to the inner man.[3]

Do not be content to skim through a chapter [of the Bible] merely to satisfy your conscience. Hide the Word of God in your heart.[4]

God does communicate with those who are willing to obey Him.
He penetrates the dark silence with free,
life-giving discoveries in nature,
the human conscience, Scripture, and the Person of Jesus Christ.[5]

Conscience is our wisest counselor and teacher,
our most faithful and most patient friend.[6]

You will never know the peace with God,
peace of conscience, peace of mind,
and peace of soul until you stand at the foot of the cross
and identify yourself with Christ by faith . . . this is peace with God.[7]

Christ can rid you of inner conflict.
Man without God is always torn between two urges.
His nature prompts him to do wrong,
and his conscience urges him to do right.[8]

In your own mind-darkened, will-paralyzed, conscience-dulled soul,
God can make the light penetrate and turn the darkness
of your own life into day, if you will let Him.[9]

We've tried calling sin "errors" or "mistakes" or "poor judgment,"
but sin itself has stayed the same.
No matter how we try to salve our conscience,
we've known all along that men are still sinners;
and the results of sin are still disease, disappointment,
disillusionment, despair, and death.[10]

Conscience tells us in our innermost being of the presence of God
and of the moral difference between good and evil;
but this is a fragmentary message,
in no way as distinct and comprehensive as the lessons of the Bible.[11]

Many a criminal has finally given himself over to the authorities
because the accusations of a guilty conscience
were worse than prison bars.[12]

Dishonesty is never justified. God will never approve,
and even your own conscience will rise up
to condemn you sooner or later.[13]

The human conscience is often beyond the grasp of a psychiatrist . . .
Humans are helpless to detach themselves from the gnawing guilt
of a heart bowed down with the weight of sin.
But where humans have failed, God has succeeded.[14]

The human conscience is reliable only when
it is guided by the Holy Spirit.[15]

Some Christians have an elastic conscience
when it comes to their own foibles—
and an ironbound conscience when it comes to the foibles of others.[16]

Sin also affects the conscience,
until one becomes slow to detect the approach of sin.[17]

There are storms in your own life: storms of
temptation, confusion, and difficulty . . .
An uneasy conscience says, "Stop before it is too late!"[18]

As a person finds God's will for his or her life, matters of conscience
can be handled with perception from the Holy Spirit.[19]

From a cleansed conscience emerges a changed life.[20]

BILLY GRAHAM ON
CONVERSION

Repent therefore and be converted, that your sins may be blotted out,
so that times of refreshing may come from the presence of the Lord.

—ACTS 3:19 NKJV

The one and only choice by which you can be converted
is your choice to believe on the Lord Jesus Christ
as your own personal Lord and Savior.
The word "conversion" means simply "turning."[1]

In every true conversion the will of man comes into line
with the will of God.[2]

True conversion will involve the mind, the affection, and the will.
There have been thousands of people who have
been intellectually converted to Christ . . .
but they have never been really converted to Him.[3]

The converted person will love the good he once hated,
and hate the sin he once loved.[4]

To be a Christian is not a pious pose. It is not a long list of restrictions.
Christianity flings open the windows to the real joy of living.
Those who have been truly converted to Jesus Christ
know the meaning of abundant living.[5]

In order to get to heaven, Jesus said that you must be converted.
I didn't say it—Jesus said it![6]

Being a Christian is more than just an instantaneous conversion—
it is a daily process whereby I grow to be more and more like Christ.[7]

There are thousands of people who have had
some form of emotional experience
that they refer to as conversion
but who have never been truly converted to Christ.
Christ demands a change in the way you live—
and if your life does not conform to your experience,
then you have every reason to doubt your experience![8]

BILLY GRAHAM ON
CONVICTIONS

Holding fast the faithful word . . . that he might be able, by sound doctrine, both to exhort and convict those who contradict.

—TITUS 1:9 NKJV

[It] is well and good when our convictions are based upon the "Thou shalts" and the "Thou shalt nots" of Scripture rather than our own ideas.[1]

When comfort and ease and pleasure are put ahead of duty and conviction, progress is always set back.[2]

It is the Holy Spirit who brings about conviction [of sin] . . . repentance cannot take place unless first there is a movement of the Holy Spirit in the heart and mind.[3]

Man seeks to excuse himself of sin,
but God seeks to convict him of it and to save him from it.
Sin is no amusing toy—it is a terror to be shunned!
Learn, then, what constitutes sin in the eyes of God![4]

Anyone who has genuinely seen God
is deeply convicted of his or her own sin.[5]

The very ones whose social pressure cause you to compromise
will despise you for it. They probably respect your convictions,
and many of them wish they had the moral stamina to stand alone.
May the Lord give you added courage to be a witness for Him,
even in a hard place.[6]

God often gives us an inner conviction or prompting
to confirm which way He wants us to go.
This prompting comes from the Holy Spirit.[7]

BILLY GRAHAM ON
CREATION

The Word gave life to everything that was created.

—JOHN 1:4

———✦———

Look up on a starry night,
and you will see the majesty and power of an infinite Creator.[1]

———✦———

A professor at the University of Michigan said to me:
"As soon as we create life in a test tube, we won't need God anymore."
I answered: "This happened once before when man ruled God out
and proposed the Tower of Babel.
It ended in frustration, confusion, and judgment."[2]

———✦———

The Bible is the one book which reveals the Creator
to the creature He created!
No other book that man has conceived can make that statement
and support it with fact.[3]

Have we just been placed here by some unknown creator or force
without any clue as to where we came from, why we are here,
and where we are going? The answer is "no."
We do have a code. We do have a key . . . the Bible.[4]

The only one who can re-create us
is the One who created us in the first place.
If your watch were out of order, you wouldn't take it to a blacksmith.
If your car needed overhauling, you wouldn't go to a machine shop.
Our spiritual problems can be solved only by the God
who created us originally.[5]

As a Christian, I believe that we are all created in the image of God.
I believe that God loves the whole world . . .
The life of no human being is cheap in the eyes of God,
nor can it be in our own eyes.[6]

There is no conclusive scientific evidence that man is "up from the ape."
While the animals were created "after their kind," we are told that
"God created man in His own image" [Genesis 1:27 NKJV].[7]

There is no point of space, whether inside or
outside the bounds of creation,
where God is not present. That is why when we ask the question,
"Who's in control?" we can answer without equivocation, "God is!"[8]

Any theory of the universe that does not take into account
the God and Creator of the universe
is not worthy of serious consideration.[9]

God is the Ruler of His mighty creation. There is no reason to despair,
because He holds in His hands the whole world,
while His Spirit is able to fill the void in man's heart.[10]

[God] has in mind a picture of what He intends to create.
He breaks, cracks, chisels, and polishes until one day
there emerges His vision . . . God has not yet finished with us.[11]

BILLY GRAHAM ON
THE CROSS

*[God] canceled the record of the charges against us
and took it away by nailing it to the cross.*

—COLOSSIANS 2:14

———

The cross has become a symbol in much of the Western world,
misused by many rock stars and others
who do not comprehend its significance.[1]

———

Sin's masterpiece of shame and hate
became God's masterpiece of mercy and forgiveness.
Through the death of Christ upon the cross,
sin itself was crucified for those who believe in Him.[2]

———

One-third of Matthew . . . one-third of Mark . . . one-fourth of Luke,
and one-half of John are given to [Christ's] death . . .
Jesus came for the express purpose of dying for sinners.
When He left heaven, He knew He was going to the cross.[3]

———

Had Satan not set himself in opposition to God . . .
there would have been no need for God to send His Son to the cross.[4]

———•—•———

Sin was conquered on the cross.
[Christ's] death is the foundation of our hope,
the promise of our triumph![5]

———•—•———

Great crowds followed our Lord . . .
as He healed the sick, raised the dead, and fed the hungry.
However, the moment He started talking about the cross . . .
"many . . . no longer followed him" (John 6:66 NIV).[6]

———•—•———

Be willing to be sneered at than to be approved,
counting the cross of Christ greater riches than all the treasures of
Washington, London, Paris, or Moscow.[7]

———•—•———

Jesus was born with the cross darkening His pathway . . .
From the cradle to the cross, [Jesus'] purpose was to die.[8]

———•—•———

The cross shows the seriousness of our sin—
but it also shows us the immeasurable love of God.[9]

———•—•———

The cross is the only way of salvation.
And the cross gives a new purpose to life.[10]

———•—•———

The law enables us to see ourselves as morally
dirty and in need of cleansing.
But it also points us to the place of cleansing: the cross of Christ.[11]

Jesus Christ opened heaven's door for us by His death on the cross.[12]

If Jesus had not risen from the dead,
no right-minded person would have glorified anything so hideous
and repulsive as a cross stained with the blood of Jesus . . .
An unopened grave would never have opened heaven.[13]

God undertook the most dramatic rescue operation in cosmic history.
He determined to save the human race from self-destruction,
and He sent His Son Jesus Christ to salvage and redeem them.
The work of man's redemption was accomplished at the cross.[14]

The cross is the suffering love of God bearing the guilt of man's sin,
which alone is able to melt the sinner's heart
and bring him to repentance for salvation.
"For he hath made him to be sin for us" [2 Corinthians 5:21 KJV].[15]

The heart of the Christian Gospel with its incarnation
and atonement is in the cross and the resurrection.
Jesus was born to die.[16]

Why is it that the cross has become the symbol of Christianity?
It is because at the cross Jesus purchased our redemption
and provided a righteousness which we could not ourselves earn.[17]

It has been said there was a cross in the heart of God
long before the cross was erected at Calvary.
As we think about it we will be overwhelmed
at the wonder and greatness of His love for us.[18]

It was not the people or the Roman soldiers
who put [Jesus] on the cross—
it was your sins and my sins that made it necessary
for Him to volunteer his death.[19]

Two thousand years ago God invited a morally corrupt world
to the foot of the cross.
There God held your sins and mine to the flames
until every last vestige of our guilt was consumed.[20]

The ground is level at the foot of the cross.[21]

When Jesus hung on the cross,
a great unseen cosmic battle raged in the heavens—and in the end,
Christ triumphed over all the forces of evil and death and hell.[22]

Though the cross repels, it also attracts.
It possesses a magnetic quality.[23]

To take up your cross means to associate yourself with Christ
and to share His rejection.
It means you take a stand for Christ even though people
make fun of you, persecute you—or even kill you![24]

The greatest vision of sin that a person can
ever receive is to look at the cross.[25]

Once you have been to the cross, you will never be the same.[26]

BILLY GRAHAM ON
DEATH

He who hears My word and believes in Him who sent Me . . .
has passed from death into life.

—JOHN 5:24 NKJV

———◆———

All mankind is sitting on Death Row.
How we die or when is not the main issue,
but where [we] go after death.[1]

———◆———

Death is not a trip, but a destination.[2]

———◆———

Someone has said that death is not a period,
but a comma in the story of life.[3]

———◆———

I have talked to doctors and nurses who have
held the hands of dying people,
and they say there is often as much difference
between the death of a Christian and a non-Christian
as there is between heaven and hell.[4]

We now have the advantage of a few years more of life,
but death is still standing at the end of the road.[5]

From the moment a child is born, the death process,
and the fight against it, begins.[6]

Death for [a Christian] is no accident.
With God there are no accidents, no tragedies, and no catastrophes
as far as His children are concerned.[7]

Death for the Christian is the doorway to heaven's glory.
Because of Christ's resurrection we can joyously say with Paul,
"Where, O death, is your victory?" [1 Corinthians 15:55 NIV].[8]

Jesus Christ was the Master Realist when He urged men
to prepare for death, which was certain to come.
Do not worry, said the Lord Jesus, about the death of the body,
but rather concern yourself with the eternal death of the soul.[9]

Death is not the end of the road—
it is merely a gateway to eternal life beyond the grave.[10]

For the Christian, death can be faced realistically and with victory,
because he knows "that neither death nor life . . .
shall be able to separate us from the love of
God" [Romans 8:38–39 NKJV].[11]

Throughout our culture we have been led to the idea
that we accept death as the end of life on earth . . .
Time bound as we are and goal oriented to achievements in our lifetime,
we find it strange to anticipate heaven.[12]

Sooner or later, we are going to face death;
should we be making preparations while we are living?[13]

If people paid more attention to death, eternity, and judgment,
there would be more holy living on earth.[14]

Death is said in the Bible to be a coronation for the Christian.[15]

It is strange that men will prepare for everything except death.
We prepare for education. We prepare for business.
We prepare for our careers. We prepare for marriage.
We prepare for old age.
We prepare for everything except the moment we are to die.[16]

Death reduces all men to the same rank.
It strips the rich of his millions and the poor man of his rags . . .
Death knows no age limits, no partiality. It is a thing that all men fear.[17]

One of the primary goals in life should be to prepare for death.
Everything else should be secondary.[18]

No matter how much you exercise, no matter how many
vitamins or health foods you eat, no matter how low
your cholesterol, you will still die—someday.
If you knew the moment and manner of your death in advance,
would you order your life differently?[19]

The word *departure* literally means to pull up anchor and set sail.
Everything that happens prior to death is a
preparation for the final voyage.
Death marks the beginning, not the end. It is our journey to God.[20]

When we all reach the end of our earthly
journey, we will have just begun.[21]

Though the Christian has no immunity from death and no claim to
perpetual life on this planet, death is to him a friend rather than a foe,
the beginning rather than the end,
another step on the pathway to heaven
rather than a leap into a dark unknown.[22]

The word *decease* literally means "exodus" or "going out."
The imagery is that of the children of Israel leaving Egypt
and their former life of bondage, slavery, and hardship for the
Promised Land. So death to the Christian is an exodus from
the limitations, the burdens, and the bondage of this life.[23]

Many people say they do not fear death, but the process of dying. It's not the destination, but the trip that they dread.[24]

Life and death is not a do-it-yourself project.[25]

Death is not the end of life; it is only the gateway to eternity.[26]

Christ did not die by accident. He died voluntarily in our place.[27]

Someday this life will end, but for the Christian death also marks a beginning—the beginning of a new life with God that will last forever.[28]

I'm not afraid to die, for I know the joys of heaven are waiting. My greatest desire is to live today in anticipation of tomorrow and be ready to be welcomed into His home for all eternity. Will you be making the journey with me?[29]

Death carries with it a certain dread.
It [is] the enemy, the great, mysterious monster
that makes people quake with fear.[30]

Someday a loving Hand will be laid upon your shoulder
and this brief message will be given:
"Come home."[31]

Death of the righteous . . . is not to be feared or shunned.
It is the shadowed threshold to the palace of God.[32]

Someday you will read or hear that Billy Graham is dead.
Don't you believe a word of it! I shall be more alive than I am now.
I will just have changed my address.
I will have gone into the presence of God.[33]

BILLY GRAHAM ON
DECEPTION

Jesus answered ... "Take heed that no one deceives you. For many will come in My name, saying, 'I am the Christ,' and will deceive many."

—MATTHEW 24:4–5 NKJV

The underlying principle of all Satan's tactics is deception.
He is a crafty and clever camouflager.[1]

Satan's method has often been to imitate God.
Satan is still using this form of deception,
and often his representatives are being
disguised as ministers of righteousness.[2]

For Satan's deceptions to be successful, they
must be so cunningly devised
that his real purpose is concealed by wiles.[3]

We see ourselves as self-sufficient, self-important, and self-sustaining.
God sees us as dependent, self-centered, and self-deceived.[4]

Thousands of uninstructed Christians are being deceived today.
False teachers use high-sounding words
that seem like the epitome of scholarship and culture.
They are intellectually clever and crafty . . .
adept at beguiling thoughtless, untaught men and women.[5]

There is a great counterfeiter who adapts himself to every culture,
even deceiving true believers at times.
He doesn't charge on the scene clothed in
red and wearing a hideous mask
but charms his way as an "angel of light."
This is how Satan operates.[6]

Believers need the gift of discernment,
or at least respect for the opinions of those who have it . . .
believers are to test the various spirits and doctrines that abound.
Most of all we are to test them against the
standard of the Word of God.[7]

Our culture will stand in roaring ovations for the illusionists,
escape artists, and magicians. Deception is
everything opposite the truth.[8]

It is important to realize that a person with the gift of discernment
can often tell the difference between what is of God and what is not.
Such a person can often point out false teachings or false teachers—
he has an almost uncanny ability to perceive
hypocrisy, shallowness, deceit, or phoniness.[9]

BILLY GRAHAM ON
DECISION

Decisions must be based on [God's] regulations.

—EZEKIEL 44:24

<hr>

By faith I accepted Him for what He claimed
to be, the Son of the Living God.
That simple decision changed my life—
and I have seen it change the lives of countless others across the world.[1]

<hr>

When my decision for Christ was made . . . I knelt in prayer.
I opened my heart and knew for the first time
the sweetness and joy of God, of truly being born again . . .
I knew in my heart that I was somehow different and changed.
That night absolutely changed the direction of my life.[2]

<hr>

Deep down inside I knew something was different . . .
I wanted to tell others what had happened to me. I didn't have any tears,
I didn't have any emotion, I didn't hear any thunder,
there was no lightning . . . but . . . I made my decision for Christ.[3]

You need to make the right decision—firmly and decisively—
and then stick with it with God's help.[4]

The journey God has set before us isn't a freeway;
we are constantly encountering forks and junctions and crossroads.
Which way will we go when we meet them?
Life is filled with decisions, and we can't avoid them.[5]

Jesus does not allow us to be neutral about Him.
Jesus demands that we decide about Him.[6]

God has a plan and the devil has a plan,
and you will have to decide which plan you are going to fit into.[7]

Men and women do make decisions wherever the Gospel is proclaimed;
whether publicly or privately,
some say yes, some say no, and some procrastinate.
No one ever hears the Gospel proclaimed
without making some kind of decision![8]

When disappointment or tragedy or suffering
strikes, we have a decision to make:
Will we turn away from God, or will we turn toward Him?
Which road will we take?
One road leads to doubt, anger, bitterness,
fear, hopelessness, and despair.
The other leads to hope, comfort, peace, strength, and joy.[9]

When we are called before God and His throne of judgment,
it will be too late to reverse our decision.
It is during our lifetime here on earth that
we decide our eternal destiny.[10]

Becoming "new" in Christ is a wonderful beginning,
but it isn't the end of pain or problems in our lives.
It is the beginning of our facing up to them.
Being a Christian involves a lifetime of hard work, dedicated study,
and difficult decisions.[11]

Part of the human makeup which distinguishes
man from other creatures
is his ability to reason and make moral
decisions. Man is a free moral agent.[12]

Once God leads you to make a decision, don't draw back.
Instead, trust His leading, and believe He goes before you—
because He does.[13]

The most important decision you will ever make
is the decision you make about eternity.[14]

BILLY GRAHAM ON
THE DEVIL/SATAN

The seed is the word of God...
the devil comes and takes away the word out of their hearts.

—LUKE 8:11–12 NKJV

The same Book that tells us over and over again of God's love warns
us constantly of the devil who would come between us and God,
the devil who is ever waiting to ensnare men's souls.[1]

The devil is the god of this world and he has blinded our eyes.[2]

Satan wants to lure us into his traps,
and he knows exactly what kind of "bait" will appeal to us.
He knows what we're like, and he will attack us
exactly where we are the weakest.[3]

Satan will do everything he can to divide
Christians and destroy our witness.
Only the Holy Spirit can subdue our old nature and
overcome it with God's love.[4]

Don't give Satan a foothold, but discipline yourself to stay close to God.
He alone is your security.[5]

Satan rejoices when old habits overwhelm [us]
and we cave in to the pressure of the crowd . . .
perhaps temptation lures [us] into sin . . .
a backsliding Christian compromises their faith
and causes unbelievers to mock the Gospel.[6]

Don't be deceived by Satan and his lies.
Instead, stay close to Christ—because the closer you are to Him,
the farther away you are from the devil.[7]

The devil and his demons really do believe
in God—and why wouldn't they?
They understand that they are engaged
in a cosmic battle of titanic proportions,
and they know they are up against the Creator of the universe—
a truth that makes them shudder. There are no atheists in hell![8]

When our minds are on Christ, Satan has little room to maneuver.[9]

The greatest roadblock to Satan's work is the
Christian who, above all else,
lives for God, walks with integrity, is filled with the Spirit,
and is obedient to God's truth.[10]

The greatest hindrance to Satan's destructive efforts
is our standing strong in the knowledge and fear of the Lord.[11]

Satan rejoices when we are inconsistent, because he knows
that an inconsistent Christian is an ineffective Christian—or worse.[12]

We constantly pass up the rich and beautiful and ennobling
experiences and seek out the tawdry, the cheap, and the degrading.
These are the works of the devil, and they flourish on every side![13]

The devil is a master at making us question God and His Word.
Twisting Scripture . . . taking a verse out of context . . .
deceiving us into thinking God is mean-spirited—
these are some of Satan's favorite tricks.[14]

Satan does not care how much you theorize about Christianity
or how much you profess to know Christ.
What he opposes vigorously is the way you live Christ.[15]

We must be constantly aware that Satan can take
any human effort and twist it to serve his own purposes.[16]

———◆———

Only God can thwart the plans of Satan and his legions.[17]

———◆———

If you are not careful you will find yourself actually in the employ
of the devil. He is powerful, slick, crafty, wily, and subtle.[18]

———◆———

One of the devil's methods is to attack everyone . . . He knows that
the Word of God is powerful, and he will try to keep you from it.[19]

———◆———

When we are filled with the Spirit of God, obeying God,
in His will and quoting Scripture, Satan will be defeated.[20]

———◆———

Jesus did not dispute [Satan] . . . our Lord quoted Scripture,
and that's one thing the devil can't stand!
The Scripture defeats him every time.[21]

———◆———

You cannot argue with [Satan], for he is the greatest debater of all time.[22]

———◆———

We are living in a topsy-turvy world, where all is confusion.
But you may be sure that it is confusion with a plan—Satan's plan![23]

———◆———

Satan is the master of the ultimate double-talk and sophistry.
He calls evil good and continues to confuse men
with his cleverly disguised untruths.[24]

Never forget: Satan's goal is to turn us away from God.[25]

Satan is masterful at using just enough of God's truth to capture
a person's attention and then mix it with his devious potion
that will lead [believers] astray.[26]

Satan is both a fashion designer and an interior designer.
He first appeals to the eye and then shouts, "Gotcha!"
Then he goes to work on the "inside job."[27]

The architect of popular culture is none other than Satan. He is
the chief designer and chief marketer, and he has been branding
worldliness since the beginning of time. His methods are shifty and
constantly in motion, changing fads and trends to keep the world
running in circles, trying to keep up with the latest and greatest.[28]

If you don't take your stand for Christ,
you will be on the wrong side, and someday when it is too late,
you'll cry out, "I've taken the wrong stand!"
You'll be in the devil's trap! You can't lick the devil.[29]

If your heart is not attuned to God, it will become
a catch basin for every device of the devil.
Yes, Satan is at work in our world. The Bible is my authority.[30]

Satan is real and is opposed to everything God is doing.[31]

———•◆•———

The cross was designed to defeat Satan,
who by deception had obtained squatters'
rights to the title of the earth.[32]

———•◆•———

Satan didn't lose any of his beguiling ways
when he became the fallen prince.
He took his charm, his subtleties, and his clever plots to use on us.[33]

———•◆•———

Satan exalted himself above God and endeavored to get man
to doubt the reliability of God's Word.[34]

———•◆•———

The devil is alive and kicking. But if you are in Christ
and follow the rules of daily Bible study, prayer, and witnessing,
he has no power over you.[35]

———•◆•———

Satan perverts everything good
by mimicking and mocking the real thing.[36]

———•◆•———

Satan is the illusive manipulator. He prances and dances and drinks
in the adulation of his worshippers as he glimmers and shimmers,
displaying all that glitters and all that attracts the shallowness of man.[37]

———•◆•———

[Satan] will create a religion without a Redeemer.
He will build a church without a Christ.
He will call for worship without the Word of God.[38]

———✦———

Your eyes should never be lent to the devil; they belong to God.
Be careful how you use your eyes![39]

———✦———

The mind is the devil's favorite avenue of attack.[40]

———✦———

I have yet to see Satan overcome a truly joyful Christian.[41]

———✦———

Before Satan there was no sin, and before sin there was no pain.[42]

———✦———

Since the Bible is God's Word,
we shouldn't be surprised if Satan tries to convince us otherwise.[43]

———✦———

Man cannot control himself, and if he will not be controlled
by Jesus Christ, then he will be controlled by Satan.[44]

———✦———

Never forget: Death was Satan's greatest victory.[45]

———✦———

Satan will thrash about in one last burst of evil,
hoping to capture as many souls as possible before his inevitable end.[46]

———✦———

The Bible teaches that Satan is the author of sin.
Sin is the reason we have afflictions, including death.
All of our problems and our suffering are a result of man's rebellion
against God. But God has provided a rescue in His Son.[47]

BILLY GRAHAM ON
DISAPPOINTMENT

This is contained in Scripture . . .
"He who believes in Him will not be disappointed."

—1 PETER 2:6 NASB

———⬥———

The time to prepare for life's disappointments and hurts is in advance.[1]

———⬥———

Don't let failure or disappointment cut you off from God
or make you think the future is hopeless.
When God closes one door, He often opens another—if we seek it.[2]

———⬥———

Don't be bound by the past and its failures.
But don't forget its lessons either.[3]

———⬥———

Many of the mysteries of God—the heartaches,
trials, disappointments, tragedies,
and the silence of God in the midst of suffering—
will be revealed in heaven.[4]

—◆—

Learn from your disappointments and failures
and with God's help seek to overcome them.
Ask yourself, could I have done anything to prevent this?
Were my hopes and dreams unrealistic, or were my motives wrong?
Is there a new path God wants me to explore?[5]

—◆—

Disappointments are part of life; we can't always have our own
way, and we need to learn to separate what is significant from
what is merely annoying. Only in heaven will we be free of all
disappointments and failures. A friend of mine says, "Oh well,
a hundred years from now it won't make any difference!"[6]

—◆—

We do not fail to enjoy the fruit of the Spirit
because we live in a sea of corruption;
we fail to do so because the sea of corruption is in us.[7]

—◆—

Pride is associated with failure, not success.
We hear a great deal about the inferiority complex,
but the superiority complex of pride is seldom spoken of . . .
The greatest act of humility . . .
was when Jesus Christ stooped to die on the cross of Calvary.[8]

—◆—

I long to see [Jesus] face to face, to hear His voice and touch Him.
In the day I go to be with Him, there will be no unfulfilled longings
or disappointments. He will welcome me into His mansion,
answer my questions, and teach me the wisdom of the ages.[9]

———⊰•⊱———

Repeated disappointment almost always triggers a series of other reactions: discouragement, anger, frustration, bitterness, resentment, even depression. Unless we learn to deal with disappointment, it will rob us of joy and poison our souls.[10]

———⊰•⊱———

If we who have the Holy Spirit living and
working within us falter and fail,
what hope is there for the rest of the world?[11]

———⊰•⊱———

[While] disappointment and failure aren't
identical, they often occur together,
and both can hold us back from God's best for our lives.[12]

———⊰•⊱———

Disappointment and failure are not signs that God has forsaken you or stopped loving you. The devil wants you to believe God no longer loves you, but it isn't true. God's love for us never fails.[13]

BILLY GRAHAM ON
DISCIPLESHIP
AND DISCIPLINE

If you abide in My word, you are My disciples indeed.

—JOHN 8:31 NKJV

<hr>

It is no accident that the words *discipline* and *disciple*
resemble each other in the English language.
The most common word in the Gospels for a Christian is *disciple*.[1]

<hr>

Christ never told his disciples that they would get an Academy Award
for their performances, but He did tell them to expect to have troubles.[2]

<hr>

Jesus Christ spoke frankly to His disciples concerning the future . . .
In unmistakable language He told them that discipleship means
a life of self-denial, and the bearing of a cross.[3]

———

Exercise and proper eating habits are very important,
since the Bible says that the body is God's holy temple,
but I don't think that superbodies equate with
committed Christian discipleship.
Some of the greatest saints I've known have
been those with physical infirmities.[4]

———

Many Christians want the benefits of their belief,
but they hesitate at the cost of discipleship.[5]

———

To be a disciple of Jesus means to learn from Him, to follow Him.
The cost may be high.[6]

———

God does not discipline us to subdue us
but to condition us for a life of usefulness and blessedness.
In His wisdom, He knows that an uncontrolled life is an unhappy life,
so He puts reins on our wayward souls
that they may be directed into the paths of righteousness.[7]

———

Our minds must be set always to seek the will of the Lord.
Following the progressive discipline revealed through the Bible
will result in a walk of obedience to God.[8]

———

To be a disciple is to be committed to Jesus Christ as Savior and Lord
and committed to following Him every day.
To be a disciple is also to be disciplined in our bodies, minds, and souls.[9]

Let us always remember that Christ calls men and women
not only to trust Him as Savior, but also to follow Him as Lord.
That call to discipleship must be part of our
message if we are to be faithful to Him.[10]

We are commissioned to make disciples,
to bring them into the same direct relationship with Christ
as those who left their nets and their fishing boats
to become "fishers of men."[11]

BILLY GRAHAM ON
ENCOURAGEMENT

Encourage me by your word.

—PSALM 119:28

———

The Bible teaches us to be more concerned
about the needs and feelings of others than our own.
We are to encourage and build self-confidence in our
loved ones, friends, and associates.[1]

———

We never gain in life by hurting others.
Sometimes we try to elevate our own insecure egos
by degrading and belittling those around us.
Yet this produces only a false sense of self-esteem.[2]

———

All around you are people whose lives are filled with trouble and sorrow,
and they need your compassion and encouragement.[3]

———

With an old head and a young heart,
you can be a source of real strength
[to others] who need your cheer and encouragement.[4]

———•••———

[The Holy Spirit] will remain with every believer right to the end.
This thought has encouraged me a thousand times
in these dark days when satanic forces are at work.[5]

———•••———

Sometimes we encourage someone without even being aware of it.
Even the example we set by attending church
may encourage someone who is searching for God.[6]

———•••———

How often do we lie simply because we are trying
to build ourselves up in the eyes of others?
How often do we gossip because we want to appear "in the know,"
or because we are trying to make ourselves
appear better than someone else?
The Bible's command is clear: ["Have regard for good things
in the sight of all men" (Romans 12:17 NKJV)].[7]

———•••———

Renewal is brought by the Holy Spirit.
Believers will learn what it means to minister to
one another and build each other up.
No longer will our lives seem ordinary and indistinguishable
from the rest of the world.[8]

BILLY GRAHAM ON
END TIMES

Write down these words . . . They will stand
until the end of time as a witness.

—ISAIAH 30:8

———⟡———

The Bible tells us that the state of the world will grow darker
as we near the end of the age.[1]

———⟡———

The book of Revelation may be difficult and demanding to read,
yet it is the only biblical book whose author promises
a blessing to those who read it.[2]

———⟡———

Revelation is a pastor's letter to his floundering flock,
an urgent telegram bearing a brilliant battle plan for a people at war.[3]

———⟡———

The end will come with the return of Jesus Christ . . .
That is why a Christian can be an optimist.
That is why a Christian can smile in the
midst of all that is happening . . .
We know what the end will be: the triumph of the Lord Jesus Christ![4]

I have become more deeply aware of the enormous problems that
face our world today, and the dangerous trends which seem to be
leading our world to the brink of Armageddon.[5]

When the "evil day" comes,
we do not have to be dependent upon the circumstances around us,
but rather on the resources of God![6]

We see the storm clouds gathering and events taking place
that herald the second coming of Jesus Christ.[7]

[Jesus Christ] is the Lord of history. Nothing is taking God by surprise.
Events are moving rapidly toward some sort of climax . . .
when His Son, Jesus Christ, returns to be rightful Ruler of the world.[8]

In the end there will be people who did the work of the Lord.
They were busy in the church. They had done many wonderful works.
But Jesus Himself says, "I never knew you" [Matthew 7:23 NKJV].[9]

We are like a people under [a] sentence of death,
waiting for the date to be set.
We sense that something is about to happen.
We know that things cannot go on as they are.
History has reached an impasse. We are now on a collision course.
Something is about to give.[10]

History is going somewhere.
And we know full well that He who does all things well will bring
beauty from the ashes of world chaos. A new world is being born.
A new social order will emerge when Christ comes back.
A fabulous future is on the way.[11]

The second coming of Christ will be so revolutionary that it will change
every aspect of life on this planet. Christ will reign in righteousness.
Disease will be arrested. Death will be modified.
War will be abolished. Nature will be changed.
Man will live as it was originally intended he should live.[12]

The world is heading for another major crisis that is being called,
even by the secular world, "Armageddon."[13]

We are told in Scripture that there will be signs
pointing toward the return of the Lord.
I believe that we see those signs in the world today.
I believe that the coming of the Lord is near.[14]

Bible teaching about the Second Coming of Christ was thought of
as "doomsday" preaching. But not anymore. It is the only ray of hope
that shines as an ever brightening beam in a darkening world.[15]

I believe that this world, as we know it, will come to an end . . .
This is not fanciful imagination
but the clear and repeated testimony of the Bible.[16]

What a moment to take the newspaper in one hand and the Bible in the other and watch the unfolding of the great drama of the ages. This is an exciting and thrilling time to be alive. I would not want to live in any other period.[17]

The Apocalypse . . . a storm warning that carries a booming jolt of truth—TROUBLE AHEAD; PREPARE TO MEET THY GOD!— followed by the voice of the Gentle Shepherd—COME![18]

The study [of Revelation] instructs us not only about the storms to come, but how to endure and come through them with great victory.[19]

A new world is coming . . . The paradise that man lost will be regained . . . One day we will live in a brand-new world.[20]

We can't go on much longer morally. We can't go on much longer scientifically. The technology that was supposed to save us is ready to destroy us. New weapons are being made all the time, including chemical and biological weapons. Today the only bright spot on the horizon of this world is the promise of the coming again of Christ.[21]

I have read the last page of the Bible. It is all going to turn out all right.[22]

BILLY GRAHAM ON
ETERNITY

Your new life will last forever
because it comes from the eternal, living word of God.

—I PETER 1:23

Life is just a schoolroom with a glorious opportunity
to prepare us for eternity.[1]

Most people are living for today with barely a thought of eternity.[2]

What you do with Christ here and now
decides where you shall spend eternity.[3]

We are so caught up with the affairs of this life
we give little attention to eternity.[4]

How do we prepare for that last day? Before we embark on our final trip,
have we left an earthly home in a state of chaos or a condition of order?[5]

[Multitudes] have never been born again.
They will go into eternity lost—while thinking they are saved
because they belong to the church, or were baptized.[6]

A Christian funeral should be a coronation ceremony,
a statement to the world about eternal life.[7]

Where will we spend eternity—
with God in that place of endless joy the Bible calls heaven,
or apart from Him in that place of endless despair the Bible calls hell?[8]

Heaven is real and hell is real, and eternity is but a breath away.[9]

God can use the fear that grips the hearts of men
today to point them to eternal truths—
the truth of God's eternal judgment, and the truth of His eternal love.[10]

Jesus taught that there is an eternal destiny for each
individual—either heaven or hell (John 5:25–29).
The eternal destiny of each individual depends on a decision made
in this life (Luke 16:19–31)—to be followed by a life of obedience.[11]

BILLY GRAHAM ON
EVANGELISM

Preach the word! Be ready in season and out of season . . .
Do the work of an evangelist.

—2 TIMOTHY 4:2, 5 NKJV

❖

An evangelist is like a newscaster on television
or a journalist writing for a newspaper . . .
except that the evangelist's mission is
to tell the Good News that never changes.[1]

❖

During all my years as an evangelist,
my message has always been the Gospel of Christ.
It is not a Western religion,
nor is it a message of one culture or political system . . .
it is a message of life and hope for all the world.[2]

❖

God called me many years ago to be an evangelist,
and I have never regretted His leading. I love the crusades,
meeting people from every country and culture all over the world.
My life has been blessed by friends from every land,
and challenges from every corner.[3]

Itinerant evangelists are the most important
ambassadors and messengers on earth.
They are a mighty army, spreading out across the world
with a vision to reach their own people for Christ.[4]

Some evangelists spend too much time thinking
and even planning about how to achieve visible results.
This is an easy trap to fall into.[5]

Nowhere do the Scriptures tell us to seek results,
nor do the Scriptures rebuke evangelists if the results are meager.[6]

The evangelist cannot bring conviction of sin, righteousness,
or judgment; that is the Spirit's work.
They cannot convert anyone; that is the Spirit's work.[7]

Evangelism is not a calling reserved exclusively for the clergy.
I believe one of the greatest priorities of the church today
is to mobilize the laity to do the work of evangelism.[8]

Philip is the only person in the Bible who was called an evangelist,
and he was a deacon![9]

He who is called to and set apart for the work of an evangelist is to
devote his time and effort single-mindedly to this God-given task.
He is not to be distracted by anything likely to deflect him from this.
Persecution will not weaken his resolution.
The persuasion of others will fall on deaf ears.
Only the clear leading of God will cause him to change his ministry.[10]

No clergyman however brilliant,
no evangelist no matter how eloquent or compelling,
can bring about the revival we need. Only the Holy Spirit can do this.[11]

The evangelistic ministry is a fight, not a frolic.[12]

The great crowds themselves are meaningless. The thing that counts is
what happens in the hearts of the people. The evangelist sows the seed,
and much inevitably falls upon stony ground and bears no fruit.
But if only a few seeds flourish, the results are manifold.[13]

Evangelism has always been the heartbeat for our ministry;
it is what God has called us to do.[14]

Evangelism is more than simply encouraging decisions for Christ.
It is urging people to become disciples—followers—of Jesus Christ.
As such, the evangelist has a responsibility to make growth in
discipleship possible for those who come to faith under his ministry.[15]

BILLY GRAHAM ON
EVIL

I have restrained my feet from every evil way, that I may keep Your word.

—PSALM 119:101 NKJV

———◆◆◆———

Evil and suffering are real . . . They aren't an illusion,
nor are they simply an absence of good.
We are fallen creatures living in a fallen world that has been
twisted and corrupted by sin, and we all share in its brokenness.
Most of all, we share in its tragic legacy of disease and death.[1]

———◆◆◆———

Evil is real—but so is God's power and love.[2]

———◆◆◆———

Guard your tongue, and use it for good instead of evil. How many
marriages or friendships have been destroyed because of criticism
that spiraled out of control? How many relationships have broken
down because of a word spoken thoughtlessly or in anger?
A harsh word can't be taken back; no apology
can fully repair its damage.[3]

———◆◆◆———

Revenge easily descends into an endless cycle of hate and violence.
The Bible says never repay evil with evil.[4]

———◆———

You cannot pray for someone and hate them at the same time.
Even if you are asking God to restrain their evil actions,
you should also be praying that He will change their hearts.
Only eternity will reveal the impact of our prayers for others.[5]

———◆———

Evil is present to cleverly disguise itself as good.
Evil is present to control and deceive us.[6]

———◆———

When the Christian or the church becomes popular
with the unbelieving world, something is seriously wrong.
Because Christ runs counter to evil and
because we are Christ-owned, we must also stand against evil.[7]

———◆———

If God were to eradicate all evil from this planet,
He would have to eradicate all evil men. Who would be exempt?
"For all have sinned and fall short of the
glory of God" [Romans 3:23 NIV].
God would rather transform the evil man than eradicate him.[8]

———◆———

Every manifestation of evil is the result of basic sin—sin that has
remained unchanged since the moment it first entered the human race.[9]

———◆———

I believe a Christian can sin, but he does not have to.
God never would have told us to reject evil acts if in point of fact
we could not help but do them.[10]

[Christ's] goodness is still a rebuke to our badness;
His purity still shows up our impurities;
His sinlessness still reveals our sinfulness;
and unless we allow [Jesus] to destroy the evil within us,
the evil within us still wants to destroy Him.
This is the conflict of the ages.[11]

BILLY GRAHAM ON
FAITH

So then faith comes by hearing, and hearing by the word of God.

—ROMANS 10:17 NKJV

❦

Faith literally means "to give up, surrender, or commit."
Faith is complete confidence.[1]

❦

Faith in Christ is voluntary.
A person cannot be coerced, bribed, or tricked into trusting Jesus.
God will not force His way into your life.
The Holy Spirit will do everything possible to disturb you, draw you,
love you—but finally it is your personal decision.[2]

❦

The Bible lists in Hebrews 11 the heroes of the faith . . .
who were tortured, imprisoned, stoned, torn
apart, and killed by the sword.
They didn't wear designer jeans but went about in animal skins,
destitute and tormented.[3]

133

There is no room for God's Word in our culture,
where our children are without reverence for God or faith in the Bible.
There is no room for our Lord's creed of purity and self-denial
when the media sends forth a constant barrage of
profanity and indecency and materialism.[4]

Discouragement is the opposite of faith.
It is Satan's device to thwart the work of God in your life.[5]

Do you want your faith to grow?
Then let the Bible begin to saturate your mind and soul.[6]

[The] inability to comprehend fully the mysteries of God does not in any
way curtail the Christian faith. On the contrary, it enhances our belief.
We do not understand the intricate pattern of the stars in their courses,
but we know that He who created them does,
and that just as surely as He guides them,
He is charting a safe course for us.[7]

The Bible teaches that faith will manifest itself in three ways.
It will manifest itself in doctrine—in what you believe.
It will manifest itself in worship—your communion with God . . .
It will manifest itself in morality—in the way you live and behave.[8]

Christians who are strong in the faith grow
as they accept whatever God allows to enter their lives.[9]

I have never been to the North Pole, and yet
I believe there is a North Pole.
How do I know? I know because somebody told me.
I read about it in a history book, I saw a map in a geography book,
and I believe the men who wrote those books. I accept it by faith.
The Bible says, "Faith cometh by hearing, and hearing
by the word of God" [Romans 10:17 KJV].[10]

Our faith can stand up to any question, but sometimes people ask
questions—and keep asking questions—just to avoid facing their
own spiritual needs and acknowledging who Jesus really is.[11]

Don't forget: Without fuel, a fire grows cold—and without the "fuel"
of the Bible, prayer, and Christian fellowship, our faith grows cold.[12]

The Bible teaches that faith is the only approach that we have to God.
No man has sins forgiven, no man goes to heaven,
no man has assurance of peace and happiness,
until he has faith in Jesus Christ.[13]

Fear can banish faith, but faith can banish fear.[14]

Faith isn't pretending our problems don't exist,
nor is it simply blind optimism.
Faith points us beyond our problems to the hope we have in Christ.[15]

Fear can paralyze us and keep us
from believing God and stepping out in faith.
The devil loves a fearful Christian![16]

If our faith isn't rooted in the Bible,
it will wither like a plant pulled out of the soil.[17]

When our faith becomes nothing more than
a series of rules and regulations,
joy flees and our love for Christ grows cold.[18]

Faith implies four things: self-renunciation, reliance with utter
confidence on Christ, obedience, and a changed life.[19]

Your faith may be just a little thread.
It may be small and weak, but act on that faith.
It does not matter how big your faith is,
but rather, where your faith is.[20]

God—the Bible's Author—loves you and wants you to be
His child through faith in Jesus Christ.[21]

Faith is loved and honored by God more than any other single thing.[22]

BILLY GRAHAM ON
FAMILY

Listen to the word of the LORD . . . all you families.

—JEREMIAH 2:4

No subject is closer to my heart than the family . . .
The moral foundation of our country is in danger of crumbling
as families break up and parents neglect their responsibilities.[1]

When the family is destroyed, society eventually disintegrates.[2]

More friction and tensions are caused in a family by tone of voice
than for any other one reason.[3]

Many times it takes just one member of a family to initiate the action
to bring a family back together again.[4]

There is something wrong when a brother or sister becomes alienated
from the rest of their family, so there is something wrong when
Christians refuse to have anything to do with their fellow Christians.
God wants us to live this Christian life together.[5]

Your own family circle knows whether Christ
lives in you and through you.[6]

We need to place God at the center of our family . . .
As a family, we need to walk with God daily.[7]

One result of family failure has been the loss of dignity.
No better example can be found than in the use of language.
[Language has been reduced to] a four-letter
word in movies, on television,
in comedy routines, and in real life.[8]

A Christian has tremendous responsibilities to his own family.
He or she has a responsibility of loving each member of the family.[9]

If people stumble, we help them get back on their feet;
if they veer off course, we urge them back.
On this journey we are all brothers and sisters in
the same family—the family of God.[10]

It is only the strong Christian family unit
that can survive the coming world holocaust.[11]

Rebellion, waywardness, lack of discipline, confusion,
and conflict prevent happy relationships within the home.
But God is interested in your family, your marriage, your children.
He shows us the ideals and the goals for the family.[12]

———◆———

God knew that children grow and mature best in a stable, loving family,
and this was one reason He gave marriage to us.[13]

———◆———

We have exchanged love of family and home for cyberfriends and
living in constant motion that robs the soul from memories—
and perhaps from that still, small voice that longs to be heard.[14]

———◆———

Not only does God give us a new relationship with Himself
and make us citizens of His kingdom,
but He also gives us a new family—the family of God.[15]

———◆———

The Bible says a great deal about entire families coming to Christ.
Rahab the harlot . . . the Philippian jailer . . .
and Cornelius, the Roman centurion.
That could be true in your family too.
You may be the one who could lead your family to Christ.[16]

———◆———

Amazing things can happen when the family of God bands together.[17]

BILLY GRAHAM ON
FOLLOWERS

I used to wander off until you disciplined me;
but now I closely follow your word.

—PSALM 119:67

————◆————

Jesus Himself was the first missionary . . .
He pledged His followers to be missionaries too![1]

————◆————

The happiest people I know are separated followers of Jesus Christ.
They are not dependent on artificial stimulants.
They do not resort to sick, dirty jokes.
They do not abuse their bodies to relax their minds.[2]

————◆————

God's followers need to know the truth He sets forth in His Word
so that we can confidently discern between His truth and Satan's lies.[3]

————◆————

As long as Satan is loose in the world and our hearts
are dominated by his evil passions,
it will never be easy or popular to be a follower of Christ.[4]

We have seen moral and religious leaders,
men who claim to be followers of Jesus,
fall into disgrace in the eyes of God and man, and worst of all
we have seen the Gospel of Jesus Christ and twisted and distorted it
by false teachers to accommodate the destructive
morals and secular behavior of these times.[5]

Salvation is free, but there is a price to pay in following Jesus.
It is never said in Scripture that we can have "Christ and . . .".
It is always "Christ or . . .". What is your "or"?[6]

In John 6 we read that when great multitudes went after Him,
He told them three times that unless they were willing to pay the price,
they could not be His followers.[7]

If [Christian leaders] do not teach Christian
principles to all followers of Christ,
we are not equipping them with God's truth that will
overcome worldly influence.[8]

[Christians] are called to distinguish themselves as Christ followers,
not community organizers.[9]

Christ warned His followers that to believe in Him
would not make them popular,
and that they should be prepared to face affliction for His sake.[10]

———◆———

[Jesus] asked [His followers] to count the cost carefully,
lest they should turn back when they met with suffering and privation.
He told His followers that the world would hate them.[11]

———◆———

Following Christ has been made too easy.
It is easy to follow Him when our world is safe and comfortable . . .
but when that world shatters, only a secure faith will sustain us.[12]

———◆———

Learn to keep close to [Jesus], to listen to His voice, and follow Him.[13]

———◆———

By faith in [Jesus] we can be forgiven of our sins
and know the joy of following Him every day.[14]

———◆———

The men who followed Jesus were unique in their generation.
They turned the world upside down
because their hearts had been turned right side up.[15]

BILLY GRAHAM ON
FORGIVENESS

Jesus said, "Father, forgive them,
for they do not know what they are doing."

—LUKE 23:34 NIV

———

God's forgiveness is not just a casual statement; it is the complete
blotting out of all dirt and degradation of our past, present, and future.[1]

———

Forgiveness does not come easily to us, especially when someone we
have trusted betrays our trust. And yet if we do not learn to forgive,
we will discover that we can never really rebuild trust.[2]

———

In one bold stroke, forgiveness obliterates the past
and permits us to enter the land of new beginnings.[3]

———

Guilt is not all bad. Without it there is nothing to drive a person
toward self-examination and toward God for forgiveness.[4]

———

Repent when you fail, and immediately seek
God's forgiveness and restoration. Sin breaks our fellowship with God.[5]

When God forgives, there is
complete change in r
Instead of hostility, there is lo
Instead of enmity, there i

Before asking God's forgiveness there is
something important you must do.
You must repent, that is, turn from the behavior
and lifestyle that [leads to sin].[7]

When God forgives us and purifies us of our sin, He also forgets it.
Forgiveness results in God dropping the charges against us.[8]

Forgiveness is one of the most beautiful words in the human vocabulary.
How much pain and unhappy consequences could be avoided
if we all learned the meaning of this word![9]

Christ can take the most sin-laden, selfish, evil person
and bring forgiveness and new life.[10]

We cannot ask forgiveness over and over again for our sins,
and then return to our sins, expecting God to forgive us.
We must turn from our practice of sin as best we know how,
and turn to Christ by faith as our Lord and Savior.[11]

BILLY GRAHAM ON
GLORIFYING GOD

The heavens declare the glory of God . . .
Their words [go out] to the end of the world.

—PSALM 19:1, 4 NKJV

◦—◦—◦

We glorify Christ when we live for God—
trusting, loving, and obeying Him.[1]

◦—◦—◦

Everything we do should glorify God![2]

◦—◦—◦

When one bears suffering faithfully, God is glorified and honored.[3]

◦—◦—◦

What greater glory can we anticipate than to
stand before the throne of God,
to humble ourselves before His great and incomparable majesty.[4]

◦—◦—◦

One of the bonuses of being a Christian is the glorious hope that
extends out beyond the grave into the glory of God's tomorrow.[5]

Prayer serves a dual purpose; the blessing of man and the glory of God.[6]

Our voices, our service, and our abilities are to be employed,
primarily, for the glory of God.[7]

One of the joys of heaven . . . will be discovering
the hidden ways that God in His sovereignty acted
in our lives on earth to protect and guide us
[that we might] bring glory to His name, in spite of our frailty.[8]

Our dress, our posture, our actions should all
be for the honor and glory of Christ.
Much of our talk as Christians is secular, not spiritual.
It is easy to fall into the conversational conformity of
the world and spend an evening discussing politics,
new cars, and the latest entertainment.
We often forget that we are to edify one another with
holy conversation and that our conversation should be on
heavenly, and not exclusively on earthly things.[9]

We glorify God by living lives that honor Him.[10]

BILLY GRAHAM ON
GOD

In the beginning was the Word, and the Word was with God,
and the Word was God.

—JOHN 1:1 NKJV

For centuries mankind has been on an incredible journey,
taking him across every generation
and through every conceivable experience in his search for God.[1]

Most of us know about God,
but that is quite different from knowing God.[2]

God says that we can learn a great deal about
Him just by observing nature.
Because He has spoken through His universe,
all men are without excuse for not believing in Him.
This is why the Psalmist said:
"The fool hath said in his heart, There is no God" [Psalm 14:1 KJV].[3]

Your yearning for God must supersede all other desires.
It must be like a gnawing hunger and a burning thirst.[4]

If God can be fully proved by the human mind,
then He is no greater than the mind that proves Him.[5]

God can be everywhere at once, heeding the prayers of all who
call out in the name of Christ; performing the mighty miracles
that keep the stars in their places, and the plants bursting up
through the earth, and the fish swimming in the sea.
There is no limit to God. There is no limit to His wisdom.
There is no limit to His power. There is no limit to His love.
There is no limit to His mercy.[6]

Talk about God can become dreary and lackluster if God isn't in you.
Church can become a drab thing and the Bible an irksome Book if the
Holy Spirit does not illuminate your soul with His indwelling presence.[7]

At this crucial point in world history,
everyone should be seeking an answer to the question,
"What is God like?" Everyone should ask it,
and everyone should make very sure of the answer . . .
The Bible says, ". . . God has shown it to them" [Romans 1:19 NKJV].[8]

Nothing in our lives takes God by surprise.[9]

God is not a bargaining God. You cannot barter with Him.
You must do business with Him on His own terms.[10]

If we read the Bible as carefully and as regularly
as we read the daily papers,
we would be as familiar with and as well informed about God as we are
about our favorite player's batting average during baseball season![11]

We have a conception that God is a haphazard God
with no set of rules of life and salvation.
Ask the astronomer if God is a haphazard God.
He will tell you that every star moves with
precision in its celestial path.[12]

If you have been trying to limit God—stop it!
Don't try to confine Him or His works to any single place or sphere.
You wouldn't try to limit the ocean.[13]

Getting to know God and being able to call on Him
is the most important step in storing up for the storms.[14]

God began by revelation to build a bridge between Himself and people.[15]

To live the life of God we must have the nature of God.[16]

God is not bound by a body, yet He is a Person.
He feels, He thinks, He loves, He forgives,
He sympathizes with the problems and sorrows that we face.[17]

Remember that "where God guides, He provides.
Where He leads, He supplies all needs."[18]

Has God designated any one person here on earth to speak
with final authority about Him?
No—the one Man who could do that lived two
thousand years ago, and we crucified Him![19]

The wheels of [God's] mercy and justice move quietly and silently,
but they do move.[20]

If we have no mercy toward others,
that is one proof that we have never experienced God's mercy.[21]

If we believe in what God made and what God said,
we will believe in the One whom God sent.[22]

We must practice the Presence of God. Jesus said,
"Lo, I am with you always" [Matthew 28:20].
Remember, Christ is always near us.[23]

There are those who say that all roads lead to God.
But Jesus said, "I am the way, the truth, and the life:
no man cometh unto the Father, but by me" [John 14:6 KJV].[24]

God holds every man accountable for his rejection of Christ.[25]

Every law that God has given has been for man's benefit.
If man breaks it, he is not only rebelling
against God; he is hurting himself.[26]

God is able to do what we can't do.[27]

God has revealed Himself in the Book called the Bible.[28]

Man would have remained forever lost if God in His infinite mercy
had not sent His Son to earth to bridge this gulf.[29]

People do not come to hear what I have to say—
they want to know what God has to say.[30]

Energy out of control is dangerous; energy under control is powerful . . .
Science takes a Niagara River with its violent turbulence and
transforms it into electrical energy to illuminate a million homes
and to turn the productive wheels of industry.
[God] does in the spiritual realm what science
does in the physical realm.[31]

When we come to the end of ourselves,
we come to the beginning of God.[32]

Denying the existence of God cannot make Him go away any
more than denying the existence of the Internal Revenue Service
can make the tax man vanish. Many people who
imagine a god of their own choosing will be horrified
when they stand before the true God of heaven.[33]

We have been told by God that if we sin against
Him and break His commandments,
He will bring judgment upon the world.
It is my responsibility and my duty
as a minister of the Gospel to [warn] people.
This is the message I must deliver.[34]

We often seek to please ourselves first, instead of God.
What is interesting is that when we seek to please God first,
very often we discover that we end up far more pleased
than we did when we put ourselves first.[35]

You will never understand who you are until
you understand who God is.[36]

[There are] seven gifts God gives you when
you commit your life to Christ:
a new relationship, a new citizenship, a new family, a new purpose,
a new power, a new destiny, and a new journey.[37]

The closer you are to God, the farther you are from the devil.[38]

Some things never change.
Not the ABC's, not the multiplication tables, not God![39]

When God speaks to us, He should have our full attention.[40]

God has paid the greatest debt you will ever incur,
and once you understand the incredible
sacrifice He has made just for you,
you will feel compelled to turn to God and
to accept Jesus Christ into your heart.[41]

Benevolent hands reach down from heaven to offer us the most
hopeful warning and remedy: "Prepare to meet your God."[42]

BILLY GRAHAM ON
GOD'S WILL

I delight to do Your will, O my God, and Your law is within my heart.

—PSALM 40:8 NKJV

———————

Do you want to know what God's will is for you?
It is for you to become more and more like Christ.
This is spiritual maturity, and if you make this your goal,
it will change your life.[1]

———————

To know the will of God is the highest of all wisdom.
Living in the center of God's will rules out all falseness of religion
and puts the stamp of true sincerity upon our service to God.[2]

———————

If you are ignorant of God's Word,
you will always be ignorant of God's will.[3]

———————

Sometimes it's best to start moving in the direction you think
God may want you to go, and then trust Him to lead you—
closing doors He doesn't want you to go through and opening up others.[4]

God's will is that we would be righteous in our living.
God is holy, and the whole scheme of
redemption has holiness for its goal.[5]

The will of God will never take us
where the grace of God cannot sustain us.[6]

The greatest barrier to knowing God's will is simply that we want to run
our own lives. Our problem is that a battle is going on in our hearts—
a battle between our wills and God's will.[7]

God wants us to know His will and He reveals
it to us both through the Bible
and through the guidance of His Holy Spirit.
Seek God's will when you pray, and He will help you know it.[8]

God will never—never—lead you to do something
that is contrary to His written Word, the Bible.[9]

God's will is for us to commit our lives to Christ and follow Him.
God's will also is that we avoid sin.[10]

When that glorious day comes, sin and death will be destroyed
and Satan will be banished. All the strife and hatred
and suffering and death that twist and scar this world
will vanish, and the Lord's Prayer will be fulfilled:
God's will *will* be done on earth as it is in heaven.[11]

BILLY GRAHAM ON
THE GOSPEL

The gospel which was preached by me is not according to man . . .
it came through the revelation of Jesus Christ.

—GALATIANS 1:11–12 NKJV

—◆—

The first hint of the Gospel comes from Genesis 3:15,
this is the first promise of salvation.[1]

—◆—

Go is the first part of the word *Gospel.*
It should be the watchword of every true follower of Christ.
It should be emblazoned on the banners of the church.[2]

—◆—

There is no such thing as a "social gospel." It is a misnomer.
There is only one Gospel. "If any man preach
any other gospel unto you . . .
let him be accursed" [Galatians 1:9 KJV].[3]

—◆—

It is impossible to believe anything into existence.
The Gospel did not come into being because men believed it . . .
The fact always precedes the faith.[4]

I realize that my ministry would someday come to an end.
I am only one in a glorious chain of men and women God has raised up
through the centuries to build Christ's church
and take the Gospel everywhere.[5]

The power to proclaim the greatest news in heaven
or on earth was not given to the angels.
It was given to redeemed men . . . Every Christian is to be a witness;
every follower of Christ is to preach the Gospel.[6]

When most major Protestant denominations have their annual councils,
assemblies, or conventions, they make pronouncements on matters
having to do with disarmament, federal aid to education, birth control,
the United Nations, and any number of social and political issues.
Very rarely are any resolutions passed that have to do with the
redemptive witness of the Gospel.[7]

The Gospel shows people their wounds and bestows on them love.
It shows them their bondage and supplies the hammer
to knock away their chains.
It shows them their nakedness and provides them the garments of purity.
It shows them their poverty and pours into
their lives the wealth of heaven.
It shows them their sins and points them to the Savior.[8]

I do not have to make the Gospel relevant;
it is always relevant in any part of the world . . .
[and] I must get the whole Gospel in [every] sermon.[9]

The Gospel should never be dull, for it is the most exciting
and relevant news we could ever receive. When we find
it dull, it is a warning sign that something is going on
inside us and we need to take action to correct it.[10]

Our chaotic, confused world has no greater need than to hear
the message of good news—the Gospel of Jesus Christ.[11]

Jesus Christ is God in human flesh, and the story of His life, death,
and resurrection is the only Good News the world will ever hear.[12]

My job is to preach the Gospel,
which has the power to change men's lives from the inside out.[13]

BILLY GRAHAM ON
GRACE

The word of the truth of the gospel . . . is bringing forth fruit . . .
since the day you heard and knew the grace of God in truth.

—COLOSSIANS 1:5–6 NKJV

———❖———

This is still the age of grace.
God's offer of forgiveness and a new life still stands.
However, the door will one day be closed. Someday it will be too late.
This is why the Bible continually warns and challenges:
"Now is the accepted time" [2 Corinthians 6:2 NKJV].[1]

———❖———

When you pick up the cross of unpopularity,
wherever you may be, you will find God's grace is there,
more than sufficient to meet your every need.[2]

———❖———

Some of the most radiant Christians I have
ever met were "wheelchair" saints.
May God give you grace to "triumph in affliction."[3]

We are living in an age of grace, in which God promises that
"whosoever will" may come and receive His Son.
But this period of grace will not go on indefinitely.
We are even now living on borrowed time.[4]

Only as we bow in contrition, confession, and repentance at the foot
of the cross, can we find forgiveness. There is the grace of God![5]

The motive of grace is the infinite,
compassionate love of a merciful God,
but the work of grace was the death of Christ on the cross.[6]

The grace of God has been tested in the crucible of human experience,
and has been found to be more than an equal
for the problems and sins of humanity.[7]

Throughout Scripture we read of warnings preceding disaster.
Such alerts from God are part of His grace and provision.[8]

Christ did not suffer and die to offer cheap grace.
Jesus did not willingly go to the cross so we could have an easy life
or offer a faith built on easy-believism. As someone said,
"Salvation is free, but not cheap." It cost Jesus His life.[9]

I look forward to seeing Christ and bowing before Him
in praise and gratitude for all He has done for us,
and for using me on this earth by His grace—just as I am.[10]

BILLY GRAHAM ON
GREED

[Jesus] said, "Beware! Guard against every kind of greed.
Life is not measured by how much you own."

—LUKE 12:15

Envy and greed always—always—exact a terrible price.
I have never met an envious or greedy person who was at peace.[1]

The Bible warns us against greed and selfishness,
it does encourage frugality and thrift.[2]

The Bible sees greed as a form of idolatry,
because a greedy person worships things instead of God.
Greed and envy have their roots in selfishness.[3]

Envy and greed starve on a steady diet of thanksgiving.[4]

Everything that we see about us that we count as our possessions
only comprises a loan from God, and it is when we lose sight of
this all-pervading truth that we become greedy and covetous.[5]

Life is not a matter of dollars and cents, houses and lands,
earning capacity and financial achievement.
Greed must not be allowed to make man the slave of wealth.[6]

What is the authority in your life? Is it your selfishness? Your lust?
Your greed? Or have you turned it all over to God and said, "Lord,
You are going to be my authority"? When you are under authority,
you are then able to assume authority.[7]

We have seen the results of unrestrained greed,
corruption, and manipulation on Wall Street, financial
mismanagement in the halls of government,
fraud and perversion at the highest levels of both church and state.
Many people sense the possibility of an even greater
unraveling in the world. We are constantly confronted
by the realities of new problems in this age of crisis.[8]

It is not wrong to want to work and earn a decent living; in fact,
God has given work to us. But this legitimate desire can very easily
cross the line into greed—especially in our materialistic society.[9]

Greed is an unreasonable or all-absorbing desire to acquire
things or wealth. One test of greed is that it is never satisfied.
Greed is repeatedly condemned in the Bible.[10]

We need to be on guard against greed . . . above all we need to
make sure our lives are centered in Christ and not things.[11]

BILLY GRAHAM ON
GRIEF

I beheld the transgressors, and was grieved; because they kept not thy word.

—PSALM 119:158 KJV

———◆———

We don't have to be on the battlefields of the
world to experience strife and conflict.
We need only to open our eyes each morning and read the headlines,
we need only to turn a keen ear when our phones ring with bad news,
we need only to open our hearts to those next door—and maybe
even in our own homes—to notice those with grieving hearts.[1]

———◆———

The facade of grief may be indifference, preoccupation, anger,
cheerfulness, or any variety of emotions. But if we try to understand it,
we may learn how to cope with it.[2]

———◆———

Grief comes with many losses.
Whatever its cause, grief will come to all of us.[3]

———◆———

Grief which is not dealt with properly
can cause us to lose our perspective on life.[4]

Grief turns us inward, but compassion turns us outward,
and that's what we need when grief threatens to crush us.
The Bible says, "Carry each other's burdens" [Galatians 6:2 NIV].[5]

When we grieve over someone who has died in Christ,
we are sorrowing not for them but for ourselves.
Our grief isn't a sign of weak faith, but of great love.[6]

Often it takes that "knife in our heart" to drive us to Him.
Our faith, our very lives, depend on God,
and when we enter the valley of grief,
we need His help or we will never climb another mountain.[7]

If there is something we need more than anything else during grief,
it is a friend who stands with us, who doesn't leave us.
Jesus is that friend.[8]

BILLY GRAHAM ON
HAPPINESS

He who heeds the word wisely will find good . . . happy is he.

—PROVERBS 16:20 NKJV

Happy is the person who has learned the secret
of being content with whatever life brings him,
and has learned to rejoice in the
simple and beautiful things around him.[1]

Do you really want happiness?
Then you will have to pay the price of humbling yourself
at the foot of the cross and receiving Christ as Savior.[2]

Happiness is a choice, but grief is a certainty.[3]

Christ said there is a happiness in that
acknowledgement of spiritual poverty
which lets God come into our souls.[4]

It is the presence of sin that prevents man from being truly happy.[5]

The "do-it-yourself" rage is spreading everywhere,
and people are being told that to be happy
all they have to do is think "happy thoughts."
Such thoughts might cheer us, but they will never change us.[6]

The mourning of inadequacy is a weeping
that catches the attention of God . . .
The happiest day of my life was when I realized that my own ability,
my own goodness, my own morality was insufficient in the sight of God;
and I publicly and openly acknowledged my need of Christ.[7]

We say, "Happy are the clever, for they shall inherit the admiration of
their friends"; "Happy are the aggressive, for they shall inherit a career";
"Happy are the rich, for they shall inherit a world of friends
and a house full of modern gadgets."
Jesus said, "[Happy] are the meek; for they shall
inherit the earth" [see Matthew 5:5].
If we want the secret of happiness . . . "meekness" is a basic key.[8]

My wife and I were invited to have lunch with
one of the wealthiest men in the world.
He was seventy-five years old. Tears came down his
cheeks. "I am the most miserable man in the world,"
he said. "I have everything anyone could ever want.
If I want to go anywhere, I have my own yacht or private plane.
But down inside I'm miserable and empty."
Shortly after, I met another man who
preached in a small church nearby.
He was vivacious and full of life, and he told us,
"I don't have a penny to my name,
but I'm the happiest man in the world!"[9]

BILLY GRAHAM ON
THE HEART

His word burns in my heart like a fire.

—JEREMIAH 20:9

When Scripture talks about the heart, it's not talking about that
life-sustaining muscle. It's talking about our entire inner being.
The heart is the seat of our emotions, the seat of decisive action,
and the seat of belief (as well as doubt).[1]

The heart symbolizes the center of our moral, spiritual,
and intellectual life. It is the seat of our conscience and life.[2]

It is possible through sin to harden our hearts against God so long
that we lose all desire for God. The Scripture says:
"God also gave them up" [Romans 1:24 KJV].[3]

Don't ever hesitate to take to [God] whatever is on your heart.
He already knows it anyway,
but He doesn't want you to bear its pain or celebrate its joy alone.[4]

Man himself is helpless to detach himself
from the gnawing guilt of a heart
weighed down with the guilt of sin.
But where man has failed, God has succeeded.[5]

Two conflicting forces cannot exist in one human heart.
When doubt reigns, faith cannot abide.
Where hatred rules, love is crowded out.
Where selfishness rules, there love cannot dwell.[6]

The heart of man, though small, is big enough for Christ to live in,
if man will only make room for Him.[7]

A true messenger lives a burdened life. If he is the Lord's vessel,
he carries in his heart a burden for souls none can share
but those who know it firsthand.[8]

Reading the Bible has a purifying effect upon the heart and mind.
As you read, the Holy Spirit will enlighten the passages for you.[9]

Christ . . . didn't come to treat symptoms.
He came to get at the very heart of man's disease.[10]

I am convinced that when a man sincerely searches for God
with all his heart, God will reveal Himself in some way.[11]

BILLY GRAHAM ON
HEAVEN

Forever, O LORD, Your word is settled in heaven.

—PSALM 119:89 NKJV

———

Heaven doesn't make this life *less* important;
it makes it *more* important.[1]

———

In heaven . . . the "communication gap" will be closed.[2]

———

God's house will be happy because Christ will be there.[3]

———

The Bible says that as long as we are here on earth, we are strangers in a
foreign land. There are enemies to be conquered before we return home.
This world is not our home; our citizenship is in heaven.[4]

———

Only in heaven will we know exactly what heaven is like.[5]

—◆—

We were equipped by our Creator not only to live on this earth,
but also to live in touch with heaven.
This was the Great Design of the Great Designer.[6]

—◆—

There are restrictions to entering heaven.
The Scripture says:
"Nothing impure will ever enter [heaven],
nor will anyone who does what is shameful or deceitful,
but only those whose names are written in the
Lamb's book of life" [Revelation 21:27 NIV].[7]

—◆—

Only one answer will give a person the certain privilege,
the joy, of entering heaven.
"Because I have believed in Jesus Christ and
accepted Him as my Savior."[8]

—◆—

Even when we allow our imaginations to run wild on the joys of heaven,
we find that our minds are incapable of conceiving what it will be like.[9]

—◆—

What a thrilling future for those of us who know that some day
we will populate the kingdom of God.[10]

—◆—

In our resurrection bodies we will know nothing of physical weakness.
Limitations imposed on us on this earth are not known in heaven.
We will have a habitation from God that is
incorruptible, immortal, and powerful.[11]

In heaven I'll wish with all my heart that I could reclaim
a thousandth part of the time I've let slip through my fingers,
that I could call back those countless conversations
which could have glorified my Lord—but didn't.[12]

Don't let the burdens and hardships of this life
distract you or discourage you,
but keep your eyes firmly fixed on what God has promised
at the end of our journey: heaven itself.[13]

The most thrilling thing about heaven is that Jesus Christ will be there.
I will see Him face to face.
Jesus Christ will meet us at the end of life's journey.[14]

Heavenly rest will be so refreshing that we will never feel that
exhaustion of mind and body we so frequently experience now.
I'm really looking forward to that.[15]

Nothing made by the hand of man has ever been so beautiful
as starlight on the water or moonlight on the snow.
And the same hand that made trees and fields and flowers, the seas and
hills, the clouds and sky, has been making a home for us called heaven.[16]

A Christian's citizenship may be in heaven,
but he has obligations as a citizen of earth. Both living with Christ
and going to be with Him in death are greatly to be desired.[17]

What is heaven? It's the home that God created and He possesses.
His throne room is His headquarters from which He
issues His commands, directions, and prophecies.
And Jesus sits at His Father's right hand.[18]

The moment we take our last breath on
earth, we take our first in heaven.[19]

Heaven is a wonderful place and the benefits for the believer
are out of this world![20]

Sometimes . . . we grow homesick for heaven. Many times in the midst
of the sin, suffering, and sorrow of this life there is a tug at our soul.
That is homesickness coupled with anticipation.[21]

I [will] not go to heaven because I am a preacher.
I am going to heaven entirely on the merit of the work of Christ.[22]

My home is in heaven. I'm just passing through this world.[23]

BILLY GRAHAM ON
HELL

I tell you . . . the gates of hell shall not prevail.

—MATTHEW 16:18 ESV

—◆—

The Bible says more about hell than about heaven.[1]

—◆—

No one spoke more about hell than Jesus did,
and the hell He came to save men from was not only a hell on earth . . .
it was something to come.[2]

—◆—

It is unbelief that shuts the door to heaven and opens it to hell.
It is unbelief that rejects the Word of God and refuses Christ as Savior.
It is unbelief that causes men to turn a deaf ear to the Gospel.[3]

—◆—

The subject of heaven is much easier to accept than the subject of hell.
And yet the Bible teaches both.[4]

———◆———

Not one word about hell in the Bible would
ever make you want to go there.[5]

———◆———

I am conscious of the fact that the subject
of hell is not a very pleasant one.
It is very unpopular, controversial, and misunderstood . . .
As a minister I must deal with it. I cannot ignore it.[6]

———◆———

Among those Christians to whom hell means little, Calvary means less.[7]

———◆———

Will a loving God send a man to hell?
The answer from Jesus and His teachings of the Bible is, clearly, "Yes!"
He does not send man willingly,
but man condemns himself to eternal hell because . . .
he refuses God's way of salvation and the hope of eternal life with Him.[8]

———◆———

The Bible teaches there is hell for every person
who willingly and knowingly rejects Christ as Lord and Savior.
Many passages could be quoted to support that fact.[9]

———◆———

Hell has been cloaked in folklore and disguised in fiction for so long,
many people deny the reality of such a place.[10]

Some teach "universalism"—that eventually everybody will be
saved and the God of love will never send anyone to hell.
They believe the words "eternal" or "everlasting"
do not actually mean forever.
However, the same word which speaks of eternal banishment from God
is also used for the eternity of heaven.[11]

A seminary professor I once knew told his students,
"Never preach about hell without tears in your eyes."[12]

BILLY GRAHAM ON
HOLINESS

Make them holy by your truth; teach them your word, which is truth.

—JOHN 17:17

———

Christians should seek after holiness—
without which no man shall see the Lord.
Let us seek ardently the kind of life that reflects the beauty
of Jesus and marks us as being what saints ought to be![1]

———

What stirs God most is not physical suffering but sin.
All too often we are more afraid of physical pain than of moral wrong.
The cross is the standing evidence of the fact that holiness is a principle
for which God would die.[2]

———

As I read the Bible, I seem to find holiness
to be [Christ's] supreme attribute.[3]

———

If you belong to Jesus Christ, you are called to live a life of purity
and holiness. God wants your mind to be shaped by Him
so that your thoughts and goals reflect Christ.[4]

Don't take the holiness of God lightly,
for it is the very essence of His character.[5]

Compassion is not complete in itself,
but must be accompanied by inflexible justice and wrath
against sin and a desire for holiness.[6]

God's holiness demands that sin be punished—
but God's love has provided the way of redemption through Christ.[7]

We cannot be satisfied with our goodness after
beholding the holiness of God.[8]

Living the Christian life means striving for holiness.[9]

BILLY GRAHAM ON
THE HOLY SPIRIT

The Helper, the Holy Spirit, whom the Father will send
in My name, He will teach you all things,
and bring to your remembrance all things that I said to you.

—JOHN 14:26 NKJV

———◆———

The Bible is clear that the Holy Spirit is God Himself.[1]

———◆———

Take care of your body; the Bible calls it "a temple of
the Holy Spirit" [1 Corinthians 6:19 NIV].[2]

———◆———

The Holy Spirit illuminates the minds of
people, makes us yearn for God,
and takes spiritual truth and makes it understandable to us.[3]

———◆———

A life touched by the Holy Spirit will tolerate sin no longer.[4]

As humans we have two great spiritual needs.
The first is forgiveness, which God has made possible
by sending His Son into the world to die for our sins.
Our second need, however, is for goodness,
which God also made possible by sending the
Holy Spirit to dwell within us.[5]

The Father is the source of all blessing,
and the Son is the channel of all blessing,
[and] it is through the Holy Spirit at work in us
that all truth becomes living and operative in our lives.[6]

The Holy Spirit not only convicts of sin
but also convinces men that Jesus is the righteousness of God.
He shows sinners that Jesus is the way, the truth, and the life.[7]

The Scripture makes it clear that this planet would already be
a literal hell on earth were it not for the presence of
the Holy Spirit in the world.[8]

The Holy Spirit can rejuvenate a tired Christian,
captivate an indifferent believer, and empower a dry church.[9]

If we feed our spiritual lives and allow the Holy Spirit to empower us,
He will have rule over us. If we starve our spiritual natures
and instead feed the old, sinful nature, the flesh will dominate.[10]

———◆———

Christians, day by day, week by week, and month by month,
are told to walk in the Spirit.
Walking in the Spirit means being led and directed by the Holy Spirit.
This comes as we progressively yield various areas of our lives
to the Spirit's control. Now desire in itself is not wrong,
it's what we desire or lust for that is wrong—and when we yield.[11]

———◆———

The Holy Spirit gives liberty to the Christian, direction to the worker,
discernment to the teacher, power to the Word,
and fruit to faithful service.
He reveals the things of Christ.[12]

———◆———

If Christians realized that God Himself
in the person of the Holy Spirit really dwells within our bodies,
we would be far more careful about what we eat, drink, look at, or read.
No wonder Paul said, "I beat my body and make it my slave"
[1 Corinthians 9:27 NIV]. This should drive
us to our knees in confession.[13]

———◆———

Faithfulness is produced by the Holy Spirit in a yielded Christian life.[14]

———◆———

It is never a question of how much you and I have of the Spirit,
but how much He has of us.[15]

———◆———

Because [the Holy Spirit] is a spirit, [He] isn't limited by time or space.
He can be everywhere at once. He is in the midst of the largest galaxy—
and the smallest atom.[16]

If you know Christ, you don't need to beg for the Holy
Spirit to come into your life; He is already there—
whether you "feel" His presence or not.
Don't confuse the Holy Spirit with an emotional feeling
or a particular type of spiritual experience.[17]

Sometimes I feel so helpless and inadequate,
and wonder if I have done enough to make the Gospel clear.
But I also know that only the Holy Spirit can
open others' eyes to the truth.[18]

We shouldn't refer to the Spirit as "it"; instead we should
always refer to the Spirit as "He"—because the Holy Spirit
is a Person. He speaks to us, He commands us,
He intercedes for us, He hears us, He guides us.[19]

BILLY GRAHAM ON
HOME

Fix these words of mine in your hearts and minds . . .
[Talk] about them when you sit at home.

—DEUTERONOMY 11:18–19 NIV

———

The home is basically a sacred institution . . .
Faith in Christ is the most important of all principles
in the building of a happy marriage and a successful home.[1]

———

Home was a refuge for me, a place I could truly relax.[2]

———

My wife Ruth once said, "If our children have the
background of a godly, happy home and this unshakeable
faith that the Bible is indeed the Word of God,
they will have a foundation that the forces of hell cannot shake."[3]

———

The Bible teaches that our homes should be hospitable and that those
who come in and out of our homes should sense the presence of Christ.[4]

The happiest Christian homes I know are those given to hospitality,
where neighbors feel at home, where young people are welcome,
where the elderly are respected, where children are loved.[5]

Cut out some of your "important social engagements,"
and make your home the center of your social life.
God will honor you, and your children will grow
up to call you "blessed" [Proverbs 31:28].[6]

In many homes and among so-called educated people—
it has become fashionable to joke about the Bible and to regard it
more as a dust-catcher than as the living Word of God.[7]

Many homes are on the rocks today because God has
been left out of the domestic picture. With the clash of
personalities in a domestic pattern, there must be an
integrating force, and the living God is that Force![8]

If there were no heaven and no hell, I would still want to be a Christian
because of what it does for our homes and our own families in this life.[9]

With the breakdown of discipline in the home
and with every source of amusement and
instruction pouring poison into daily life,
it is not to be wondered that the minds of people
are ready to receive anything but the truth
and that they are ready to believe lies and ultimately *the lie*.[10]

———◆———

The world is not a permanent home, it is only a temporary dwelling.[11]

———◆———

It is far easier to live an excellent life among your friends,
when you are putting your best foot forward
and are conscious of public opinion,
than it is to live for Christ in your home.[12]

———◆———

The broken home has become the number
one social problem of America,
and could ultimately lead to the destruction of our civilization . . .
it does not make screaming headlines; but, like termites,
it is eating away at the heart and core of the American structure.[13]

———◆———

If you are a true Christian, you will not give way at home to bad
temper, impatience, fault-finding, sarcasm, unkindness, suspicion,
selfishness, or laziness.[14]

———◆———

How many homes are broken because of men
and women who are unfaithful!
God will not hold you guiltless! There is a day of reckoning.
"Be sure your sin will find you out" (Numbers 32:23 ESV). They will find
you out in your own family life here in your relationship with your mate;
they will find you out in the life to come.[15]

The home only fulfills its true purpose when it is God-controlled.
Leave Jesus Christ out of your home and it loses its meaning.
But take Christ into your heart and the life of your family,
and He will transform your home.[16]

When we are young and restless to be free,
home is the place from which we long to escape.
But if there is still a home intact when trouble arises
and life becomes a battlefield,
home is the place to which we yearn to return.[17]

In some ways, Christians are homeless.
Our true home is waiting for us, prepared by the Lord Jesus Christ.[18]

The Bible takes the word *home* with all of its tender
associations and sacred memories, and applies it to the
hereafter and tells us that heaven is home.[19]

God does not want an apartment in our house.
He claims our entire home from attic to cellar.[20]

The Lord Jesus Christ is preparing a home fit for all who live for Him,
a place designed for the church triumphant.
Let's exemplify the work of His hands, for they are busy, on our behalf,
building a city large enough to encompass His people of faith—
an eternal home for the soul.[21]

One final reason for choosing God's path is of supreme importance: It leads us home.[22]

BILLY GRAHAM ON
HOPE

Your word is my source of hope.

—PSALM 119:114

⟞⬥⟝

Perhaps the greatest psychological, spiritual,
and medical need that all people have is the need for hope.[1]

⟞⬥⟝

For the believer there is hope beyond the grave,
because Jesus Christ has opened the door to heaven for us
by His death and resurrection.[2]

⟞⬥⟝

Christ wants to give you hope for the future.
He wants you to learn what it means to walk with Him every day.
When you come to Christ, God gives you eternal life—
which begins right now as you open your heart to Him.[3]

⟞⬥⟝

Faith points us beyond our problems to the hope we have in Christ.[4]

Christ's second coming reminds us that ultimately our hope
is not in this world and its attempts to solve its problems,
but in Christ's promise to establish His perfect rule over all the earth.[5]

Man has no ability to repair this damaged planet.
The flaw in human nature is too great. God is our only hope![6]

Earth's troubles fade in the light of heaven's hope.[7]

My hope does not rest in the affairs of this world.
It rests in Christ who is coming again.[8]

Only because Jesus is God and we have
confessed Him as Savior and Lord,
can He bestow and we receive these benefits,
this blessed assurance and hope (see Romans 10:9).[9]

Our world today desperately hungers for hope, and yet uncounted people
have almost given up. There is despair and hopelessness on every hand.
Let us be faithful in proclaiming the hope that is in Jesus![10]

BILLY GRAHAM ON
HUMAN NATURE

[Jesus] did not need anyone to bear witness concerning man . . .
for He Himself knew what was in human nature.

—JOHN 2:25 AMP

———◆◆◆———

We have two natures within us, both struggling for mastery.
Which one will dominate us? It depends on which one we feed.[1]

———◆◆◆———

We are to feed the new nature on the Word of God constantly,
and we are to starve the old nature,
which craves the world and the flesh.
We are told to "make not provision for the flesh" [Romans 13:14 KJV].[2]

———◆◆◆———

The greatest need in the world is the transformation of human nature.
We need a new heart that will not have lust and greed and hate in it.
We need a heart filled with love and peace and joy,
and that is why Jesus came into the world.[3]

———◆◆◆———

Men cannot help that it is their nature to respond to the lewd,
the salacious, and the vile.
They will have difficulty doing otherwise until they are born again.[4]

One of the ironies of human nature is that it often
has a way of rejecting the best and accepting the worst.[5]

Acknowledge that there is a defect in human nature,
a built-in waywardness that comes from man's rebellion against God.[6]

Man is a rebel, and a rebel is naturally in confusion.
He is in conflict with every other rebel.
For a rebel by his very nature is selfish.
He is seeking his own good and not the good of others.[7]

Some people have said that man has improved . . .
[and] that if Christ came back today, He would not be
crucified but would be given a glorious reception.
Christ does come to us every day in the form
of Bibles that we do not read,
in the form of churches that we do not attend, in the form of human
need that we pass by. I am convinced that if Christ came back today,
He would be crucified more quickly than
He was two thousand years ago.
Sin never improves. Human nature has not changed.[8]

The deepest problems of the human race are spiritual in nature.
They are rooted in man's refusal to seek God's way for his life.
The problem is the human heart, which God alone can change.[9]

Flesh is the Bible's word for unperfected human nature.
Leaving off the "h" and spelling it in reverse, we have the word *self*.
Flesh is the self-life:
it is what we are when we are left to our own devices.[10]

Man's nature and destiny are revealed in the Scriptures.[11]

Science, they say, can tap the brain of man and alter his desires.
But the Bible, which has withstood the ravages of time . . . says that
we are possessed of a sinful, fallen nature which wars against us.[12]

Our worldly wisdom has made us calloused and hard.
Our natural wisdom, as the Scriptures teach, comes not from God,
but is earthly, sensual, and devilish.[13]

In taking our human nature upon Himself,
[Jesus] showed us what we might become, what God intended us to be.[14]

BILLY GRAHAM ON
IMAGINATION,
ENTERTAINMENT,
AND FUN

We ought not to think that the divine being is like gold or silver
or stone, an image formed by the art and imagination of man . . .
Now [God] commands all people everywhere to repent.

—ACTS 17:29–30 ESV

———◆———

God is concerned with our imaginations,
for they in a large measure determine what kind of persons we are to be.[1]

———◆———

Jesus invited us not to a picnic, but to a pilgrimage;
not to a frolic, but to a fight.
He offered us not an excursion, but an execution.[2]

All transgressions begin with sinful thinking . . . guard against
the pictures of lewdness and sensuality that Satan flashes upon
the screen of your imagination, select with care the books
you read, choose discerningly the kind of entertainment you
attend, the kind of associates with whom you mingle, and
the kind of environment in which you place yourself.[3]

Never has there been a time when men tried
so desperately to have fun as they do today.[4]

We have arrived at the point where we are flippant about God.
We tell jokes about Him.
God's name is used so often in profanity in the entertainment world
that sometimes it is embarrassing to watch television.[5]

God gives us a glimpse of what heaven will be like for the believer.
It will have the characteristics of a happy home, a holy city,
a glorious garden, and a beautiful bride. This staggers the imagination![6]

Our schedules are so hectic we can't get everything done, or else we
are bored and restless, constantly looking for something to amuse us.
We are the most frantic generation in history—
and also the most entertained.
The Bible tells us that both extremes are wrong.[7]

Our imaginations are so stilted.
The very thought of being like Jesus is breathtaking.[8]

BILLY GRAHAM ON
INFLUENCE

If you speak good words . . . you will be my spokesman.
You must influence them; do not let them influence you!

—JEREMIAH 15:19

———————

I would not change places with the wealthiest and
most influential person in the world.
I would rather be a child of the King, a joint-heir with Christ,
a member of the Royal Family of heaven![1]

———————

Your life is intricately woven into the lives of scores
and hundreds of others around you.
Consider the variety of lives that you influence in one day.
Somewhere within your circle of contacts someone is being hurt.
Are you aware of it?[2]

———————

Apart from religious influence,
the family is the most important unit of society.[3]

God will never lead contrary to His word—
so get acquainted with the Word of God, the Bible. Pray.
He leads through the illumination of the Holy Spirit in our hearts.
Use whatever you have and be faithful.
We are called to serve Christ in our sphere of influence.[4]

It doesn't take great wealth or social influence to be faithful,
but it does take obedience and endurance.[5]

The way in which we react to hurts and disappointments
influences the shaping of our personalities.[6]

Salt and light speak of the influence
Christians can exercise for good in society.[7]

BILLY GRAHAM ON
INTEGRITY

Joyful are people of integrity, who follow the instructions of the LORD.

—PSALM 119:1

———◆———

Integrity means that if our private life was suddenly exposed,
we'd have no reason to be ashamed or embarrassed.
Integrity means our outward life is consistent
with our inner convictions.[1]

———◆———

Integrity is the glue that holds our way of life together.
What our young people want to see in their elders is
integrity, honesty, truthfulness, and faith.
What they hate most of all is hypocrisy and phoniness . . .
Let them see us doing what we would like them to do.[2]

———◆———

[Integrity] means a person is the same on the inside
as he or she claims to be on the outside.
He is the same person alone in a hotel room
a thousand miles from home
as he is at work or in his community or with his family.
A man of integrity can be trusted.[3]

Being pure in conduct also includes honesty and integrity
in dealing with our fellowmen.
A Christian should be known in his neighborhood or place of business
as an honest person.[4]

A godly person—one who serves Christ
and exhibits purity and integrity in his life—
is not necessarily welcomed or admired by those who live differently.
They may even react in scorn, or refuse to include a Christian in their
social gatherings because his very presence is a rebuke to them.[5]

God's standard is expressed in the Bible,
and the ultimate example of that standard is Jesus Christ.
When we live by the truth, we possess integrity.[6]

Integrity means that we are trustworthy and dependable,
and our character is above reproach.[7]

Unless men of purpose, integrity, and faith stand together in unswerving
loyalty to Jesus Christ, the future of the world is dark indeed.[8]

I believe integrity can be restored to a society one person at a time.
The choice belongs to each of us.[9]

Our world today is looking for men and women with integrity,
for communicators who back up their ministry with their lives.
Our preaching emerges out of what we are.
We are called to be a holy people—
separated from the moral evils of the world.[10]

The truth is that others judge us. More than that, they evaluate
the truth of the Gospel by what they see of our lives and our
integrity. [We] must make every effort to be above all suspicion in
the matter of finances and statistics. We are not only accountable
to God's people, but also to our Master (see Acts 24:16).[11]

BILLY GRAHAM ON
JESUS

For [Jesus] is sent by God. He speaks God's words,
for God gives him the Spirit without limit.

—JOHN 3:34

❖

The central message of the Bible is Jesus Christ.[1]

❖

Jesus made everything so simple and we have made it so complicated.
He spoke to the people in short sentences and everyday words,
illustrating His messages with never-to-be forgotten stories.[2]

❖

When Jesus needed friends, they left Him.[3]

❖

Not everyone Jesus tried to turn back from the
brink of destruction responded—nor will they with us.[4]

———

Many people are willing to have Jesus as part of their lives—
as long as it doesn't cost them anything.
They may even profess faith in Jesus and join a church.
But Jesus to them is almost like an insurance policy—
something they obtain and then forget about until they die.
What keeps you from being His disciple?[5]

———

Though [Jesus'] words were profound, they were plain.
His words were weighty, yet they shone with a luster and simplicity
of statement that staggered His enemies.[6]

———

Every word that [Jesus] spoke was historically true.
Every word that He spoke was scientifically true.
Every word that He spoke was ethically true.
There were no loopholes in the moral conceptions
and statements of Jesus Christ.
His ethical vision was wholly correct,
correct in the age in which He lived
and correct in every age that has followed it.[7]

———

A Roman soldier . . . thrust a spear into Jesus' side
and out came blood and water.
Physicians say that a mixture of blood and water indicates
that Jesus died of a broken heart.
He poured out the last ounce of His blood to redeem us.[8]

———

I trust Jesus with all my tomorrows,
knowing that He will solve the mystery of life beyond the grave.[9]

Jesus knows the intentions of our hearts and what we do in secret.[10]

Sin diverts some. Pleasure diverts others.
Social service and "religious" activity divert others.
We are told to be occupied with Jesus Christ Himself.[11]

"What shall I do, then, with Jesus who is called
the Christ?" (Matthew 27:22 NIV).
This is the most important question that has ever been asked.
It is also the question you must ask yourself.[12]

We should be about our Father's business by pouring His
compassionate love into aching and parched souls that have
nowhere to turn, no one to love, and no one to care.
Let them see Jesus in us. That is a living testimony.[13]

If you want to know what God is like, then take a look at Jesus Christ.[14]

BILLY GRAHAM ON
JOY

*The people went . . . to celebrate with great joy because
they had heard God's words and understood them.*

—NEHEMIAH 8:12

———————◆———————

We have to be tuned to God. We will never be free
from discouragement and despondency until we know
and walk with the very fountainhead of joy.[1]

———————◆———————

Pleasures are the things that appeal to our flesh and to our lust.
But joy is something else. Joy runs deep.[2]

———————◆———————

The ability to rejoice in any situation is a sign of spiritual maturity.[3]

———————◆———————

Without dark clouds in our lives
we would never know the joy of sunshine.
We can become callous and unteachable if we do not learn from pain.[4]

Only the forward-looking Christian remains
sincerely optimistic and joyful,
knowing that Christ will win in the end.[5]

Without Him our daily routine would become tiresome and tedious,
a drudgery rather than a joy.[6]

I have found in my travels that those who keep heaven in view
remain serene and cheerful in the darkest day.
Forward-looking Christians remain optimistic and joyful,
knowing that Christ someday will rule.[7]

This "I" was made in the image of God for fellowship with God.
Without God it is miserable, empty, confused, and frustrated.
Without God life has no meaning;
but with God at its center there is life,
an inner strength and peace, a deep satisfaction,
an unfading joy known only to those who know Jesus Christ.[8]

No matter what the climate is, what the troubles are,
what the difficulties are, there is joy for the child of God,
because joy is produced supernaturally by the Holy Spirit in us.[9]

[As a young man] I sought thrills! I found them in Christ.
I looked for something that would bring perfect joy! I found it in Christ.
I looked for something that would bring pleasure and that would
satisfy the deepest longing of my heart! I found it in Christ.
And my life has never been the same.[10]

BILLY GRAHAM ON
JUDGMENT

The entirety of Your word is truth,
and every one of Your righteous judgments endures forever.

—PSALM 119:160 NKJV

We will be judged according to the secret motives
and the character of our work.
If we have done our work for selfish motives or personal gain,
even if the results looked noble to our friends and family,
God knows our hearts.[1]

Hundreds of passages point to a time of judgment for every person who
has ever lived—none will escape.
If you took all the references to judgment out of the Bible,
you would have little Bible left.[2]

When we all stand before the judgment seat of Christ,
we will have our true motives revealed.[3]

———⊷•⊶———

God has already set the date [for judgment].
You may make and break appointments in this life,
but this is one appointment you are going to keep.[4]

———⊷•⊶———

People judge us not by what we think or believe,
but by what we do—and when our lives don't measure up,
we lose their respect and they conclude our faith isn't real.[5]

———⊷•⊶———

I believe that one of the reasons for crime, perversion,
and the evils of modern mankind is that we have lost belief
in the certainty of God being just, holy, and righteous,
and that He will judge the world.[6]

———⊷•⊶———

A call for national and individual repentance is urgently needed today,
or judgment is certain to fall.[7]

———⊷•⊶———

God judges mankind by the standard of the only God-man
who ever lived, Jesus Christ. Jesus, the innocent Lamb of God,
stands between our sin and the judgment of God the Father.[8]

———⊷•⊶———

God's judgment echoes the sound of hoofbeats,
but God's love quietly convicts.[9]

We will be judged according to our ability. The retired couple who count the offering every Sunday, never divulging the amount anyone in the congregation contributes, will not be tested in the same way as the millionaire who wants an inscription on the stained glass window, so everyone will know who donated it. Some of the most severe tests will be given to the [preachers] for the way in which they handled the Word of God. There will be no reward for leading others astray in lifestyle or in doctrine through false teaching.[10]

None of us deserves God's love.
All of us deserve His righteous judgment and
wrath (John 3:18, 36; Romans 3:9–12).
It is easy to think of an evil and depraved man like
Adolf Hitler deserving divine judgment . . .
But think of the kind and good people that you know . . .
They too will be lost if they refuse and neglect God's offer of
mercy and forgiveness. God's judgment applies to them too.[11]

But the judgment of God is not only an event that may take place some day in history when war or conflict might bring death to millions. His judgment is more than death—it is eternal banishment from the presence of God (2 Thessalonians 1:6–10; Revelation 20:11–15).[12]

BILLY GRAHAM ON
KNOWLEDGE

According to your word ... teach me knowledge and good judgment.
—PSALM 119:65–66 NIV

Science is learning to control everything but man.[1]

The blessing of knowledge becomes a curse when we pervert it.[2]

If ever a generation was bequeathed the knowledge of God, we were.
Yet we are throwing away
this glorious heritage on our lust and passions.[3]

The more man learns, the less he knows.[4]

Today an educated, civilized society is turning its face
while thousands of unborn babies are being killed.
God Himself, if not history, will judge this greater holocaust.[5]

Much of the world in search of knowledge and fulfillment ignores God![6]

———◆———

Today we have more knowledge than at any other time in history.
In seconds our laptops or PCs can call up information
about a topic that would have taken years to collect.
Young people graduate with more knowledge than ever before—
but in spite of their knowledge, they are confused, bewildered, frustrated,
and without moral moorings.[7]

———◆———

It is the absence of the knowledge of God and man's refusal to
obey Him that lie at the root of every problem which besets us.[8]

———◆———

We are the most informed people in the history of civilization—
and yet the most confused.
Though our heads are crammed with knowledge, our hearts are empty.[9]

BILLY GRAHAM ON
LIFE

Turn my eyes from worthless things, and give me life through your word.

—PSALM 119:37

<hr>

Every journey has a starting point . . . and it has an end.
God meant for [life] to be filled with joy and purpose.
He invites us to . . . take the rest of our journey with Him.[1]

<hr>

There comes a moment when we all must realize that life is short,
and in the end the only thing that really
counts is not how others see us,
but how God sees us.[2]

<hr>

A century ago man's chief concern was his spiritual life;
today his chief concern is with his physical and temporal affairs.[3]

<hr>

Sometimes life touches one person with a bouquet
and another with a thorn bush.
But the first may find a wasp in the flowers,
and the second may discover roses among the thorns.[4]

The one who made the Ford knew how to make it run.
God made you and me, and He alone
knows how to run your life and mine.
We could make a complete wreck of our lives without Christ.[5]

Sometimes we get a little tired of the burdens of life,
but it is exhilarating to know that
Jesus Christ will meet us at the end of life's journey.[6]

End your journey well. Don't waste your life,
and don't be satisfied with anything less than God's plan.[7]

Many a life has come forth from the furnace of affliction
more beautiful and more useful than before.[8]

The legacy we leave is not just in our possessions,
but in the quality of our lives.[9]

I could recall countless illustrations of men and women
who have encountered Jesus Christ . . .
Their whole lives have been transformed.[10]

Our life is not of this world.[11]

No matter how advanced its progress,
any generation that neglects its spiritual and moral life
is going to disintegrate.[12]

Instead of giving God His rightful place at the center of our lives,
we have substituted the "god" of Self.
Only Christ can change our hearts—
and through us begin to change our world.[13]

Walk into any bookstore and you'll find hundreds of books
telling you how to live. Don't be misled, and don't be deceived.
Instead, build your life on the truth God has given us in His Word.[14]

Though cultures differ and times change,
the Word of our God stands forever as an
unchanging source of answers to all of life's problems.[15]

Don't waste your life on things that have no eternal value.[16]

A life without God is like a boat without an anchor.[17]

One of the most important things God wants to teach us
from the Old Testament is how *not to live*.[18]

God calls us to live lives of purity.[19]

———⋙◆⋘———

Ask God to reveal hypocrisy in your life—
an inconsistency between what you profess and what you practice.
Then ask God to bring you so close to Christ
that you won't have any desire to live an inconsistent, deceitful life.[20]

———⋙◆⋘———

Jesus demands to be Master and Lord of every part of your life.
Is He Lord of your mind, of what you think, read, and believe?
Of what you dream about, meditate on, and entertain yourself with?
Do your eyes belong to Christ? Can [you] ask God's blessing on it?
Can [you] do this to the glory of God?[21]

———⋙◆⋘———

I believe this is one of the tests of the Spirit-filled life.
Is Christ becoming more and more evident in my life?
Are people seeing more of Him, and less of me?[22]

———⋙◆⋘———

The way we live often speaks far louder than our words.[23]

———⋙◆⋘———

A tame horse contributes much more to life than a wild one.
Energy out of control is dangerous; energy under control is powerful.[24]

———⋙◆⋘———

The Bible has much to say about the brevity of life
and the necessity of preparing for eternity.
I am convinced that only when a man is prepared to die
is he also prepared to live.[25]

Our interests are centered in ourselves.
We are preoccupied with material things.
Our supreme god is technology; our goddess is sex. Most of us are
more interested in getting to the moon than in getting to heaven,
more concerned about conquering space
than about conquering ourselves.
We are more dedicated to material security than to inner purity.
We give much more thought to what we wear, what we eat, what we
drink, and what we can do to relax than we give to what we are.
This preoccupation with peripheral things
applies to every area of our lives.[26]

If anything has been accomplished through my life,
it has been solely God's doing, not mine,
and He—not I—must get the credit.[27]

We must learn to live triumphantly
amid the traumas and pressures we face daily.[28]

How often do you cave in to the pressures of the crowd,
seeking the approval of others instead of the approval of God?
We all like to be liked—but that can be a very dangerous thing.
Make it your goal to live for Christ and be faithful to Him,
regardless of what the crowd demands.[29]

Our natural desire is to be doing something;
but there are times in our lives when it is wiser to wait and just be still.[30]

———

As life hits us head-on we can respond with resentment, resignation, acceptance, or welcome. We are the living examples of our responses.[31]

———

Because God is the giver and source of our life,
He has a legitimate claim upon our lives.[32]

———

We are to be catch basins for the fullness of God.
Like a freshly running spring, we are to overflow and let
our lives touch the lives of those around us.[33]

———

Life is a glorious opportunity if it is used to condition us for eternity.[34]

———

The Bible teaches that life does not end at the cemetery.
There is a future life.[35]

———

Don't be a prude, or snobbish, but let your life "glow" for Christ.
We are lamps shining in the darkness.[36]

———

God's Word is not a book of human ideas . . .
it is given to us by [God] to teach us how to live.[37]

———

Life is sacred and given to us by God; for that reason
we must never condone the deliberate, unnatural taking of life.[38]

Only by a life of obedience to the voice of the Spirit, by a daily denying of self, by full dedication to Christ, and by constant fellowship with Him are we enabled to live a godly life and an influential life in this present ungodly world.[39]

Supporters of the [environmental] movement often appear to worship not the God of heaven, but the god of nature. This is a dangerous form of idolatry. Anytime animal life becomes more sacred in our view than human life, we have lost sight of our proper priorities.[40]

When I received Jesus Christ as my Lord and Savior, I found the secret of life![41]

Jesus Christ said the gate that leads to destruction is wide and the way is broad, but the gate which leads to life is straight and the way narrow.[42]

You can't change the past.
But with God's help you can change the future.
No matter what your life has been like so far,
God wants to put your feet on a new path . . .
a better path . . . His path.[43]

[We] are not here by chance or by accident;
God put us on this journey called life. We came from Him,
and our greatest joy will come from giving ourselves back to Him and learning to walk with Him every day until we return to Him.[44]

An architect draws the plans for a new
building—but it still has to be built.
A composer writes a new piece of music—but it still has to be played.
A chef devises a new recipe—but the ingredients still have to be cooked.
In the same way, God has given us a blueprint for living—
but we must know what it is and then put it into action.[45]

Some day our journey through this life will be over
and we will embark on another journey—one that will last forever.[46]

If we don't know who we are, we'll never know how we ought to live.[47]

I am still learning, for the Christian life is one of constant growth.[48]

Do others see something of Christ in your life?
Do they see a "family resemblance" to Him by the way you live?[49]

God's goal isn't just to remove the bad things in our lives;
He wants to replace them with good things.
His plan is to remake us from within, by His Holy Spirit.[50]

The Christian life isn't a playground but a battlefield.[51]

Why are our inner lives so important?
One reason is because our thoughts determine our actions.[52]

———◆———

We need to know what the Bible teaches about right and wrong.
Every day we are battered by messages—from the media,
advertising, entertainment, celebrities, even our friends—
with one underlying theme: "Live for yourself."[53]

———◆———

Sometimes we face "gray areas," things that aren't necessarily
forbidden by the Bible but still may not belong in our lives.[54]

———◆———

Sin, like a deadly cancer, has invaded every area of our lives:
our bodies, our minds, our emotions, our wills—everything.[55]

———◆———

Life [can] become unbalanced, and in the process God gets
pushed to the fringes. Instead of staying at the center of our lives,
Christ gradually gets relegated to the shadows.
Don't let this happen to you![56]

———◆———

The self-life manifests itself in self-indulgences, such as self-love,
self-will, self-seeking, self-pride . . . It takes self-denial to turn off the
television and spend [time] in prayer . . . and read the Scriptures . . .
the only object in life is that Christ may be honored.[57]

———◆———

Make it your goal to build strong foundations for your life—
foundations constructed from prayer and the truths of God's Word.[58]

———◆———

Because of the brevity of life,
the Bible warns that we should be prepared to meet God at all times.[59]

———◆———

Becoming a Christian takes only a single step;
being a Christian means walking with Christ the rest of your life.[60]

———◆———

Mark my word, the day is coming when it's
going to cost to live for Jesus Christ.
We are, more and more, a minority,
and that's exactly what it was like in the first century.[61]

———◆———

What do others see when they look at your life?
What do those who know you best say about you—your spouse,
your children, your friends, your coworkers?
Do they see inconsistencies in any area of your life—
money, relationships, speech, possessions?[62]

———◆———

I've known the thrill of winning a tough ball game
and of winning a golf match on the last hole.
But to me the biggest thrill is to win the big one—
the spiritual battle of life.[63]

———◆———

The light of God's presence in our lives
is a purifying flame that will draw us near to Him.[64]

BILLY GRAHAM ON
LIVING THE
CHRISTIAN LIFE

We instructed you how to live in order to please God . . . For you know
what instructions we gave you by the authority of the Lord Jesus.

—1 THESSALONIANS 4:1–2 NIV

———◆———

Authentic Christian living has its own order of priority in our lives:
God first, others second, self third.[1]

———◆———

All believers are called to be holy in mind, body, and spirit (1 Peter 1:15).[2]

———◆———

If we are living according to what we believe, we may be falsely accused.[3]

———◆———

Make it your goal to become more like Christ
by refusing to let sin have its way,
and pursuing instead that which is pure and good in the sight of God.[4]

———◆———

There must be no discrepancy between what we say
and what we do, between our walk and our talk.[5]

———⋯———

I am engaged in spiritual warfare every day.
I must never let down my guard—I must keep armed.[6]

———⋯———

"Being" is far more important than "doing."
When we are what we should be inside, we will bring forth fruit.[7]

———⋯———

Submission . . . involves getting rid of everything
which hinders God's control over our lives.[8]

———⋯———

Whatever is unlike Christ in conduct, speech,
or disposition grieves the Spirit of grace.[9]

———⋯———

To be Spirit-filled is to be controlled or dominated
by the Spirit's presence and power.[10]

———⋯———

The lives of many reflect the practices and standards
of this present world . . .
they are more interested in imitating the world system
dominated by Satan than in imitating Christ.[11]

———⋯———

Every area of our lives is to be under the Lordship of Jesus Christ.
And that means the searchlight of God's Word
must penetrate every corner of our lives.[12]

The world doesn't really have much respect for Christians
who adopt its fashions and ideas.
It is inclined to regard them with contempt—
to write them off either as cowards who are ashamed of their
faith or as frauds whose profession is not sincere.[13]

Popularity and adulation are far more dangerous
for the Christian than persecution.
It is easy when all goes smoothly to lose our
sense of balance and perspective.[14]

Extremes should be avoided.[15]

[Our] minds are molded in many different ways—
often in ways we are not aware of at the time.
I am convinced that many things—the films we watch,
the television we see, the music we listen to,
the books we read—have a great effect on us.[16]

The more we yield to pressure, the more easily we will yield next time.[17]

Delighting in the Lord alters the desires.[18]

Confidentiality is the essence of being trusted.[19]

———•———

The Bible teaches that you have three enemies . . .
the devil . . . the world . . . the flesh.[20]

———•———

You cannot build a superstructure on a cracked foundation.[21]

———•———

The [twentieth century] could well go down in history not so much
as a century of progress but as "the century of superficiality."[22]

———•———

Christians are to be "the light of the world" [Matthew 5:14],
illuminating the darkness caused by sin and giving guidance
to a world that has lost its way.[23]

BILLY GRAHAM ON
LONELINESS

God sets the lonely in families.

—PSALM 68:6 NIV

———❦———

Loneliness is no respecter of persons.
It invades the palace as well as the hut.[1]

———❦———

One kind of loneliness is the loneliness of solitude. If you have
repented, surrendered, and committed your heart and life to Him,
Christ forgives . . . and takes you into His family; He brings you to
the hearth, and you feel the warmth of the fire. If you are lonely
today, seek Christ and know the fellowship that He brings.[2]

———❦———

I am never lonely when I am sharing [Christ] with others.
There is a great exhilaration in talking to others about [Him].[3]

———❦———

There are thousands of lonely people who carry heavy and
difficult burdens of grief, anxiety, pain, and disappointment;
but the loneliest of all is one whose life is steeped in sin.[4]

I am never lonely when I am praying, for this brings me
into companionship with the greatest friend of all—Jesus Christ.
He said, "I call you not servants; . . . but . . . friends" [John 15:15 KJV].[5]

The kind of society we live in can contribute to loneliness.
Mobility and constant change tend to make some individuals
feel rootless and disconnected.[6]

God didn't make Adam and Eve because He was lonely
or because He needed someone to love Him in return.
God is complete in Himself; He lacks nothing.
God's love compelled Him to create [humanity].
His love was expressed in the creation of the human race.[7]

I have often said that loneliness is the
predominant attitude in our culture.
A person can be lonely in the midst of a party;
he can be lonely in a crowd.
Loneliness may be experienced by the rich and famous
or the poor and unknown.[8]

With Christ as your Savior and constant Companion,
you, although alone, need never be lonely.[9]

I am never lonely when I am reading the Bible.
Nothing dissolves loneliness like a session with God's Word.[10]

BILLY GRAHAM ON
LOVE

Those who obey God's word truly show how completely they love him.

—1 JOHN 2:5

❖

I am convinced the greatest act of love we can ever perform
for people is to tell them about God's love for them in Christ.[1]

❖

When Christ's love fills our hearts, it puts selfishness on the run.[2]

❖

The mystery of God's love would not be a mystery
if we knew all the answers.[3]

❖

God has not changed. His laws have not changed.
He is still a God of love and mercy.
But He is also a God of righteousness and judgment.[4]

❖

God is sending forth His message of love, but you must tune in.
You must be willing to listen and to receive
His message and then to obey it.[5]

Don't make the mistake of thinking that because God is love
everything is going to be sweet, beautiful, and happy
and that no one will be punished for his sins . . .
God's love provided the cross of Jesus,
by which we can have forgiveness and cleansing.[6]

A God of love must be a God of justice.
It is because God loves that He is just.
His justice balances His love and makes His acts of both
love and justice meaningful.[7]

God could not consistently love men
if He did not provide for the judgment of evildoers.[8]

[The] love of God that reaches to wherever
a man is, can be entirely rejected.
God will not force Himself upon anyone against his will.
It is your part to believe. It is your part to receive.
Nobody else can do it for you.[9]

God's love is unchangeable;
He knows exactly what we are and loves us anyway.[10]

God's love did not begin at the cross.
It began in eternity before the world was established,
before the time clock of civilization began to move.[11]

It was God's love which knew that men were
incapable of obeying His law,
and it was His love which promised a Redeemer, a Savior,
who would save His people from their sins.[12]

No one can grasp the love of the God of the universe
without knowing His Son.[13]

Speak about the love of God and faces light up,
but speak of God as a Judge, and our attitudes change.[14]

There is one thing God's love cannot do.
It cannot forgive the unrepentant sinner.[15]

Our popular music talks constantly about love,
and yet divorce rates skyrocket.[16]

"God is love" means that He tries constantly
to block your route to destruction.[17]

What relationships need strengthening in your life?
Don't wait for them to grow cold or bitter, but ask God to help you
strengthen them by putting God's love into action—begin today.[18]

[Christians] are commanded to love our neighbors, and the first step in
doing this is to show a watching world that Christ reigns within us.[19]

Agape love is selfless love . . . the love God wants us to
have isn't just an emotion but a conscious act of the will—
a deliberate decision on our part to put others ahead of
ourselves. This is the kind of love God has for us.[20]

Until the Good News of Jesus Christ burst onto the human scene,
the word *love* was understood mostly in terms of seeking one's
own advantage. Loving the unlovely was incomprehensible.
A loving God reaching down to sinful humans was unthinkable.[21]

Scripture makes it clear that our first love is always to be for our Lord.[22]

When you truly love someone,
you want to please and honor them by the way you act.
How you treat someone
shows whether or not you really care about them.[23]

If we truly love Christ, we will want to please and honor Him by the
way we live. Even the thought of hurting Him or bringing disgrace
to His name will be abhorrent to us.[24]

True love is an act of the will—a conscious decision to do what is best
for the other person instead of ourselves.[25]

BILLY GRAHAM ON
LUST

You have heard that it was said, "Do not commit adultery."
But I tell you that anyone who looks at a woman lustfully
has already committed adultery with her in his heart.

—MATTHEW 5:27–28 NIV

———※———

An unbelieving world may say otherwise, but so-called "sexual
liberation" is actually sexual slavery—slavery to our own lusts.[1]

———※———

Pornography is anything that depicts lewdness in such a way
as to create impure thoughts and lusts.
However, the sewers continue to flow,
destroying the moral fabric of our society.[2]

———※———

It has always been a mark of decaying civilizations
to become obsessed with sex. When people lose their way, their purpose,
their will, and their goals, as well as their faith . . . they go "a whoring."
It is a form of diversion that requires
no thought, no character, and no restraint.[3]

Why shouldn't we have laws forbidding pornography and obscenity?
Many heroic leaders have tried, but they have stumbled
over even the definition of the word "obscenity."
If we cannot agree on the length of a foot,
it is because we have lost our yardstick.[4]

[Satan] has hundreds of agents writing pornographic literature and
producing sex movies to pollute [the mind]. He has intellectuals in
high positions teaching a hedonistic and permissive philosophy . . .
They lack an anchor for their real self.[5]

We are going through a sexual tempest, a bombardment
provided by unprecedented exploitation of cheap
sex by moviemakers, theater owners,
publishers, and producers of pornography. [There is more] openness
of talk about sex, acceptance of public nudity . . . homosexuality.
Sex revolution, no! But sex pollution? Yes!!![6]

Sex-centered magazines litter our newsstands . . . each edition
trying to escape new laws from the bottom of the sewers.
We put lids on sewer holes. Ought we not to do
something about the pornography which is spewing out
a polluted river of filth which can destroy us faster
than any chemical pollution we seem so worried about?[7]

The serious student of the Bible cannot dismiss
homosexual behavior simply as an alternate lifestyle.
Nor can it be argued that homosexuals were
"born this way" or that such behavior is an illness.[8]

No matter how we may rationalize the practice [of homosexuality] . . .
Romans 1 makes it clearly the product of a reprobate mind . . .
I am not exonerating all heterosexual activity . . . When we
come to Christ, we are called upon to repent of our sins and
no longer to practice the ungodly patterns of living.[9]

In the face of legalized pornography, the conscience of America seems
to be paralyzed. More serious than our fakery in art, literature,
and pictures is the collapse of our moral standards and the
blunting of our capacity as a nation for righteous indignation.[10]

It is a source of encouragement that many homosexuals report
being transformed through the power of the Gospel.[11]

Society has become so obsessed with sex
that it seeps from all the pores of our national life.[12]

The word *lust* [can] mean "selfish desire." . . .
It is wanting something so badly you will do anything
to get it. That is one of the tricks of the devil.
It is too high a price to pay.[13]

BILLY GRAHAM ON
MARRIAGE

Blessed are those who are invited to the marriage supper . . .
These are true words of God.

—REVELATION 19:9 NASB

———◆———

The Bible stresses that a marriage ideally should be a
picture or a reflection of Christ's love for His people.[1]

———◆———

Marriage is a holy bond because it permits two people to help each other
work out their spiritual destinies. God declared marriage to be good.[2]

———◆———

Marriage is the most serious long-term contract a
couple will make in their lifetime,
but many enter into it with a lack of maturity and knowledge.
The growing number of divorces shows how imperative it is
that young people be adequately prepared for marriage.[3]

———◆———

Nothing brings more joy than a good marriage,
and nothing brings more misery than a bad marriage.[4]

———

Thousands of young couples go through with a loveless marriage
because no one ever told them what genuine love is.
If people today knew that kind of love,
the divorce rate would be sharply reduced.[5]

———

The perfect marriage is a uniting of three persons—
a man and a woman and God. That is what makes marriage holy.[6]

———

Gardens don't grow by themselves;
they need to be tended and cultivated and weeded.
The same is true of a marriage.[7]

———

The secret of domestic happiness is to let God,
the party of the third part in the marriage contract,
have His rightful place in the home.
Make peace with Him,
and then you can be a real peacemaker in the home.[8]

———

If young people could only realize that a happy marriage depends not
only on the present, but upon the past, they would be more reluctant
to enter into loose, intimate relations with anyone and everyone.[9]

———

Every divorce represents a broken dream,
a shattered hope, a ruined expectation.[10]

———

My wife often said that "a good marriage
consists of two good forgivers."[11]

When a husband and wife are concerned only
about their own individual desires,
the stage is set for conflict.[12]

I have been asked the question,
"Who do you go to for counsel, for spiritual guidance?"
My answer: My wife, Ruth. She is the only one I completely confide in.[13]

[My wife] is a great student of the Bible.
Her life is ruled by the Bible more than any person I've ever known.
That's her rule book, her compass.[14]

[Ruth's] disposition is the same all the time—
very sweet and very gracious and very charming.
When it comes to spiritual things,
my wife has had the greatest influence on my ministry.[15]

Without Ruth's partnership and encouragement over the years,
my own work would have been impossible.
We were called by God as a team.[16]

A loving God ordained monogamous marriage
and the sanctity of what we call the traditional family.[17]

It's amazing how we can hurt others, especially those close to us . . .
subtle and not-so-subtle ways in which
wives belittle husbands and vice versa.[18]

=>◆<=

I get many letters every day from people who got married
because they wanted their own selfish needs satisfied,
and have only later come to realize that this does not work.[19]

=>◆<=

Marriage is not a reform school . . .
Instead of you reforming [your spouse],
[he or she] will instead influence you.[20]

=>◆<=

As husband and wife, to have a happy life together,
you must have confidence and respect,
and you must have substantial agreement in your faith.[21]

=>◆<=

The only really sound marriages are those based on mutual respect.[22]

=>◆<=

Our culture puts feelings first, but true love isn't based on feelings.
That is why there are so many divorces today.
When the early romantic feelings in a marriage
do not remain constant . . .
many people believe divorce is the answer.[23]

=>◆<=

[God] can help you begin to rebuild your marriage and your life
if you will let Him rule in your life.[24]

=>◆<=

While God's will is that every marriage will endure,
man's sin has poisoned many relationships.[25]

I'm afraid many young people today have very
romantic ideas about marriage—
ideas that do not necessarily reflect the truth . . .
Romantic feelings alone are not enough when the
problems and strains come—as they inevitably do.[26]

Many people today have discarded the Bible's clear teaching on
sexual relations outside of marriage,
simply because they are absorbed only in
their own pleasures and desires.[27]

A good marriage is not "made in heaven," but on earth.
Love is a fragile commodity which needs to be
cultivated and nourished constantly.[28]

Marriage is God's invention, not ours!
Society didn't establish it; God did.[29]

Satan's first appearance in the Bible included an attack on a marriage—
trying to divide Adam and Eve. His tactics have not changed.
He wants our marriages to flounder and fail,
because he knows that few things will discourage us more.[30]

I know of few families today that aren't touched to some extent
by the heartache of divorce, including our own.[31]

A marriage based only on physical attraction or romantic emotions is almost certainly doomed to failure right from the start.[32]

Too many husbands and wives enter into marriage with the idea that their spouse exists for one purpose: to make them happy.[33]

Young people, look to your Bible when thinking about any matter, including getting married.[34]

BILLY GRAHAM ON
MONEY

Don't love money; be satisfied with what you have.
For God has said, "I will never fail you."

—HEBREWS 13:5

———◆———

Tell me what you think about money,
and I will tell you what you think about God,
for these two are closely related.
A man's heart is closer to his wallet than anything else.[1]

———◆———

Money represents your time, your energy, your talents,
your total personality converted into currency.
We usually hold on to it tenaciously, yet it is uncertain in value
and we cannot take it into the next world.[2]

———◆———

The Bible warns that money cannot buy happiness!
Money cannot buy true pleasure. Money cannot buy peace of heart.
And money certainly cannot buy entrance into the kingdom of God.[3]

———❖———

We have tried to enthrone the false gods of money, fame,
and human intelligence; but however we try, the end is always the same:
"It is appointed unto men once to die" [Hebrews 9:27 KJV].[4]

———❖———

The Internal Revenue Service wants a record
of how you spend your money,
but that is nothing compared to the books God is keeping.[5]

———❖———

Money takes our minds off God.[6]

———❖———

Covetousness puts money above manhood.
It shackles its devotee and makes him its victim.
It hardens the heart and deadens the noble impulses
and destroys the vital qualities of life.[7]

———❖———

Today we are putting our hopes in materialism,
in technological progress, and in freedom from moral absolutes.
They have all failed.
They've failed because they've been powerless
to change the human heart.
What is the answer? There is hope, if we will turn to God.[8]

———❖———

If we allow our Christian faith to be adulterated with materialism,
watered down by secularism, and intermingled with a bland humanism,
we cannot stand up to a system that has vowed to bury us.[9]

———

Part of our problem with debt is that we
have confused needs with wants.
Yesterday's luxuries are today's necessities.[10]

———

There are two ways of being rich—have a lot, or want very little.
The latter way is the easier for most.[11]

———

There are those who have made their fortunes
on other people's misfortune.
The Bible never promised that life would be fair.[12]

———

Many young people are building their lives on the rock of materialism.
I find across the country a deep economic discontent
among people in every walk of life.[13]

———

Can people tell from the emphasis we attach to material things
whether we have set our affection on things above,
or whether we are primarily attached to this world?[14]

———

Materialism may do what a foreign invader
could never hope to achieve—
materialism robs a nation of its spiritual strength.[15]

———

We can possess nothing—no property and no person . . .
It is God who owns everything, and we are but stewards of
His property during the brief time we are on earth.[16]

———✦———

God does not need our money.
He owns everything, including "our" money.
What He wants [us] to discover
is where our central focus of worship lies.
Is that focus on God or our money?[17]

———✦———

Materialism and self-centeredness are the great vices of our age.[18]

———✦———

There are things which money cannot buy; which no music can bring;
which no social position can claim; which no personal influence
can assure; and which no eloquence can command.[19]

———✦———

We are only stewards of the world's resources.
They are not ours; they are God's.
When we find our security in Him, we can then give generously
from what He has entrusted to us. This is our Christian duty.[20]

———✦———

There is nothing wrong with men possessing riches.
The wrong comes when riches possess men.[21]

———✦———

Pleasure depends on circumstances, but Christian joy is
completely independent of health, money, or surroundings.[22]

BILLY GRAHAM ON
MORALS

Make every effort to respond to God's promises.
Supplement your faith with a generous provision of moral excellence.

—2 PETER 1:5

———◆———

New morality is nothing more than
the old immorality brought up to date.[1]

———◆———

We have changed our moral code to fit our behavior
instead of changing our behavior to harmonize with God's moral code.[2]

———◆———

We have glamorized vice and minimized virtue.
We have played down gentleness, manners, and morals—
while we have played up rudeness, savagery, and vice . . .
and the philosophy of "might is right."[3]

———◆———

We do not need a new moral order;
the world desperately needs the tried and tested moral order
that God handed down at Sinai.[4]

The Bible teaches that man can undergo a radical spiritual
and moral change that is brought about by God Himself.[5]

What happens when lying and stealing and immorality and murder
become the norm? The result can be summarized in one word: chaos.[6]

Immorality is glorified today.
The Scripture teaches that God hates immorality!
The ideal of purity is scorned, immorality is laughed at in school—
"God is old-fashioned!"
What else can we expect but that thousands of our
young people are growing up to be immoral?[7]

The first and second commandments are the only therapy the
world has ever needed. "Thou shalt love the Lord thy God with all
thy heart, and with all thy soul, and with all thy mind . . .
Thou shalt love thy neighbor as thyself" [Matthew 22:37, 39 KJV].[8]

This is a high-strung, neurotic, impatient age. We hurry when there
is no reason to hurry, just to be hurrying. This fast-paced age has
produced more problems and less morality than previous generations,
and it has given us jangled nerves. Impatience has produced a crop
of broken homes, ulcers, and has set the stage for more world wars.[9]

Moral living sometimes demands difficult choices.
It requires selflessness.[10]

The fact that immorality is rampant throughout the nation
doesn't make it right![11]

Movie and television stars lay down the law of
fashions, manners, speech, and even moral behavior.
It has been proven that a movie or a television program can brainwash.[12]

The Ten Commandments are just as valid today
as they were when God gave them. They reflect the moral character of
God, and they also provide the foundation of right living with others.[13]

BILLY GRAHAM ON
PARENTS

Obey your parents in the Lord, for this is right. "Honor your father and mother," which is the first commandment with promise.

—EPHESIANS 6:1–2 NKJV

—◆—

Both my parents had a great influence on me.
I never heard my father use a profane or even a slang word.
I always respected him because of his complete integrity.
In his business dealings his handshake was like a contract.
He was as good as his word.
Of all the people I have ever known,
my mother had the greatest influence on me.[1]

—◆—

If God gives you responsibility for aging parents,
seek what is best for them, not what is most convenient
for you. And keep contact with them![2]

—◆—

Parents, pray that God may crown your home with grace and mercy.[3]

In searching for ways to bridge the generation gap, there is no doubt that we, as parents, will have to practice what we preach, by striving more to bring our conduct into line with our code of beliefs.[4]

If ever we needed to put the Golden Rule into action,
it's with our aging parents.[5]

Although the testimony of my mother's life helped mold me
and taught me how to live,
the testimony of her last years and her death
gave me insight into how to die.[6]

What a comfort it was for me to know that no matter where I was
in the world, my mother was praying for me.[7]

The greatest tribute a boy can give to his father is to say,
"When I grow up, I want to be just like my dad."
It is a convicting responsibility for us fathers and grandfathers.[8]

Parents have bought into the world's pastimes chock-full of
pop culture, and it is searing the souls of our children.
Parents have allowed electronic babysitters to infiltrate their homes
and minds; young people's sense of right and wrong is being
choked by wild and rank weeds in a moral wasteland.[9]

Only God Himself fully appreciates the influence of a Christian mother
in the molding of character in her children.[10]

The influence of a mother upon the lives of
her children cannot be measured.
They know and absorb her example and attitudes
when it comes to questions of
honesty, temperance, kindness, and industry.[11]

Many parents preach to their children but do not set good examples.
Parents want the children to do as they say, not as they do.[12]

Parenting is the most important responsibility most of us will ever face,
and none of us does it perfectly.[13]

My father-in-law . . . was a great inspiration to me
both in life and in his preparation for death.[14]

What a blessing it is for parents to believe in their children.[15]

Billy Graham on
Patience

Honest, good-hearted people who hear God's word,
cling to it, and patiently produce a huge harvest.

—Luke 8:15

———※———

Our lives are to be characterized by patience,
for it is important in developing the mature, stable character
which God wants to produce in His people.[1]

———※———

Patience . . . speaks of a person's steadfastness under provocation . . .
enduring ill-treatment without anger or
thought of retaliation or revenge.[2]

———※———

Patience is the transcendent radiance of a
loving and tender heart which,
in its dealings with those around it,
looks kindly and graciously upon them.[3]

The Christian . . . way of daily living must be distinct from the world.
While some will think you "peculiar," do not let this disturb you,
for just as many others will secretly admire you for your stand.
It is possible you will be persecuted by jokes and be misunderstood . . .
but if you accept this with patience and in the spirit of love,
God can use this very thing to help you win
some of your friends [to Christ].[4]

Patience includes perseverance—the ability to bear up under
weariness, strain, and persecution when doing the work of the Lord.[5]

Patience graciously, compassionately and with understanding,
judges the faults of others without unjust criticism.[6]

God allows difficulties, inconveniences, trials,
and even suffering to come our way for a specific purpose:
They help develop the right attitude for the growth of patience.[7]

Patience is part of true Christlikeness, something we so often
admire in others without demanding it of ourselves.[8]

Patience in our lives springs from God's power
based upon our willingness to learn it.[9]

BILLY GRAHAM ON
PEACE

These things I have spoken to you, that in Me you may have peace.

—JOHN 16:33 NKJV

———◆———

If the United Nations could bring lasting peace, man could say to God,
"We do not need You anymore. We have brought peace on
earth and have organized humanity in righteousness."
All of these schemes are patchwork remedies that a sick and
dying world must use while waiting for the Great Physician.[1]

———◆———

Only Christ can meet the deepest needs of our world and our hearts.
Christ alone can bring lasting peace—
peace with God, peace among men and nations,
and peace within our hearts.
He transcends the political and social boundaries of our world.[2]

———◆———

I call upon the leaders of all nations to work for peace,
even when the risks seem high.
I call upon Christians to pray and work for peace
in whatever constructive ways are open to them.
I do not believe this is only a political issue; it is a moral one as well.[3]

Peace conferences are held almost daily by governments,
civic organizations, and churches.
But the Scripture teaches that peace and safety will not come
in any lasting way until the Prince of Peace, the Messiah,
Jesus Christ, comes and rules and reigns in our world.[4]

If we are at peace with this world,
it may be because we have sold out to it and compromised with it.[5]

For the Christian, peace is not simply the absence of conflict,
or any other artificial state the world has to offer.
Rather it is the deep, abiding peace only
Jesus Christ brings to the heart.[6]

There is going on in the world today a quiet, bloodless revolution.
It has no fanfare, no newspaper coverage, no propaganda;
yet it is changing the course of thousands of lives.
It is restoring purpose and meaning to life as men of all races
and nationalities are finding peace with God.[7]

When everyone does what is right in his own eyes,
there is no possibility of order and peace.[8]

Peace with God and the peace of God in a man's heart and the joy
of fellowship with Christ have in themselves a beneficial effect
upon the body and mind and will lead to the development
and preservation of physical and mental power.[9]

The world thinks peace would come if everyone made a lot of money,
but people haven't found peace in possessions.
They have thought the world would have
peace if all arms were destroyed.
Yet Cain killed Abel without a handgun.
It is man's heart that is the problem.[10]

Jesus didn't leave a material inheritance to His disciples.
All He had when He died was a robe. But Jesus willed
His followers something more valuable than gold.
He willed us His peace.
He said: "My peace I give to you; not as the
world gives" [John 14:27 NKJV].[11]

The war that exists between you and God can be over quickly,
and the peace treaty is signed in the blood of [God's] Son Jesus Christ.[12]

Peacemaking is a noble vocation . . .
To be a peacemaker, you must know the Peace-Giver.[13]

We're not going to have peace—permanent peace—
until the Prince of Peace comes. And He is coming.[14]

Your future does not hinge on the world situation,
however grim it might become.
It depends on what happened 2,000 years ago at the cross
and your acceptance or rejection of the Prince of Peace.[15]

The world doesn't give peace, for it doesn't have any peace to give.
It fights for peace, it negotiates for peace, it maneuvers for peace,
but there is no ultimate peace in the world.
But Jesus gives peace to those who put their trust in Him.[16]

The promoters of change offer a grand vision of world unity.
While the globalists and international affairs specialists continue
their chant for "peace, peace," we are reminded that the Bible says
that there can be no lasting peace until Christ returns.
So the world remains restless and uncertain.[17]

I know where I've come from. I know why I'm here.
I know where I'm going—and I have peace in my heart.
His peace floods my heart and overwhelms my soul![18]

Most people yearn for one thing more than anything else: inner peace.
Without it they have no lasting happiness or security.[19]

Peace—[the ability] to sleep in the storm![20]

Until you actually possess true peace with God,
no one can describe its wonders to you.[21]

BILLY GRAHAM ON
PEOPLE

All the people answered . . .
"All the words which the L ord has spoken we will do."

—EXODUS 24:3 NASB

———◆———

God can take anything that happens to us—even bad things—
and use it to shape us and make us into a better,
more Christlike person—if we will let Him.[1]

———◆———

There are three of you. There is the person you think you are.
There is the person others think you are.
There is the person God knows you are and can be through Christ.[2]

———◆———

Our personalities, our intelligence, and our capabilities are gifts from
[God's] own bountiful hand. If we divert their use for our own profit,
we become guilty of selfishness.[3]

———◆———

Almost nothing is as complex as the human personality, and no
simple formula will ever cover every situation or every relationship.[4]

People are little creatures with big capacities,
finite beings with infinite desires,
deserving nothing but demanding all.
God made people with this huge capacity and desire in order that
He might come in and completely satisfy that desire.[5]

Man is not growing better! Man is not climbing upward.
Instead of progress in man himself there is degeneracy—
degeneracy of body, mind, and spirit. Man is going downhill.[6]

I am becoming aware of the truth that people change people as much
as ideas change people. The power of personality is strong . . .
often personality is greater than the idea.[7]

The Bible says that God sees two classes of men.
He sees the saved and the lost,
those who are going to heaven and those who are going to hell.[8]

Lying is one of the worst of all sins and can be committed
by a thought, word, or deed.
Anything that is intended to deceive another person is lying.[9]

As men and women seek to find independence from God,
they have lost a sense of purpose in life.
The worth of human personality is often equated with
what we do for a living. However, a person's occupation,
community standing, or bank account is not
what is important in God's eyes.[10]

Tell me why the gardener trims and prunes his rosebushes,
sometimes cutting away productive branches,
and I will tell you why God's people are afflicted.
God's hand never slips.[11]

All around you are people who need Christ: your family, your neighbors,
people you work with or go to school with every day.
Are you praying for them,
asking God to open the door of their hearts to His truth?[12]

Someday all of us will give account of the way we have used the
gifts God has given. The person to whom much has been given
will find much required of him.[13]

I have never met a person who didn't have problems of some kind.
This is why we need one another's encouragement.[14]

No area of human life is so full of difficulties and heartaches as
relationships. If you listed everything that upset you during the
past week, I suspect most had to do with other people.
People can be selfless and kind, but they can also be difficult,
stubborn, ego-driven, thoughtless, mean, selfish, manipulative.
But the problem is not just other people; it's also ourselves.[15]

Instead of manipulating [people] for our own purposes, we'd help them
achieve what is best for them. We'd also try to see life through their eyes.
Treat others the way you would want them to treat you.[16]

"If the other person would just do things my
way, we could get along," one says,
when the other person is probably thinking the
same about us—that leads to conflict.
Our deepest problems are within ourselves.[17]

Man boasts of his nobility, his ideals, and his progress.
Man's goal is imitation, not redemption.[18]

Man persists in waywardness.
If one institution fails [he says], try another—anything but God's plan.[19]

Some of the most miserable people I have ever met
have been people who are very popular with the public,
but down inside are empty and miserable.[20]

In our day many people are broad but shallow.
Agnosticism, anxiety, and emptiness have gripped much of our world.[21]

Compared to when I was a boy, we now live in reverse.
The people are locked up in their homes at night
and criminals are outside on the loose!
When I was young, the criminals were locked up and
the people were free to move about.
That time has passed for many cities.[22]

———◆———

The central theme of the universe
is the purpose and destiny of every individual.
Every person is important in God's eyes.[23]

———◆———

I have never known a man who received Christ and ever regretted it.[24]

BILLY GRAHAM ON
PERSECUTION

Persecution comes because of the word.

—MATTHEW 13:21 NIV

———————

Persecution is one of the natural consequences
of living the Christian life.
It is to the Christian what "growing pains" are to the growing child.
No pain, no development. No suffering, no glory.
No struggle, no victory.
No persecution, no reward![1]

———————

No Christian has the right to go around wringing his hands,
wondering what we are to do in the face of the present world situation.
The Scripture says that in the midst of persecution, confusion, wars,
and rumors of wars, we are to comfort one another with the knowledge
that Jesus Christ is coming back in triumph, glory, and majesty.[2]

———————

We should not covet or expect the praise of ungodly men . . .
the very fact that they are inclined to persecute us is proof that
we are "not of the world."[3]

—=⧫=—

Bearing our cross does not mean wearing gunny sacks and long faces.
Some people . . . wear the look of a martyr
every time they hear criticism.
Sometimes we deserve the criticism we receive; however,
we are blessed only when men speak evil
against us *falsely* for Christ's sake.[4]

—=⧫=—

Persecution may wear an insulting face.
Insults may come as a result of a Christian's lifestyle,
which should be different from that of the secular world.[5]

—=⧫=—

Throughout the world today there are people who are enduring
cruelties and persecution because of their Christian faith.
We must pray for them, and for ourselves,
so that in our own dying hour God will give us grace to endure
until the end, anticipating the certainty of His glory to come.[6]

—=⧫=—

In a country where Christians were looked upon with suspicion
and disfavor, a government leader said to me with a twinkle in his eye,
"Christians seem to thrive under persecution.
Perhaps we should prosper them, and then they would disappear."[7]

—=⧫=—

While Christians in America have worshipped without the
fear or threat of physical abuse for their beliefs,
thousands of their brothers in Christ throughout the world
have been tortured and martyred for confessing the name of Christ.[8]

The Bible clearly says that faithfulness and persecution
often go hand in hand.[9]

———◆———

Subtle persecution may happen to you in your office, school,
or social gathering. You may not be "with it," or be "one of the crowd."
No suffering that the Christian endures for Christ is ever in vain.[10]

———◆———

If you take a stand [for God] and mean it,
you may suffer persecution. Some of your friends will drift away.
They don't want to be with people like you.
You speak to their conscience.
They feel uncomfortable in your presence
because you live for God.[11]

———◆———

We can take persecution because we know the purpose behind it.
The purpose is to glorify God.[12]

BILLY GRAHAM ON
PLEASURE

In the last days . . . men will be . . .
lovers of pleasure rather than lovers of God.

—2 TIMOTHY 3:1–2, 4 NASB

❧

The more worldly pleasure we enjoy,
the less satisfied and contented we are with life.[1]

❧

Today our world is mad in its obsession with pleasure, sex, and money.
Its ear is too dull to hear the truth. Most men's eyes are blind.
They do not want to see. They do not want to hear.
They hurry to their doom.[2]

❧

Many of us have no appetite for spiritual things
because we are absorbed in the sinful pleasures of this world.
We have been eating too many of the devil's delicacies.[3]

❧

[Mankind has] allowed worldly desires and pleasures to fill the heart and
mind. Whatever the sin, we need to repent and
turn to Jesus Christ in faith for forgiveness and new life.[4]

We have at our fingertips every pleasure that man is capable of enjoying,
and man has abused every gift God ever gave him.[5]

There is legitimate pleasure, which is not wrong,
but we are not to become so preoccupied with its activities
that it takes the place of God.[6]

How do we get our values so mixed up?
We look for shortcuts to happiness.
Our lust for immediate pleasure prompts us to think of evil as good.[7]

We are like a restless sea,
finding a little peace here and a little pleasure there,
but nothing permanent and satisfying. So the search continues![8]

Billy Graham on
PRAYER

We will give ourselves continually to prayer and to the ministry of the word.

—ACTS 6:4 NKJV

Heaven is full of answers to prayer
for which no one ever bothered to ask![1]

Many times I have been driven to prayer.
When I was in Bible school I didn't know what to do with my life.
I used to walk the streets . . . and pray, sometimes for hours at a time.
In His timing, God answered those prayers,
and since then prayer has been an essential part of my life.[2]

I have never met anyone who spent time in daily prayer,
and in the study of the Word of God, and was strong in faith,
who was ever discouraged for very long.[3]

If there are any tears shed in heaven,
they will be over the fact that we prayed so little.[4]

In the morning, prayer is the key that opens to us
the treasures of God's mercies and blessings;
in the evening, it is the key that shuts us up
under His protection and safeguard.[5]

Sometimes I'm asked to list the most important steps in preparing
for an evangelistic mission, and my reply is always the same:
prayer . . . prayer . . . prayer.[6]

Prayer is crucial in evangelism:
Only God can change the heart of someone
who is in rebellion against Him.
No matter how logical our arguments or how fervent our appeals,
our words will accomplish nothing unless God's Spirit prepares the way.[7]

We should not pray for God to be on our side,
but pray that we may be on God's side.[8]

We must repent of our prayerlessness. We must make prayer our priority.
Even our churches today have gotten away from prayer meetings.[9]

You cannot pray for someone and hate them at the same time.[10]

Prayer is for every moment of our lives,
not just for times of suffering or joy. Prayer is really a place,
a place where you meet God in genuine conversation.[11]

No matter how dark and hopeless a situation might seem,
never stop praying.[12]

Prayers have no boundaries.
They can leap miles and continents
and be translated instantly into any language.[13]

True prayer is a way of life, not just for use in cases of emergency.
Make it a habit, and when the need arises you will be in practice.[14]

Persecution, whether it is physical, social, or mental,
is one of the worst types of pain,
but those who persecute us are to be the objects of our prayers.[15]

Prayer is powerful, but if our prayers are aimless, meaningless,
and mingled with doubt, they will be of little hope to us.[16]

Prayer is more than a wish; it is the voice of faith directed to God.[17]

Prayer should not be merely an act, but an attitude of life.[18]

[Jesus] prayed briefly when He was in a crowd;
He prayed a little longer when He was with His disciples;
and He prayed all night when He was alone.
Today, many in the ministry tend to reverse that process.[19]

[Jesus] had only three years of public ministry,
but He was never too hurried to spend hours in prayer . . .
No day began or closed in which He was not
in communion with His Father.[20]

If we are to depend on prayer during tough times,
we should be people of prayer before the crisis hits.[21]

Have you ever said, "Well, all we can do now is pray"? . . .
When we come to the end of ourselves,
we come to the beginning of God.[22]

I realize more than ever that this ministry has been a team effort.
Without the help of our prayer partners, our financial supporters,
our staff, and our board of directors—
this ministry and all of our dreams to spread the Good News of
God's love throughout the world would not have been possible.[23]

No matter where we are, God is as close as a prayer.
He is our support and our strength.
He will help us make our way up again from
whatever depths we have fallen.[24]

The most eloquent prayer is often prayed
through hands that heal and bless.[25]

When we know Him, we can be sure God hears our prayers.[26]

When troubles come may prayer be your automatic response.[27]

We were created to live a life of prayer.[28]

We can change the course of events
if we go to our knees in believing prayer.[29]

Someone has said,
"Prayer is the highest use to which speech can be put."[30]

I firmly believe God continues to answer the prayers of His people
even after He has taken them to heaven.
Never forget that God isn't bound by time the way we are.
We see only the present moment; God sees everything.
We see only part of what He is doing; He sees it all.[31]

Prayer is key to our effort to communicate the Gospel
and win men and women to Christ.[32]

Prayer is the Christian's greatest weapon.[33]

I believe we should pray that God will take possession
of our lives totally and completely.
We should pray that we will be emptied of self—
self-love, self-will, self-ambition—
and be placed completely at His disposal.[34]

Long after you and I are gone, God will still be at work—
and many of the things we prayed for will finally come to pass.[35]

Prayer is not just asking. It is listening for God's orders.[36]

Nothing will drive us to our knees quicker than trouble.[37]

Our prayers must be in accordance with [God's] will.
He knows better what is good for us than we know ourselves.[38]

The Book of Psalms is the Bible's hymnbook.
It will show you what it means to walk with God in prayer and praise.[39]

The devil will tremble when you pray.[40]

We are to pray in times of adversity,
lest we become faithless and unbelieving.
We are to pray in times of prosperity, lest we become boastful and proud.
We are to pray in times of danger, lest we become fearful and doubting.
We need to pray in times of security, lest we become self-sufficient.[41]

A prayerless Christian is a powerless Christian.[42]

If [Jesus] felt that He had to pray, how much more do we need to pray![43]

You cannot afford to be too busy to pray.[44]

As I close my eyes in prayer,
let me see the faces of those who need to know You, beloved Savior.[45]

Whether prayer changes our situation or not, one thing is certain:
Prayer will change us![46]

Prayer is more than a plea, it is a place where we must spend time
if we are to learn its power.[47]

It is not the posture of the body,
but the attitude of the heart that counts when we pray . . .
The important thing is not the position of the body
but the condition of the soul.[48]

This should be the motto of every follower of Jesus Christ.
Never stop praying no matter now dark and hopeless it may seem.[49]

Our prayers must be in accordance with the will of God
for the simple reason that God knows better
what is good for us than we know ourselves.[50]

At its deepest level, prayer is fellowship with
God: enjoying His company,
waiting upon His will, thanking Him for His mercies . . .
listening in the silence for what He has to say to us.[51]

Pray frequently as you read [the Bible]
and you will discover a fellowship with God.[52]

That "the Spirit Himself intercedes" indicates that it is actually
God pleading, praying, and mourning through us.[53]

God Himself is the power that makes prayer work.[54]

The men upon whose shoulders rested the initial responsibility of
Christianizing the world came to Jesus with one supreme request.
They did not say, "Lord, teach us to preach";
"Lord, teach us to do miracles";
or "Lord, teach us to be wise" . . .
but they said, "Lord, teach us to pray."[55]

To the Son of God prayer was more important
than the assembling of great throngs . . .
He often withdrew into the wilderness and prayed [Luke 5:15–16].[56]

———

The reason many . . . close their eyes while
praying is to shut out the affairs
of the world so that their minds can be
completely concentrated on God . . .
it certainly lends itself to the attitude of prayer.[57]

———

Prayer is more than a wish turned heavenward . . .
it is the voice of faith directed Godward.[58]

———

Obedience is the master key to effectual prayer.[59]

———

If we are to have our prayers answered, we must give God the glory.[60]

———

Prayer and Bible study are inseparably linked. Effective prayer is
born out of the prompting of God's Spirit as we read His Word.[61]

———

Too often we use petty little petitions, oratorical exercises,
or the words of others rather than the cries of our inmost being.
When you pray, pray![62]

———

Those you know the least may need your prayers the most. Don't let the
fact that you don't know someone keep you from praying for them.[63]

———

Prayer by itself is like a diet without protein!
Prayer is important to our spiritual growth—
but of even greater importance is God's Word, the Bible.[64]

Often, we try to tell God what we want Him to do—
but ask Him to help you guard against this, and to seek His will
instead of your own. Pray and ask God to guide you.[65]

How can you keep your mind from wandering when you pray?
Remember what you are doing: talking to God.
If you had the opportunity to talk with the president,
I doubt if your mind would wander.
[We] have the privilege of talking to someone far greater:
the King of kings![66]

Prayer is not our using of God;
it more often puts us in the position where God can use us.[67]

God welcomes our prayers.
He is much more concerned about our hearts than our eloquence.[68]

A friend of mine defines prayer as "a declaration of dependence."[69]

Ask God to give you a greater hunger for Himself and
a deeper desire for His fellowship.
Then be honest about whatever is keeping you from prayer,
and ask God to help you deal with it.[70]

Pray because Christ died to give us access to the Father.
Pray because God is worthy of our praise.
Pray because we need His forgiveness,
cleansing, guidance, and protection.
Pray because others need our prayers.[71]

Nothing can replace a daily time spent alone with God in prayer.
We can also be in an attitude of prayer throughout the day—
sitting in a car or at our desks, working in the kitchen,
even talking with someone on the phone.[72]

Prayer is speaking to God—
but sometimes He uses our times of prayerful silence
to speak to us in return.[73]

Be sure that your motive in praying is to glorify God.[74]

Jesus demonstrated the importance of prayer by His own example.
His whole ministry was saturated with prayer.[75]

We have not yet learned that we are more powerful on our knees
than behind the most powerful weapons that can be developed.[76]

A life taught in the Scriptures, and tuned in to God in prayer,
produces an outflowing of grace and power.[77]

God urges us to bring our concerns to Him—not just petitions about our own needs, but also intercessions for others. [The apostle] Paul said . . . "Brothers, pray for us" [1 Thessalonians 5:25 NIV].[78]

Many doctors today prescribe yoga as a helpful stress reliever but would not consider prescribing prayer to the One who calms our fears and anxieties.[79]

Why do we need to pray? Because the Christian life is a journey, and we need God's strength and guidance along the way.[80]

[God] says to pray for our enemies. How many of us have ever spent time praying for our enemies?[81]

A survey reported that the majority of the seminaries [in the United States] had no classes on prayer. That really shouldn't surprise us when we consider how many local churches offer classes on gardening and the "Art of Conversation" instead of the study of God's Word and prayer.[82]

Prayer is our lifeline to God.[83]

Prayer is not an option but a necessity.[84]

Prayer is the most powerful weapon we have in our spiritual arsenal to stand against the world's greatest enemy, the one who presents himself as an angel of light [2 Corinthians 11:14].[85]

———

The best way to pray is to open the Bible and pray Scripture back to the Lord, claiming His promises and asking that He strengthen and guide [us] in obeying His Word.[86]

———

Prayer shouldn't be a burden but a privilege—
God wants our fellowship.[87]

———

Prayer is the companion of Bible study.[88]

———

Before prayer changes others, it first changes us.[89]

———

I listened to a discussion of religious leaders
on how to communicate the Gospel.
Not once did I hear them mention prayer.
And yet I know of scores of churches that win many converts
each year by prayer alone.[90]

BILLY GRAHAM ON
PREACHING

O Lord . . . give us, your servants,
great boldness in preaching your word.

—ACTS 4:29

———❖———

Oh God, if You want me to preach, I will do it.[1]

———❖———

I'm not a great preacher, and I don't claim to be a great preacher . . .
I'm an ordinary preacher,
just communicating the Gospel in the best way I know how.[2]

———❖———

As the people came to a desert place to hear John the Baptist proclaim,
"Thus saith the Lord,"
so [man] in his confusions, frustrations, and bewilderment
will come to hear the minister who preaches with authority.[3]

———❖———

We preach Christ crucified.
The cross is the focal point in the life and ministry of Jesus Christ.
It was no afterthought or emergency measure with God.
Christ was "the Lamb slain from the foundation
of the world" [Revelation 13:8 KJV].[4]

—◆—

Preachers are not salesmen, for they have nothing to sell.
They are bearers of Good News.[5]

—◆—

God's strength is made perfect in weakness.
The weaker I became, the more powerful became the preaching.[6]

—◆—

Preach with authority. The authority for us is the Word of God.
Preach with simplicity . . .
Preach with urgency . . . heaven and hell are at stake.
Preach for a decision.[7]

—◆—

I have had the privilege of preaching the Gospel on every continent
in most of the countries of the world,
and I have found that when I present the simple message
of the Gospel of Jesus Christ,
with authority, quoting from the very Word of God—
He takes that message
and drives it supernaturally into the human heart.[8]

—◆—

I preach a Gospel not of despair but of hope for the individual,
hope for society, and hope for the world.[9]

—◆—

Nowhere in Mark 16:15—"Go ye into all the world,
and preach the gospel to every creature" [KJV]—
nor in any similar Scripture did Christ command us
to go only into the Western or capitalist world.
Nowhere did He say to exclude the Communist world.[10]

When I preach—no matter where it is in the world—
I can always count on five areas of human need that afflict all peoples.
Emptiness, loneliness, guilt, fear of death, deep-seated insecurity.[11]

I am counting totally and completely on the Lord Jesus Christ,
and not on Billy Graham.
I am not going to heaven because I've read the Bible,
nor because I've preached to a lot of people.
I'm going to heaven because of what Christ did.[12]

I know that many of the things I have said from
the Scriptures have offended some,
but I cannot afford to tone down the message.
As Paul said in 1 Corinthians 9:17,
"I have a stewardship entrusted to me" (NASB), and that is
to preach the pure and simple Gospel in whatever culture I am in.[13]

Many churches have their eyes on the culture instead of on Christ.
Many pastors preach on *common unity*
instead of calling the *community* to repent.[14]

When we preach or teach the Scriptures,
we open the door for the Holy Spirit to do His work.
God has not promised to bless oratory or clever preaching.
He has promised to bless His Word.[15]

———⊰◆⊱———

I must ask myself, "Billy Graham, are you prepared to
meet the Master at any moment?" Yes, I am—
but not because I have preached or tried to help people,
but solely because I am trusting Christ as my Lord and Savior.
Stop right now and ask yourself that question.[16]

———⊰◆⊱———

Effective preaching must be biblical preaching,
whether it is the exposition of a single word in the Bible,
a text, or a chapter.
The Word is what the Spirit uses.[17]

———⊰◆⊱———

Thousands of pastors, Sunday school teachers, and Christian workers
are powerless because they do not make the Word
the source of their preaching or teaching.[18]

———⊰◆⊱———

Proclaiming "the whole will of God" should be the goal—and the joy—
of every church and every preacher.[19]

BILLY GRAHAM ON
PRIDE

As the Scriptures say, "God opposes the proud but favors the humble."

—JAMES 4:6

———❈———

Man has rejected the revelation of the Bible concerning the true and living God of his fathers, and he has substituted gods of his own making. In actuality modern man has decided to dethrone God and enthrone himself in all of his nuclear glory.[1]

———❈———

Pride comes from looking only at ourselves;
meekness comes through looking at God.[2]

———❈———

There may have been a time when pride was the very center of your life. You had ambitious thoughts of yourself, your powers, desires, and aims; but now that will begin to change . . . you have been born again.[3]

———❈———

Pride consists not in wanting to be rich,
but in wanting to be richer than your neighbor.
It is not in wanting to be noticed but in wanting to be the most noticed.
It is not in wanting to have things
but in wanting more things than others.[4]

The destructive power of pride is that it countenances
nothing higher than itself.
Because of an inherent fault in our nature,
man's bias is on the side of error.
In our willful desire to live independently of God,
we have severed the lifeline that flows from the source of all life.[5]

We must not build up ourselves at the expense of others.[6]

Pride always puts [self] above others—and cuts
[itself] off from them as a result.
No one likes an arrogant, prideful person.[7]

Pride flees when we compare ourselves to
God instead of [to] other people.[8]

BILLY GRAHAM ON
RACE

[The Lord] was given authority, honor, and sovereignty
over all the nations of the world, so that people of every
race and nation and language would obey him.

—DANIEL 7:14

———※———

We have some of the finest civil rights laws in the world,
but they have not solved our racial problems. Why?
Because we need a change of heart and attitude,
Jesus said, "You must be born again" [John 3:7].[1]

———※———

The human race has the power right now to destroy itself.
Jesus Christ is going to save us from ourselves.[2]

———※———

There is only one possible solution to the race problem
and that is a vital personal experience with Jesus Christ
on the part of [all] races.[3]

———※———

God prescribes the remedy for the ills of the human race.
That remedy is personal faith and commitment to Jesus Christ.
The remedy is to be born again.[4]

In Christ the middle wall of partition has been broken down.
There is no Jew, no Gentile—no black, white, yellow, or red.
We could be one great brotherhood in Jesus Christ.
However, until we come to recognize Him as the Prince of Peace
and receive His love in our hearts, the racial tensions will increase,
racial demands will become more militant,
and a great deal of blood will be shed.
The race problem could become another flame out of control![5]

I had not been preaching long before I decided that
I would never preach to another segregated audience
in any situation over which we had control.
This was long before the Supreme Court decision of 1954.
I felt this was the Christian position and I could do no other.[6]

How can men boast that they control their own destiny when they
cannot solve the problems of war, racism, poverty, sickness, or suffering?[7]

Only God can break down the national and racial barriers that divide
men today. Only God can supply that love that we must have for our
fellowman. We will never build brotherhood of man upon earth
until we are believers in Christ Jesus.[8]

Down through the ages man's heart has remained unchanged.
Whatever the color of his skin,
whatever his cultural or ethnic background,
he needs the Gospel of Christ.[9]

Ancient historians tell us that one of the symptoms of a declining civilization is a desexualization of the human race, with men becoming more effeminate and women becoming more masculine, not only in physical [appearance] but in their basic characters.[10]

The closer the people of all races get to Christ and His cross, the closer they will get to one another.[11]

Here is the judgment toward which every person outside [of] Christ is headed. The date has already been set by God. All men of all races and nationalities, both past and present, will be there. You may make and break appointments in this life— but this is one appointment you will keep.[12]

No personality in history stands above Jesus Christ . . . He alone is able to meet every need of the human race.[13]

The human race is called on throughout the Bible to repent of sin and return to God.[14]

BILLY GRAHAM ON
RELIGION

Be doers of the word . . . Pure and undefiled religion before God and
the Father is this . . . to keep oneself unspotted from the world.

—JAMES 1:22, 27 NKJV

━━◆━━

Christianity is not a white man's religion
and don't let anybody ever tell you that it's white or black.
Christ belongs to all people; he belongs to the whole world.[1]

━━◆━━

In order to compete with God for the dominion of the world, Satan,
whom Christ called "the prince of this world,"
was forced to go into the "religion" business.[2]

━━◆━━

Some Christian leaders . . . are willing to give up some of the teachings
of the Bible in order to harmonize Christianity with the other religions.[3]

━━◆━━

Something distinguishes Christianity from all the religions of the world.
Not only does it carry the truth of the redemption,
by the death of our Savior for our sins on the cross,
but it carries the fact that Christ rose again.[4]

———

I never try to defend religion. Religion has spawned
wars. Many so-called religious people have been
characterized by prejudice, pride, and bickering . . .
I would call you to a simple faith in Jesus, who said,
"Love your neighbor as yourself."[5]

———

There are many bibles of different religions; there is the Mohammedan
Koran, the Buddhist Canon of Sacred Scripture, the Zoroastrian Zend-
Avesta, and the Brahman Veda . . . they all begin with some flashes
of true light, and end in utter darkness. Even the most casual observer
soon discovers that the Bible is radically different. It is the only Book
that offers redemption to us and points the way out of our dilemma.[6]

———

Christianity is being compared with other religions as never before.
Some so-called Christian leaders even advocate the
working out of a system of morals, ethics, and religion that
would bring together all the religions of the world.
It cannot be done. Jesus Christ is unique.[7]

———

Only God knows the future and that we are to look to Him—
not to the stars or the tea leaves or the lines on the palms of our hands—
for our confidence in the future.[8]

———

We see that humanism has become for many a polite
name for a vocal, aggressive, influential crusade against
religion in the name of social and moral advance.
There is nothing new about humanism.
It is the yielding to Satan's first temptation of Adam and Eve:
"Ye shall be as gods" [Genesis 3:5 KJV].[9]

———••———

"Religion," [some] argue, "may be all right for certain emotional people,
but you can't beat a man who believes in himself."
But this self-confident generation has produced
more alcoholics, more dope addicts,
more criminals, more wars, more broken homes,
more assaults, more embezzlements,
more murders, and more suicides than any
other generation that ever lived.
It is time for all of us to take stock of our
failures, blunders, and costly mistakes.
It is about time that we put less confidence in ourselves
and more trust and faith in God.[10]

———••———

Astrology can never give you the answers to life's deepest questions—
especially where you will spend eternity. Commit your life to Christ.
It will give you joyous confidence that your
future is securely in His hands—
tomorrow and forever.[11]

———••———

People of the West have various forms of democracy based on a
belief in God as well as on a general acceptance of moral law.
However, in practice we are beginning to resemble the Marxists,
who have little respect for moral law or religion.[12]

———••———

Hundreds of philosophies and scores of religions
have been invented to circumvent the Word of God.
Modern philosophers and psychologists are still trying to make it
appear that there is some way out other than the path of Jesus.[13]

Students today want to know about the devil, about witchcraft, about the occult. Many people do not know they are turning to Satan. They are being deluded.[14]

You can have religion but not know Christ. It's having Christ that counts.[15]

While the West had lulled itself to sleep with the comforting doctrine of man's achievements, a great revolution had been in progress in Russia. The hammer pounded and the sickle gleaned until a new social order called Communism emerged as one of the most powerful ideologies of all time. It challenged every concept man had ever held. It threatened the life of the whole world. It became the greatest challenge Christianity had faced in 2,000 years. It was a fanatic religion that asked questions and demanded answers.[16]

Religion can be anything! But true Christianity is God coming to man in a personal relationship.[17]

Man suppresses the truth, mixes it with error, and develops the religions of the world.[18]

Nothing seems to satisfy. Not politics, not education, not material goods. Some who refuse to turn their hearts toward God have created the New Age movement, with all of its aberrations. This is actually not new but only the latest attempt by man to place something other than Christ inside himself in a futile attempt to satisfy spiritual longings.[19]

——◆——

From the ghetto to the mansion, from community
leader to prisoner on death row,
man wonders if there is a God. And if there is, what is He like?
Whatever period of history we study, whatever culture we examine,
if we look back in time we see all peoples, primitive or modern,
acknowledging some kind of deity.
Some people give up the pursuit of God in frustration,
calling themselves "atheists" or "agnostics," professing to be irreligious.[20]

——◆——

Many evidences and arguments suggest God's existence,
yet the plain truth is that God cannot be proved
by intellectual arguments alone.
If the human mind could fully prove God,
He would be no greater than the mind that proves Him![21]

——◆——

Idolatrous beliefs have eroded the foundations of truth.
Whether ancient or modern, all have posed alternatives
to the biblical way of approaching God.[22]

——◆——

Men and women may devise plans to satisfy their inner longings,
but in the midst of all the "religions" of the world, God's way is
available in the Bible for all who will come to Him on His terms.[23]

——◆——

Today . . . when Satan worship is increasing at an alarming rate,
we had better be aware of him,
his origin, his aims, his abilities, and his limitations.[24]

Many people have just enough natural religion
to make them immune to the real thing.[25]

Nothing could be more wrong than the old cliché that says
any religion will do just as long as one is sincere.
In no other area of life is there so much error, deception,
and charlatanism as in religion.[26]

The Bible differentiates clearly between true faith and mere religiosity.[27]

Man has naturally and universally a capacity for religion—
and not only a capacity, for the vast majority of the human race
practices or professes some form of religion.[28]

All false religions cut away parts of God's revelation,
add ideas of their own, and come out with various viewpoints
that differ from God's revelation in the Bible.[29]

A false religion is like the imitation of high fashion.
The very presence of counterfeits proves the existence of the real.
There would be no imitations without a genuine product.
God's original design has always had imitators and counterfeits![30]

We want to be relevant . . . However, the more relevant we become to a
sin-dominated world, the more irrelevant we actually are to God.[31]

———◆———

There is a strong movement, especially in Protestantism, to recast the Christian message in order to make it acceptable to modern man.[32]

———◆———

Jesus tells us not to be misled by the voices of strangers.
There are so many strange voices being heard
in the religious world of our day.
We must compare what they say with the Word of God.[33]

———◆———

We read every day about the rich, the famous,
the talented who are disillusioned.
Many of them are turning to the occult, or Transcendental Meditation,
or Eastern religions. Some are turning to crime.
The questions they thought were answered are left dangling:
What is man? Where did he come from?
What is his purpose on this planet? Where is he going?
Is there a God who cares? If there is a God,
has He revealed Himself to man?[34]

———◆———

Satan has slaughtered, plundered, and bludgeoned his way through the centuries, manifesting himself in every false ideology, sect, and cult.[35]

———◆———

In this age of humanism, man is seduced by society with
the lie that he can become his own god . . .
the New Age movement is polluted with self
and it will never bow before God—
at least not until Christ returns.[36]

Modern Western culture has become a mixture
of paganism and Christianity.
We are a blend of both. We talk of God,
but we often act as though we are atheists.[37]

New Agers are terrified of their own mortality,
and they want to believe that somehow the soul will survive.
Of course it will, but not as they imagine.[38]

There are many religions in the world, and they have developed
because various people have had various ideas about God.
Christianity makes a unique claim . . . we can know God because
He came to us in human form in the person of His Son, Jesus Christ.[39]

Many Christian leaders are willing to give up
some of the teachings of the Bible
in order to harmonize Christianity with the other religions.[40]

I am convinced that hundreds of religious leaders throughout the
world today are servants not of God, but of the Antichrist.
They are wolves in sheep's clothing; they are tares instead of wheat.[41]

BILLY GRAHAM ON
REPENTANCE

The Lord G OD . . . has said, "In repentance . . . you will be saved."

—ISAIAH 30:15 NASB

The word *repentance* is sadly missing today from the average pulpit.
It is a very unpopular word. The first sermon Jesus ever preached was
"Repent: for the kingdom of heaven is at hand" [Matthew 4:17 KJV].[1]

Repentance is mentioned seventy times in the New Testament . . .
the Bible says God commands repentance . . . it is a command . . .
God says, "Repent! Or perish!"[2]

The only sin God cannot forgive is the sin of rejecting Christ.
Turn to Him in repentance and faith—and He will forgive.[3]

True repentance is a turning from sin . . .
Humanly speaking, it is our small part in the plan of salvation.
Our part is repenting. God will do the converting,
the transforming, and the forgiving.[4]

It is entirely possible to be deeply sorry because of the devastation which sin has wrought in our lives—and yet not repent.[5]

Repent means to renounce sin . . .
and by God's grace to fill my mind with things that honor Him.[6]

You and I, God's ambassadors, are called to sound the warning,
to call sinners to repentance,
to point the way to peace with God and the hope that is in Christ.[7]

Confession and repentance might be described
as the negative side of submission;
this involves getting rid of everything which
hinders God's control over our lives.
Yielding to God might be described as the positive side . . .
placing ourselves totally into the hands of God.[8]

We can be convicted of sin—we can pray and confess our sin—
we can repent—but the real test is our willingness to obey.[9]

Understanding the consequence of sin and arrogance should
motivate every Christian to pray for repentance and revival.[10]

[Christians] are commanded to warn the nations of the world that
they must repent and turn to God while there is yet time.[11]

I have been preaching repentance for seventy years;
there are thousands of ministers of the Gospel all over this planet
preaching repentance this very hour . . . and most of the time
the world has laughed in the face of the King of kings.[12]

What does repentance mean? It means to change—
to change your mind, change the way that you're living—
and to determine that with God's help you will live for Christ.[13]

A transformed life is the greatest of all miracles.
Every time a person is "born again" by repentance of sin
and faith in Jesus Christ, the miracle of regeneration is performed.[14]

BILLY GRAHAM ON
THE RESURRECTION

Jesus said . . . "I am the resurrection and the life."

—JOHN 11:25 NASB

———◆◆◆———

The resurrection of Christ changed the
midnight of bereavement into a sunrise of reunion;
it changed the midnight of disappointment into a sunrise of joy;
it changed the midnight of fear to a sunrise of peace.[1]

———◆◆◆———

Because of what Jesus Christ did for us
through His cross and resurrection,
we know that we have hope for the future.[2]

———◆◆◆———

By [Christ's] resurrection life,
He gives us the power over the tendency to sin
as we allow Him to control our lives.[3]

———◆◆◆———

Never forget that the resurrection of Christ is in many ways
the central event of all history.[4]

———◆———

At the return of Christ the resurrection of believers will take place.
It will take the unbelieving world by surprise.[5]

———◆———

Death has two stages, first the separation of the body from the spirit . . .
for a purely spiritual existence, and second, reunion with the body
and a glorious resurrection at the Second Coming of Christ.[6]

———◆———

The resurrection is our great hope.[7]

———◆———

The resurrection blasts apart the finality of death,
providing an alternative to the stifling,
settling dust of death and opens the way to new life.[8]

———◆———

Christ broke the bonds of death by His resurrection,
and from that moment on, Satan was a defeated foe.[9]

———◆———

The most important events in human history were
the death and the resurrection of Jesus Christ.[10]

———◆———

Without the resurrection, the cross is meaningless.[11]

BILLY GRAHAM ON
RIGHT AND WRONG

All Scripture is inspired by God . . .
It corrects us when we are wrong and teaches us to do what is right.

—2 TIMOTHY 3:16

Before one can know what is right and wrong,
he must first align himself with God.
Only then is one in a position to do right.[1]

Right is right, and wrong is wrong,
in small things as well as in big things.[2]

When something brings profit or pleasure to us,
we are inclined to call evil good, even if we know it is dead wrong.[3]

We live in an upside-down world. People hate when they should love,
quarrel when they should be friendly,
fight when they should be peaceful,
wound when they should heal, steal when they should share,
do wrong when they should do right.[4]

Truly, the world is in need of moral leadership . . .
that teaches the difference between right and wrong
and teaches us to forgive one another even as we are forgiven
by our Father in heaven.[5]

Christians need to take a stand for what is right
and not let evil go unchallenged.[6]

Our relationship must be right with God
before it can be right with man.[7]

There is a right way and a wrong way to make contact with God.[8]

To find the right path, we first need to remember
why we are on the wrong path. The reason can be put in one word: sin.[9]

If evil were not made to appear attractive,
there would be no such thing as temptation.
It is in the close similarity between good and evil,
right and wrong, that the danger lies.[10]

———◆———

When I have a problem of deciding right from
wrong, I always give it three tests.
First, I give it the common-sense test, and ask if it is reasonable.
Then, I give it the prayer test. I ask God if it is good and edifying.
Then, I give it the Scripture test. I see if the Bible
has anything to say for or against it.[11]

———◆———

When we do good—even when others are doing wrong—
God will bless us.[12]

BILLY GRAHAM ON
SALVATION

Let Your mercies come . . . O LORD—
Your salvation according to Your word.

—PSALM 119:41 NKJV

❖

Salvation is free! God puts no price tag on the Gift of gifts.[1]

❖

Salvation is an act of God. It is initiated by God,
wrought by God, and sustained by God.[2]

❖

Salvation is not just repairing the original self.
It is a new self created of God in righteousness and true holiness.[3]

❖

[God] holds in His omnipotent hand the priceless,
precious, eternal gift of salvation,
and He bids you to take it without money and without price.[4]

⟡

Is it not arrogance or narrow-mindedness to claim that there is only one
way of salvation or that the way we follow is the right way? I think not.
After all, do we fault a pilot for being narrow-minded when he
follows the instrument panel [while] landing in a rainstorm?
No, we want him to remain narrowly focused![5]

⟡

Man stands on the brink of hell.
The forces building up in our world are so overwhelming
that man everywhere is beginning to cry out in desperation:
"What must I do to be saved?"[6]

⟡

Millions today want salvation, but on their own terms.
They want to come their own way,
and so we have hundreds of schemes and plans
devised by men to regain paradise.[7]

⟡

God longs for men to be saved.
God is at work to get men to stop their downward plunge in sin.[8]

⟡

The blood of Christ justifies and saves us . . .
The word *justification* means "just as if you had never sinned."[9]

⟡

God's grace—His goodness and love toward us in spite of our sin—
is the wellspring of our salvation.[10]

⟡

Believers in Christ owe nothing to God in payment for salvation . . .
but they do owe God a life of undivided devotion and service.[11]

———⟞•⟝———

Your salvation depends on what [Christ] has done
for you, not on what you do for Him.
It isn't your hold on God that saves you; it's His hold on you.[12]

———⟞•⟝———

If Satan can't keep you away from Christ,
he will at least try to make you doubt your salvation.[13]

———⟞•⟝———

The Bible is primarily concerned with the story of man's redemption
as it is in Jesus Christ.
If you read Scripture and miss the story of salvation,
you have missed its message and its meaning.[14]

———⟞•⟝———

God doesn't say to be perfect and you'll get to heaven.
He says to confess that you're a sinner and come to the cross,
and whosoever shall call upon the name of the Lord
shall be saved.[15]

———⟞•⟝———

Your salvation is a free gift,
made possible only because God planned it . . .
Christ paid for it . . . and the Holy Spirit assures you of it.[16]

———⟞•⟝———

Salvation is always "good news."
It is news of God's love and forgiveness—adoption into His family—
fellowship with His people—freedom from the penalty of sin—
liberation from the power of sin.[17]

BILLY GRAHAM ON
SERVICE

Be obedient . . . doing the will of God from the heart . . .
doing service, as to the Lord.

—EPHESIANS 6:5–7 NKJV

———◆—◆———

Take your eyes and your ears and your hands and your feet
and your thoughts and your heart:
Give them completely and unreservedly to Christ.[1]

———◆—◆———

As Christians we have a responsibility toward the poor,
the oppressed, the downtrodden,
and the many innocent people around the world who are caught
in wars, natural disasters, and situations beyond their control.[2]

———◆—◆———

The Bible teaches that we have a Christian duty
to help our neighbors in their time of need.
We are called by God to bring the water of life for both soul and body.
God created them both, and His purpose is to redeem them both.[3]

———◆—◆———

May our gratitude find expression in our prayers and our service
for others, and in our commitment to live wholly for Christ.[4]

Be honest about your weaknesses
and ask God to help you overcome them
so you can serve Christ more effectively.[5]

God wants to use you right where you are.
Every day you probably come in contact with people
who will never enter a church, or talk with a pastor, or open a Bible—
and God wants to use you to point them to Christ.
You may be the "bridge" God would use to bring them to Himself.[6]

Oh God, if You want me to serve You, I will.
I'll be what You want me to be.
I'll go where You want me to go.[7]

If we are going to touch the people of our communities,
we too must know their sorrows, feel for them in their temptations,
stand with them in their heartbreaks.
Jesus Christ entered into the arena of our troubles,
and He wept with them that wept and rejoiced with them that rejoiced.[8]

Many Christians would prefer to hear
"What a great guy" from the crowd rather than
"Well done, good and faithful servant" from the Master [Matthew 25:23].[9]

One of Satan's most effective ways of blocking God's work is to convince
us God can't use us to make an impact for Christ. But it isn't true.
All around you are people no one else
will ever be able to reach with the Gospel.[10]

Jesus, by example, tells us that every true leader should be a helper, a servant, or even a bondslave. This is a command, not a suggestion, and applies with special force to leaders.[11]

The strain of Christian service can result in sickness . . . I have known Christian workers who have risked their lives and health in serving the Lord.[12]

Thinking of and serving with others can be an antidote to negative and unhealthy introspection.[13]

God never calls a person [into His service] without equipping him. I know that from experience.[14]

BILLY GRAHAM ON
SIN

The Scripture declares that the whole world is a prisoner of sin.

—GALATIANS 3:22 NIV

—◆—

Sin is the great clogger, and the blood of Christ is the great cleanser.[1]

—◆—

The Bible says there is a certain pleasure in sin.
However, it is short-lived and fatal.[2]

—◆—

Gratitude is one of the greatest Christian virtues;
ingratitude, one of the most vicious sins.[3]

—◆—

There is a difference between sin and sins.
Sin is the root; sins are the fruit.[4]

—◆—

The cause of all trouble, the root of all sorrow,
the dread of every man lies in this one small word—sin.
It has crippled the nature of man . . .
It has caused man to be caught in the devil's trap.[5]

Be assured that there is no sin you have ever committed
that the blood of Jesus Christ cannot cleanse.[6]

We have largely lost sight of the holiness and purity of God today.
This is one reason why we tolerate sin so easily.[7]

True freedom consists not in the freedom to sin,
but the freedom not to sin.[8]

Our magazine covers frequently feature the immoral,
the perverted, the psychologically sick.
Sin is "in." People don't like to be told they are sinners.[9]

Sin—plain, old-fashioned sin, the self-same sin which
caused Adam's downfall—is what we are all suffering from
today, and it will do us far more harm than good to try
to dress it up with a fancy, more attractive label.[10]

There is less teaching about sin, and very little warning of judgment.[11]

Neither the devil nor the world,
nor even our own evil heart can compel us to sin.
It must be by our own consent and will.[12]

We don't need to be crippled any longer by the disease of sin—
because God has provided the cure.[13]

———◆———

When we use the word "sin," we usually think of our misdeeds—
actions or habits we know are wrong.
But those are specific sins, and they are the result of sin,
the deeper spiritual disease that infects our souls.
Sin is the cause; sins are the effect.
Sin is the tree; sins are the fruit.
Sin is the disease; sins are the symptoms.[14]

———◆———

The sin of self is a deadly sin.[15]

———◆———

Sin is serious—so serious it sent Jesus Christ to the cross.
Flee from [sin] and stay close to Christ.[16]

———◆———

Superficial views of God and His holiness will produce
superficial views of sin and atonement. God hates sin.
It is His uncompromising foe.
Sin is vile and detestable in the sight of God . . .
The sinner and God are at opposite poles of the moral universe.[17]

———◆———

Sin pierced the very heart of God.
God felt every piercing nail and spear thrust. God felt the burning sun.
God felt the mocking derision and the body blows.[18]

———◆———

As much as we hate to admit it, we are sinners by birth.
We are also sinners by choice. We are also sinners by practice.[19]

BILLY GRAHAM IN QUOTES

We all have a terminal disease far worse than cancer
that will kill us morally and spiritually.
It's called sin.[20]

We cannot come to Christ
unless the Holy Spirit convicts us of our sin.[21]

Sin is often, if not always, the perversion of something good.
In the midst of all our sinning, though,
God is willing to forgive us, change us,
and give us a new power to overcome that sin.[22]

Only [God] can convict nonbelievers of their sins;
only He can convince them of the truth of the Gospel.[23]

Galatians 5:21 constitutes the most serious warning
to those who may think they can sin that grace may abound.[24]

Sooner or later we must leave our dream world and face up
to the facts of God, sin, and judgment.
The Bible says, "All have sinned and come short
of the glory of God" [Romans 3:23 NIV].[25]

Sin is a revolt against God.[26]

Sinful pleasure can ruin our appetite for the things of God.[27]

The Bible teaches that whosoever is born of God does not practice sin.[28]

Sin has progressed and gained momentum;
[man] seems to have lost his ability to be shocked.
Behavior that was once considered abominable is now acceptable.[29]

Only the Holy Spirit can open our eyes.
Only He can convict us of the depth of our sin,
and only He can convince us of the truth of the Gospel.[30]

The Gospel of Jesus Christ is not anti-intellectual.
It demands the use of [the] mind, but the mind is affected by sin.[31]

The essence of sin is self-will—
placing ourselves at the center of our lives instead of Christ.[32]

In all of these centuries there has not been the slightest
shadow of change in the nature of God or in His attitude toward sin.
The Bible teaches from the beginning to the end
that adultery and fornication are sin,
and the attitude of churchmen does not alter its character.[33]

The Bible does not teach that sin is completely eradicated
from the Christian in this life,
but it does teach that sin shall no longer reign over you.[34]

The influence of sin touches the innocent as well as the guilty.[35]

Can the sin of one or a few cause suffering for many?
The answer, of course, is yes,
for no sin is isolated in the life of the sinner.
It spreads like poison gas into every available crevice.[36]

There are many new sinners today,
but there aren't any new sins, just the old ones clothed in different rags.[37]

We do not have a paradise on earth;
it is riddled with so much sin and disease.[38]

Learn to take sin seriously—be on guard against
it and resist its tug, fight its power.
But most of all learn to take the Holy Spirit seriously,
calling on Him to help you overcome sin's power
and live a holy and godly life.[39]

Man got into difficulty when he lifted his will against God's.
He gets out of trouble when he bows to the divine superiority,
when he repents and says humbly: "God be merciful to me a sinner."
Man's extremity then becomes God's opportunity.[40]

⸻◆⸻

Sin is rebellion against God.[41]

⸻◆⸻

Perversion is considered a biological abnormality rather than a sin.
These things are contrary to the teaching of God's Word.
And God has not changed. His standards have not been lowered.
God still calls immorality a sin and the Bible
says God is going to judge it.[42]

⸻◆⸻

We make a mockery of God's forgiveness when we deliberately
engage in sin because we think He will forgive it later.[43]

⸻◆⸻

The unpardonable sin involves the total and irrevocable
rejection of Jesus Christ.[44]

⸻◆⸻

Sin has tarnished every area of life,
and [Christ] wants to erase its stain everywhere.[45]

⸻◆⸻

[The Bible] warns us about "the little foxes, that
spoil the vines" [Song of Solomon 2:15 KJV].
This is a picture of the way "little" sins
can destroy our fruitfulness for the Lord.[46]

⸻◆⸻

Scripture has the remedy for sinfulness.[47]

Why did Jesus Christ leave heaven's glory
and enter this sin-infested world?
For one reason: to make our eternal salvation possible.[48]

Nothing can alter the fact that God calls perversion *sin*.[49]

Sin lies at the heart of chaotic world conditions as we now know them
and as they have existed through the centuries.[50]

The tragedy of sin reached its crescendo when
God in Christ became sin . . .
He was offering Himself as the sacrifice required
by the justice of God if man was to be redeemed.[51]

God can break the chain of every sin that binds
you if you are willing to give it up.
He comes into your heart and gives you power to overcome sin.[52]

It would be the greatest tragedy if I didn't tell you that unless you
repent of your sins and receive Christ as your Savior,
you are going to be lost.[53]

Sinners, pray to a merciful God for forgiveness.[54]

BILLY GRAHAM ON
SOCIETY

What society sees and calls monumental,
God sees through and calls monstrous.

—LUKE 16:15 MSG

Are you disappointed with society? If you are,
I challenge you to take the first step. I challenge you to look at yourself.[1]

Jesus indicated that there will be a permissive society just before He
comes back . . . the world today is on an immoral binge such as has not
been known since the days of Rome. We are in a hedonistic society, and
what we are seeing is human nature expressing itself without God.[2]

The world does need changing, society needs changing,
the nation needs changing,
but we never will change it until we ourselves are changed.[3]

In a decadent society the will to believe, to resist, to contend, to fight,
to struggle is gone. In place of this will to resist,
there is the desire to conform, to drift,
to follow, to yield, and not give up.[4]

The same conditions that prevailed in Rome prevail in our society.
Before Rome fell, her standards were abandoned,
the family disintegrated, divorce prevailed,
immorality was rampant, and faith was at a low ebb.[5]

Sometimes I think the truly committed Christian is in conflict with
society around him more than any other person.
Society is going one direction, and the Christian is going in the
opposite direction. This brings about friction and conflict.
But God has promised, in the midst of trouble and conflict,
a genuine peace, a sense of assurance and security,
that the worldly person never knows.[6]

Our society has traded strength of character for makeovers that deceive.[7]

Today we see social evil, terrorism, and gross immorality
throughout the world. Someone has said,
"A wrong deed is right
if the majority of people declare it not to be wrong."
By this principle we can see our standards shifting
from year to year according to the popular vote!
This new permissiveness is condoned by intelligent men and women,
many of whom are found in the churches.[8]

The focus on self has led our society into a fascination with pleasure,
emotional and sexual stimulation, and "personal fulfillment."
America's compulsion for "maximum personhood"
is evidenced everywhere.[9]

Sickness is deep within the soul of our society—
and that has always been God's exclusive territory.[10]

BILLY GRAHAM ON
THE SOUL

Humbly accept the word God has planted in your hearts,
for it has the power to save your souls.

—JAMES 1:21

———❖———

Jesus said our souls are more valuable
than all the rest of the world put together.[1]

———❖———

Our souls have a disease.
It causes all the troubles and difficulties in the world.
It causes all the troubles, confusions,
and disillusionments in your own life.
The name of the disease is . . . sin.[2]

———❖———

We spend all our time and energy pampering our bodies and minds,
but if we ignore our souls,
we will end up spiritually starved and malnourished.[3]

———❖———

Take care of your soul—your inner self—
by feeding on the Word of God
and letting His Spirit transform you from within.[4]

———

Christ taught that in the sight of God
one soul is worth the entire materialistic world!
In God's sight the individual is all-important.
When Christ calls a man to follow Him,
He calls him "out" from the "group."
Christ can fill the vacuums. He can restore your personal identity.
He can become THE TRUTH to your generation.[5]

———

Nothing can calm our souls more or better prepare us for life's challenges
than time spent alone with God.[6]

———

You should no more allow sinful imaginations to accumulate in your
mind and soul than you would let garbage collect in your living room.[7]

———

[God] knows that an uncontrolled life is an unhappy life,
so He puts reins on our wayward souls that
they may be directed into the
"paths of righteousness."[8]

———

I have not known of too many people who found Christ on their
deathbeds. When we come to Christ in our youth, a life is saved.
When we come in old age, a soul is salvaged and life eternal is assured;
but the opportunity to live a life for Christ has been lost.[9]

———

Someday your life will be over,
no matter how much attention you give to your health.
Will you look back with regret,
because you nourished your body but starved your soul?[10]

We spend enormous amounts of time and money on fad diets,
expensive exercise machines, and health clubs.
For many people, these things only demonstrate their preoccupation
with the physical side of life . . . but even more important is
taking care of our souls.[11]

Partial education throughout the world is far worse than none at all
if we educate the mind but not the soul.[12]

Unless the soul is fed and exercised daily, it becomes weak and shriveled.
It remains discontented, confused, restless.[13]

God requires something of us. We must confess our spiritual poverty,
renounce our sins, and turn by faith to His Son, Jesus Christ.
When we do that, we are born again. He gives us a new nature.
He puts a little bit of heaven down in our souls.[14]

The Bible teaches that whether we are saved or lost,
there is conscious and everlasting existence of the soul and personality.[15]

May we all storm the gates of heaven for the souls of the anguished,
that in their greatest time of need they will hear
the gentle voice of God's Spirit calling them to repentance.[16]

The Bible teaches that you are an immortal soul.
Your soul is eternal and will live forever . . .
the real you—the part of you that thinks, feels,
dreams, aspires; the ego, the personality—
will never die . . . your soul will live forever in one of two places—
heaven or hell.[17]

Even in the darkest moment, before death snatches man's last breath,
God is willing to save a lost soul.[18]

It is a time for soul-searching, a time to see if our anchor holds.[19]

The soul actually demands as much attention as the body . . .
the soul was made for God,
and without God it is restless and in secret torment.[20]

The searchlight of [God's] Spirit will probe
the inner depths of your soul and reveal things
that you think you have already yielded, but you have not.[21]

The Bible teaches whether we are saved or lost,
there is an everlasting existence of the soul.[22]

Hardship is not our choice; but if we face it bravely,
it can toughen the fiber of our souls.[23]

Our soul is that part of our being which possesses intelligence,
conscience, and memory—the real personality.
Your body will die, but your soul lives on.
And that soul has a "sixth sense"—
the ability to believe, to have faith.[24]

Our souls set us apart from every other living creature,
and that makes us unique. It also makes us fully human.[25]

Let [Christ] transform your life so that you will have a glow on your face,
a spring in your step, and joy in your soul.[26]

BILLY GRAHAM ON
SPEECH

The Spirit of the LORD *spoke by me, and His word was on my tongue.*

—2 SAMUEL 23:2 NKJV

Each of us has a tongue and a voice.
These instruments of speech can be used
destructively or employed constructively.[1]

Some of the most healing words in any language are,
"I'm sorry. Will you forgive me?"
How much more we need that confession to our Father in heaven.[2]

Our daily conversation when we meet each other,
whether it be in the office or on the campus or in the shop,
should be concerned with the things of God.[3]

We should say nothing that we would not wish to say in His Presence.
We should do nothing that we would not do in His Presence.[4]

The Scripture warns about evil communications
that corrupt good manners.
Off-color jokes and dirty stories have no place in the Christian life.
Thousands of people are engaging in immorality by the way they talk.
Keep your talk pure. Ask God to purify your tongue.[5]

You can use your tongue to slander, to gripe,
to scold, to nag, and to quarrel;
or you can bring it under the control of God's Spirit
and make it an instrument of blessing and praise.[6]

Cursing, telling smutty stories, smearing the good name of
another, and referring irreverently to God and the Scriptures may
be considered as coming under the expression *corrupt speech*.
Our speech is to be clean, pure, and wholesome.[7]

Double-mindedness means the faculty of
holding two contradictory beliefs
in one's mind and accepting both of them.
We talk out of both corners of our mouths at once.[8]

We insult God by speaking to Him with our lips
while our hearts are far from Him.[9]

The Bible teaches that a man who can control his tongue
can control his whole personality.[10]

God speaks to those who are prepared in their hearts to listen.
Discern the voice from heaven
above the noisy din of earth's confusion.[11]

Suppose there was no anger, no profanity,
no lying, no grumbling or complaining;
suppose there were no dirty stories told,
no unjust criticism—
what a different world this would be![12]

Pain has many faces . . .
the unseen part of man is often the victim
of the most debilitating of pains . . .
a man can endure excruciating physical pain,
and yet he can be felled by one unkind word.[13]

Are you willing to follow [Christ] with a disciplined mind and tongue?[14]

How many relationships have broken down because of
gossip or a word spoken thoughtlessly or in anger?
A harsh word can't be taken back;
no apology can fully repair its damage.[15]

BILLY GRAHAM ON
STRENGTH

Strengthen me according to Your word.

—PSALM 119:28 NKJV

———◆———

A muscle becomes weak if it is not used.
To become strong, a muscle must push against something.[1]

———◆———

Grief can kill a person emotionally and physically.
If not counteracted with God's strength and power,
our personal weakness may debilitate us.[2]

———◆———

God is in control.
He may not take away trials or make detours for us,
but He strengthens us through them.[3]

———◆———

God takes the weak and makes them strong.
He takes the vile and makes them clean.
He takes the worthless and makes them worthwhile.
He takes the sinful and makes them sinless.[4]

———◆———

God will give us the strength and resources we need
to live through any situation in life that He ordains.[5]

———◆———

We shouldn't think about ourselves and how weak we are.
Instead, we should think about God and how strong He is.[6]

———◆———

Are your beliefs anchored in a faith that can withstand emotionalism,
the drug culture, social and peer pressure, and material temptations?
The world is seething with demonic energy.
Only supreme inner strength can resist its ceaseless hassling.[7]

———◆———

We must learn to let the Word of God feed us
and strengthen us in our faith in God its author,
Christ its message, and the Holy Spirit its teacher.[8]

———◆———

Our ministries are strengthened,
sometimes more than we realize,
by our devotional life. [9]

BILLY GRAHAM ON
SUCCESS

*Do not let this Book . . . depart from your mouth; meditate on
it day and night, so that you may be careful to do everything
written in it. Then you will be . . . successful.*

—JOSHUA 1:8 NIV

Where do we get the notion that our idea of
success and God's are the same?
You have written a book; you are a clever manager and promoter;
you are a talented artist; you are independently wealthy;
you have achieved fame and fortune.
Without the gifts of intelligence, imagination, personality,
and physical energy—which are all endowed by God—
where would you be?[1]

Our world is obsessed with success.
But how does God define success?
Success in God's eyes is faithfulness to His calling.[2]

Regardless of our cleverness, our achievements, and our gadgets,
we are spiritual paupers without God.[3]

In our desire to achieve success quickly
it is easy to get our values mixed up and call evil good and good evil.[4]

A true servant of God is someone who helps another succeed.[5]

Success stories may be great motivational material for sales seminars,
but we are not always successful.[6]

Time and tide and the ravages of sin take their toll
on the most noble achievements of man.[7]

Our job in life is not to be successful, but to be faithful.[8]

This age is interested in success, not suffering . . .
Our Lord was ridiculed, insulted, persecuted, and eventually killed.
In the face of opposition, He went about "doing good."[9]

Many of the wicked are receiving their wages now.
Many Christians who may not be succeeding according to the
world's standards now, will reap great rewards in heaven.[10]

The Western world's sole objective seems to be
success, status, security, self-indulgence, pleasure, and comfort.[11]

Success or failure cannot be measured by any human standard.[12]

God measures people by the small dimensions of humility
and not by the bigness of their achievements
or the size of their capabilities.[13]

BILLY GRAHAM ON
SUFFERING

God is not blind. He knows about you and your problems.
He knows of those who are suffering . . .
and His love for His children will never leave in times of trouble.[1]

Nowhere does the Bible teach that Christians are to be exempt from
the tribulations and natural disasters that come upon the world.
It does teach that the Christian can face tribulation, crisis, calamity,
and personal suffering with a supernatural power that
is not available to the person outside of Christ.[2]

Some of the happiest Christians I have met have been life-long
sufferers. They have had every reason to sigh and complain,
being denied so many privileges and pleasures that they see others enjoy,
yet they have found greater cause for gratitude and joy
than many who are prosperous, vigorous, and strong.[3]

When suffering comes, learn to trust each day into God's hands . . .
let your lips be filled with prayer and praise.[4]

The most remarkable thing about suffering is that
God can use it for our good.[5]

Our sufferings may be hard to bear, but they teach us lessons which,
in turn, equip and enable us to help others.[6]

Tens of thousands of God's saints and sufferers through the ages have
found their dark nights lightened and tortured souls strengthened
because they found help from the Spirit in the Word of God.[7]

A suffering person does not need a lecture—he needs a listener.[8]

In my years of global travels, I have seen a world in pain . . .
Without God's guidance, our response to suffering is a futile
attempt to find solutions to conditions that cannot be solved.[9]

We can react with bitterness and hate God, as some do,
or we can accept suffering as a natural part of life
and a condition that comes with living in this world.
We cannot avoid suffering, but we can determine our response to it.[10]

In His thirty-three years on earth, Jesus suffered with man;
on the cross He suffered for man.[11]

———

We enjoy the sense of God's presence in the
midst of suffering here and now.
I have talked to people who are experiencing
deep pain or severe difficulties,
and they have said, "I feel God is so close to me."[12]

———

Jesus suffered more than any other person in human history.[13]

———

The book of Job does not set out to answer the problem of suffering,
but to proclaim a God so great that no answer is needed.[14]

———

I believe one reason that God allows poverty and suffering is so that His
followers may demonstrate Christ's love, mercy, and comfort to [others].[15]

———

Being a Christian does not exempt us from tough training,
which may mean suffering. If the training were easy,
we would not be prepared for the tough days ahead.[16]

———

To suffer for the faith is not a penalty; it is a privilege.[17]

———

The beginning of all pain and suffering in the
world started with one act of disobedience.
Christian and non-Christian alike have inherited the consequences
from our common ancestors, Adam and Eve—
our polluted environment and flawed human nature.[18]

May we store up the truths of God's Word in our hearts
as much as possible, so that we are prepared for
whatever suffering we are called upon to endure.[19]

—◆—

[The Lord] does go with us through our sufferings, and He awaits
us as we emerge on the other side of the tunnel of testing—
into the light of His glorious presence to live with Him forever![20]

—◆—

True faith and suffering frequently go hand-in-hand . . .
Living for Christ, walking in His way, will not be an easy path.[21]

—◆—

The Bible and the history of the church both demonstrate
that God's way for the suffering of His people
has not always been the way of escape, but the way of endurance.[22]

—◆—

We don't deliberately look for trouble in life. It comes.
Suffering is a universal fact; no one can escape its claws.[23]

—◆—

God has prescribed the remedy for the spiritual sickness of the human
race. The solution is personal faith and commitment to Jesus Christ . . .
if we deliberately refuse it, we must suffer the horrible consequences.[24]

—◆—

No one is exempt from the touch of tragedy:
neither the Christian nor the non-Christian;
neither the rich nor the poor; neither the leader or the commoner.
Crossing all racial, social, political, and economic barriers,
suffering reaches out to unite mankind.[25]

———✦•✦———

Suffering in life can uncover untold depths of character and
unknown strength for service. People who go through life
unscathed by sorrow and untouched by pain tend to be shallow
in their perspectives on life. Suffering, on the other hand,
tends to plow up the surface of our lives to uncover the depths
that provide greater strength of purpose and accomplishment.
Only deeply plowed earth can yield bountiful harvests.[26]

———✦•✦———

Ours may be the heritage of the withheld promises.
We have been blessed through the endurance and
faithfulness of those who have suffered in the past;
the people around us, or those who will succeed us,
may be blessed through our trials and suffering
and how we react to them.[27]

———✦•✦———

Suffering can give us opportunities to witness. The world is a gigantic
hospital; nowhere is there a greater chance to see the peace and joy of
the Lord than when the journey through the valley is the darkest.[28]

———✦•✦———

The Bible teaches that we are to be patient in suffering.
Tears become telescopes to heaven, bringing eternity a little closer.[29]

BILLY GRAHAM ON
SURRENDER

I am not ashamed of the Gospel . . . for it is God's power
working unto salvation . . . to everyone who believes
with a personal trust and a confident surrender.

—ROMANS 1:16 AMP

We must understand what the word *believe* implies.
It means "commit" and "surrender."[1]

We can hold nothing back [from God].
He must control and dominate us [wholly].
It is a surrender without any conditions attached.
This surrender is a definite and conscious act on our part
in obedience to the Word of God.[2]

There is not one verse of Scripture that indicates you can be a
Christian and live any kind of a life you want to.
When Christ enters into the human heart,
He expects to be Lord and Master. He commands complete surrender.[3]

Faith actually means surrender and commitment to the claims of Christ.
It means an acknowledgment of sin and a turning to Christ.[4]

Jesus expects one hundred percent surrender,
and when that is accomplished He rewards a thousandfold.[5]

Surrendering to Christ is like signing your name to a blank check
and letting the Lord put in the amount.[6]

In our spiritual pilgrimage we see sins which
mar our relationship with God,
but beneath it is a commitment which seeks
to move beyond to a higher life,
based on wholehearted surrender to God.[7]

BILLY GRAHAM ON
TEMPTATION

[Jesus] said to them, "Pray that you may not enter into temptation."

—LUKE 22:40 NKJV

Don't savor temptations;
don't dwell on them or toy with them
or replay them over and over in your mind.
The more you think about a particular temptation,
the more enticing it becomes.[1]

We can't flee from temptation in our own strength—
but God will give us the strength we need, if we'll only seek it.
A friend of mine says, "When the devil knocks,
I just send Jesus to the door!"[2]

It is not the temptations you have,
but the decision you make about them that counts.[3]

Everyone has temptations but some folks entertain them . . .
Get your eyes off the temptation and onto Christ![4]

—⊰•⊱—

I know that many of the things I have said
from the Scriptures have offended,
and I have sometimes been tempted to tone down the message.
But, God helping me, I never will!
I would become a false prophet. I would also betray my Lord.[5]

—⊰•⊱—

God promises no easy life or days without troubles, trials, difficulties,
and temptations. He never promises that life will be perfect.
He does not call His children to a playground, but to a battleground.[6]

—⊰•⊱—

Every stage of life has its own temptations and dangers,
and Satan will do all he can to exploit them . . .
the time to prepare is now, not when it arrives.[7]

—⊰•⊱—

The devil doesn't need to invent any new temptations;
the old ones work as well as they ever have.[8]

—⊰•⊱—

Be very sure that you do not deliberately place yourself
in a position to be tempted.[9]

—⊰•⊱—

Temptation requires definite, decisive action.[10]

—⊰•⊱—

Be sure that Satan will tempt you at your weak point, not the strong.[11]

Many Christians give in to various temptations through peer
pressure and find themselves surrendering to worldly passions,
justifying pleasures the world offers.[12]

When Jesus was tempted, He didn't debate the devil.
He quoted Scripture:
"It is written . . . It is written . . . It is written" (Matthew 4:4–10 NKJV).
And each time the devil was defeated.[13]

All of us are not subjected to the same weaknesses and temptations.
To one, alcohol may be the temptation;
to another, it may be impure thoughts and acts;
to another, greed and covetousness;
to another, criticism and an unloving attitude.[14]

Temptation is not a sin. It is the yielding that is sin.
All temptation is from the devil.[15]

Only a strong faith—a faith based on God's Word—
will protect us from temptation and doubt.[16]

A thought enters; we pamper it;
it germinates and grows into an evil act.[17]

The Bible is intensely practical, and one of the reasons
God gave it to us is so we'll be better prepared to
deal with life's problems and temptations.
All too often we respond to these in ways that don't reflect Christ . . .
when we do that, Satan is the winner and the cause of Christ suffers.[18]

Temptation: Recognize it for what it is,
and then reject it—immediately and without compromise.[19]

BILLY GRAHAM ON
TESTIMONY

This is [the] report of the word of God and the testimony of Jesus Christ.

—REVELATION 1:2

———❖———

Our creativity, our inner sense of right and wrong,
our ability to love and to reason—
all bear witness to the fact that God created us in His image.
The Bible says God "has not left himself
without testimony" [Acts 14:17 NIV].[1]

———❖———

The devil will try to discourage you, to divert you;
he will seek to dilute your testimony; he will attempt anything to
destroy your relationship to Christ and your influence upon others.[2]

———❖———

The greatest testimony to this dark world today would be a band of
crucified and risen men and women, dead to sin and alive unto God,
bearing in their bodies "the marks of the Lord Jesus"
[Galatians 6:17 NKJV].[3]

———❖———

I urge new converts to take plenty of time in Bible study and prayer
before getting on a public platform to testify.[4]

Man has not changed. Man still rejects the testimony of the Scripture.[5]

The unbelieving world should see our testimony lived out daily because it just may point them to the Savior.[6]

BILLY GRAHAM ON
THANKFULNESS

Let the word of Christ dwell in you richly . . .
with thankfulness in your hearts to God.

—COLOSSIANS 3:16 ESV

———◆———

A spirit of thankfulness is one of the most distinctive marks
of a Christian whose heart is attuned to the Lord.
Thank God in the midst of trials and every persecution.[1]

———◆———

We should not let a day go by without thanking God
for His mercy and grace to us in Jesus Christ.[2]

———◆———

When thanksgiving is filled with true meaning
and is not just the formality of a polite "thank you,"
it is the recognition of dependence.[3]

———◆———

Thanksgiving is recognition of a debt that cannot be paid. We express
thanks, whether or not we are able otherwise to reimburse the giver.[4]

Why should we give God thanks?
Because everything we have comes from God.[5]

Grumbling and gratitude are, for the child of God, in conflict.
Be grateful and you won't grumble. Grumble and you won't be grateful.[6]

As you think about the future . . . give thanks and trust God . . .
Even when life may be difficult,
we should thank God for all He does for us—which we do not deserve.[7]

BILLY GRAHAM ON
TIME

Truthful words stand the test of time.

—PROVERBS 12:19

——◆——

It is not just becoming a Christian;
it is also being a Christian all the time,
24 hours a day.[1]

——◆——

Time is running out. The seconds are ticking away toward midnight.
The human race is about to take the fatal plunge . . .
Is there any authority left? Is there a path we can follow?
Can we find a code book that will give us the key to our dilemmas?
We do have authoritative source material.
It is found in the ancient and historic Book we call the Bible.[2]

——◆——

We are accountable to [God] for the way we use our time.[3]

——◆——

Once a minute passes it can never be reclaimed.[4]

Heaven has no clocks or calendars, and time
will be no more [Revelation 10:6].[5]

We relegate God to our spare time—
but end up never having any spare time!
Jesus said, "Seek first his kingdom" [Matthew 6:33 NIV].[6]

Life is short; none of us knows how long we have.
Live each day as if it were your last—for someday it will be.[7]

The greatest waste in all of our earth
is our waste of the time God has given us each day.[8]

We all have exactly the same number of minutes in a day.
The question is, how will we use them?
Most people today are either too busy—or not busy enough.
The Bible tells us that both extremes are wrong.[9]

There is for each man a day, an hour, a minute.
The Bible talks in many places about the brevity of life,
and the Bible warns that we should be
prepared to meet God at all times.[10]

God has given us a message that is not only for past times and this time,
but for all time.[11]

Every day has exactly 1,440 minutes;
can't you find even ten of them to be with your heavenly Father?
Doesn't God deserve the best minutes of your day?[12]

God can do more with a few days of your time if
given completely to Him, than He can with a whole
life characterized by a half-hearted service.[13]

You can trust Christ at this moment.
The Bible says, "Now is the accepted time" [2 Corinthians 6:2 KJV].
Don't put it off. Don't say, "I'll think about
it." Don't say, "I'll do it tomorrow."
Do it right now. At this moment, say yes to Jesus Christ.[14]

Allow the resurrected Christ to allocate your time as His own
. . . and have complete right-of-way throughout your being.[15]

If ever we are to study the Scriptures,
if ever we are to spend time in prayer,
if ever we are to win souls for Christ,
if ever we are to invest our finances for His kingdom—it must be now.[16]

BILLY GRAHAM ON
TRUTH

The very essence of your words is truth.

—PSALM 119:160

❖

Truth is timeless. Truth does not differ from one age to another,
from one people to another,
from one geographical location to another . . .
the great all-prevailing Truth stands for time and eternity.[1]

❖

Because truth is unpopular does not mean
that it should not be proclaimed.[2]

❖

Our emotions can lie to us,
and we need to counter our emotions with truth.[3]

❖

I have met men who are habitual liars.
They have lied so long that they no longer can distinguish
between the truth and a lie.
Their sensitivity to sin has been almost completely deadened.[4]

Where there is truth and error there is always compromise.
Within some churches there is a movement
to reshape the Christian message
to make it more acceptable to man.[5]

If our minds and hearts are not filled with God's truth,
something else will take His place:
cynicism, occultism, false religions and philosophies, drugs—
the list is endless.[6]

At the end of his life Buddha said: "I am still searching for truth."
This statement could be made by countless thousands of scientists,
philosophers, and religious leaders throughout all history.
However, Jesus Christ made the astounding claim:
"I am . . . the truth" [John 14:6]. He is the embodiment of all truth.
The only answer to man's search is found in Him.[7]

It is Satan's purpose to steal the seed of truth
from your heart by sending distracting thoughts . . .
The difference between a Christian and a non-Christian is:
though they both may have good and evil thoughts,
Christ gives His followers strength to select
the right rather than the wrong.[8]

The Holy Spirit can take God's word of truth
and minister it to our deepest needs.[9]

It is far better to know God's truth than to be ignorant of it.[10]

———◆———

Honesty means exactly what it says.
We are honest and trustworthy in all our dealings.
People can trust our word, because we refuse to lie or shade the truth.[11]

BILLY GRAHAM ON
WAR

By wise counsel you will wage your own war.

—PROVERBS 24:6 NKJV

———◆———

How can men boast that they control their own destiny
when they cannot solve the problems of war?[1]

———◆———

Modern war is the most highly developed of all sciences.
We have perfected our weapons but failed to
perfect the men who use them.[2]

———◆———

The Charter of the United Nations said in its preamble:
"We the people determined to save succeeding generations from war . . ."
Can the United Nations save the world from war? The answer is No!
It was conceived and created by statesmen who knew little of the
significance of the biblical concept of history and the nature of man.
When the perspective is wrong, the whole viewpoint will be wrong.[3]

The Garden of Eden was somewhere in present-day Iraq.
The turmoil and war [we are witnessing] in that part of the world . . .
is occurring in the land where God
established the first perfect civilization.[4]

If the human race would turn from its evil ways and return
to God, putting behind its sins of disobedience, idolatry,
pride, greed, and belligerence, and all the various aberrations
that lead to war, the possibility of peace exists.[5]

Scripture indicates that deception,
false religions, and apostasy lead to war,
and that war in turn leads to famine and pestilence.[6]

Philosophically, war is an extension of man's struggle
with sin and evil in the world.[7]

War is only one facet of the larger problem of evil
which has been with the human race since the beginning . . .
This same evil tried to destroy
the greatest human being who ever lived, nailing Him to a cross.[8]

BILLY GRAHAM ON
WITNESSING

This stone will be a witness . . . It has heard all the words the LORD has said to us. It will be a witness against you if you are untrue to your God.

———◆———

What is your story?
Be ready to share it when the Lord gives you the opportunity.[1]

———◆———

Be a good witness by the way you live.
The way we live is often more convincing than the words we say.[2]

———◆———

One faithful witness is worth a thousand mute professors of religion . . .
Our faith grows by expression . . . we must share it—we must witness.[3]

———◆———

We witness in two ways: by life and by word . . . God's purpose . . .
after we have been converted is that we
be witnesses to His saving grace and power.
We are to be commandoes for Christ.
We are to be minute-men for Him.[4]

When brothers and sisters in Christ unite in the common bond of the
Word of God and prayer, they are strengthened
in their faith and witness.[5]

We are stewards of the Gospel.
The power to proclaim the greatest news in heaven and earth
was not given to the angels; it was given to redeemed men.
Every Christian is to be a witness.[6]

The Spirit goes ahead of us when we witness—
preparing the way, giving us the words, and granting us courage.[7]

The lukewarm Christian can accomplish nothing with
a whole life in which to do it. If you have lived for sin and self . . .
your witness will have [a] telling effect on all who have known you.[8]

Christians ought to carry written in our hearts the solemn truth of
how short is our opportunity to witness for Christ and live for Him.[9]

Satan will do everything he can to divide Christians and destroy
our witness. Only the Holy Spirit can subdue our old nature
and overcome it with God's love.[10]

While separation does not mean disengagement from the world,
there are certain activities and places that God clearly wants us
to avoid not only to protect ourselves from spiritual harm
but so that the witness we have will not be tarnished.[11]

The greatest way to witness is through the life you live.
Let the radiance of your Christian life be such that it will
make [others] ask questions about your [faith].[12]

BILLY GRAHAM ON
THE WORD OF GOD

Blessed are all who hear the word of God and put it into practice.

—LUKE 11:28

When I quote Scripture,
I know I am quoting the very Word of God.[1]

The Spirit of God takes the Word of God and makes the child of God.[2]

Through the written Word
we discover the Living Word—Jesus Christ.[3]

Some, who doubt that the Bible is the true Word of God,
doubt it because they are unwilling to ascribe to God anything
they cannot themselves achieve.[4]

[God the Spirit] will never lead you contrary to the Word of God.
I hear people saying, "The Lord led me to do this . . ."
I am always a little suspicious
unless what the Lord has said is in keeping with His Word.[5]

Your spiritual life needs food . . . where do you find [this]?
In the Bible, the Word of God. The Bible reveals Christ,
who is the Bread of Life for your hungry soul,
and the Water of Life for your thirsty heart.[6]

God has not promised to bless my thoughts,
but He has promised to bless His Word.[7]

Faith grows when it is planted in the fertile soil of God's Word.[8]

As Christians, we have only one authority, one compass:
the Word of God.[9]

Nothing will help us grow spiritually more
than spending time alone with God every day,
reading His Word and praying.
Time alone with God is essential to our spiritual welfare.[10]

God's Word not only gives authority to one's ministry;
it provides a solid foundation for one's life.[11]

The Old Testament may not seem relevant to us today—but it is,
because it is part of God's Holy Word,
and He has much to teach us through its pages.[12]

I look upon it as a lost day when I have not had a good time
over the Word of God.[13]

God never leads us to do anything that is contrary to His Word.
But the opposite is also true:
God always leads us to do everything that
is in agreement with His Word.[14]

The Word of God is God's authoritative message to us.
It is [the] infallible Book.[15]

While we read the Word, its message saturates our hearts,
whether we are conscious of what is happening or not.[16]

The Word of God hidden in the heart is a stubborn voice to suppress.[17]

Who can tell us how to get along with each other better than God?
Where can we turn for wisdom better than God's Word, the Bible?[18]

The saddest words I can ever imagine would be to hear the Lord say,
"I never knew you. Away from Me" [Matthew 7:23 NIV].[19]

O God! There are many things in [the Bible] I do not understand . . .
I am going to accept this as Thy Word—by *faith*!
I'm going to allow faith to go beyond my
intellectual questions and doubts,
and I will believe this to be Your inspired Word.[20]

A computer . . . has no worth unless it is programmed . . .
The believer has tremendous potential, but that potential cannot
be used until he is programmed with the Word of God.[21]

We need to fortify ourselves with the Word of God.[22]

Don't argue with [a professor],
but test everything he says in the light of God's Word.[23]

Scientific discoveries (not theories) are found more and more
to fit into the record God has given us in His Word.[24]

The fact that God is infinite
makes the study of His Word a lifetime occupation.[25]

Oh that we would hunger to be filled with the Word of God;
for there is no greater armor, no greater strength,
no greater assurance that He is with us, and in us,
when we go forth in battle equipped and nourished by His instruction
and determined to stand firm on His promises.[26]

It often takes a tragedy to open our hearts, minds,
and wills to the truth of God's Word.[27]

While those around you are filling their minds with the bad news
about man in their daily papers,
steep yourself in the good news about God in His precious Word![28]

God and God's Word are inseparable.[29]

The Bible teaches that
there will be a famine of the Word of God in the last days . . .
spiritual starvation leads to spiritual death.[30]

Wherever the Word of God is hidden or ignored,
there will be certain destruction.[31]

We need to encourage new believers to feed on God's Word—
it is nourishment for the soul.[32]

BILLY GRAHAM ON
WORK

Do your best to present yourself to God . . .
a workman who . . . correctly handles the word of truth.

—2 TIMOTHY 2:15 NIV

───※───

Jesus worked all His life.
But the greatest work that Jesus did was not in the carpenter's shop . . .
His greatest work was achieved
in those three dark hours on Calvary . . . dying for us.[1]

───※───

Calloused hands were the badge of the pioneer,
while furrowed brows are the insignia of modern man.[2]

───※───

[Every] believer will receive a reward for his works.
The New Testament teaches these rewards are called "crowns."
We will surely be surprised to note who receives the crowns and who
doesn't. The lowliest servant may sparkle with more jewels than
the philanthropist who endowed the church and
whose name is engraved on the plaque in the narthex.[3]

Work isn't only earning a living;
work gives us a sense of purpose and worth
and opportunities for companionship.[4]

One of the Christian's responsibilities in following Christ
is to have a new attitude toward work.
So many young people want Christ without responsibility . . .
whatever work a Christian does . . . he should do his best.[5]

Think of working forever at something you love to do,
for [the] one you love with all your heart, and never getting tired!
We will never know weariness in heaven.[6]

God did not intend for us to be idle and unproductive.
There is dignity in work.[7]

Often volunteer work leads to employment.[8]

Often our self-esteem is tied to our work. In our culture,
men and women often define themselves by the jobs they hold . . .
But a person's job tells you nothing about a person's character or value.[9]

Many people who have lost jobs . . .
find that this was God's way of redirecting their lives.[10]

———❖———

We face a dark time in the history of God's people . . .
the forces of evil seem to be gathering for a colossal
assault on the work of God in the world.
In the darkest hour God can still revive His people,
and by the Holy Spirit breathe new vigor and power
into the body of Christ.[11]

———❖———

The devil's overriding goal is to block God's work—
and if he can convince you God doesn't really love you,
or that you can't fully trust Him,
then he has blocked God's work in your life and achieved his goal.[12]

———❖———

Do your work with honesty and integrity, and don't compromise
God's moral standards. It may be difficult, but it's far better to do right
than to do wrong. God is with you, and He will not abandon you.[13]

———❖———

Christians at work in the world are the only real spiritual light
in the midst of great spiritual darkness.
This places a tremendous responsibility on all of us.[14]

———❖———

Any work done by a follower of Christ to the glory of God is
"gold, silver, precious stones." But if any follower of Christ works
with any self-interest or personal ambition involved,
it will be "wood, hay, and stubble" and will be burned.[15]

BILLY GRAHAM ON
THE WORLD

Because . . . the word of God abides in you . . .
Do not love the world nor the things in the world. If anyone loves
the world, the love of the Father is not in him.

—1 JOHN 2:14–15 NASB

———◆———

It is strange that the world accepts enthusiasm
in every realm but the spiritual.[1]

———◆———

We don't live in an ideal world,
but in a world dominated by sinful, selfish desires.[2]

———◆———

Much of the world believes little or nothing.
People are broad but shallow.
Agnosticism, anxiety, emptiness, and meaninglessness have gripped
much of the world—and even the church . . .
By contrast, our Pilgrim forebears stand as shining examples
of men who were narrow but deep, certain of what they believed,
unswerving in their loyalty,
and passionately dedicated to the God they trusted,
and for whom they would willingly have died.[3]

Worldliness is an inner attitude
that puts self at the center of life instead of God.[4]

Too many times we are concerned with how much, instead of how little,
like this [world] we can become.[5]

We act as if it doesn't matter how we live or what we think or say.
We have moved in with the world,
and we have allowed the world to penetrate the way we live.
So the things that we used to call sin no longer seem to be sin to us.[6]

As Christians, we are not to get our worlds mixed up . . .
We are not to mingle with the world, but we are to witness to the world.[7]

I have heard the hollow, shallow laughter of the world.
I have heard the genuine laughter of the beaming young Christian.
I know there is a difference.[8]

When you are unsure whether or not something is wrong,
ask yourself these questions: Does this glorify God?
Can I offer a prayer of thanksgiving for it?
Does it draw me closer to Christ,
or does it make me preoccupied with this world?
Will it harm my health or hurt me in some other way?
Will it cause someone else to stumble spiritually or morally?
I have never forgotten what a wise Christian said to me many years ago:
"When in doubt—don't!"[9]

As for the world system of evil, we are to be separated from it.
This then is our problem: to associate with and love
those who are involved in the world without being
contaminated, influenced, or swayed by them.
This distinction can be achieved only by a close walk with Christ,
by constant prayer, and by seeking
the Holy Spirit's leadership every hour of the day.
We are in the world, but the world is not to be in us.[10]

Any history of the political events of our time
which does not also include a discussion of the Bible,
the impact of Christianity,
and the role of faith in changing the hearts and minds of people
all over the world is an incomplete and invalid study.
For what is taking place in the world today is not just a protest,
but a revolution in the sphere of the human heart.[11]

Any Christian whose interest is directed toward himself is worldly.[12]

When we come to Christ,
God calls us out of this world's sin and confusion.
But then He sends us back into the world—
not to share any longer in its sin and spiritual darkness,
but to bear witness to the light of Christ.[13]

Jesus told His disciples that the "world," meaning the world system,
the political and social order organized apart from God,
will despise Christians.[14]

It is easy for Christians to allow themselves to be
squeezed into the world's mold . . .
When nonbelievers see nothing different in the lifestyle of believers,
they wonder if our profession of faith is sincere.[15]

Those who believe [in Christ] are expected
to be different from the world . . .
they are members of a new society.[16]

Jesus invited us not to a picnic, but to a pilgrimage.
He offered us, not an excursion, but an execution.
Our Savior said that we would have to be ready to die
to self, sin, and the world.[17]

Have you fallen into the world's trap,
following its self-indulgent goals and driven by its self-centered motives?
It can happen without you even being aware of it.
Make sure Christ is first in your life,
and make it your goal to live according to His Word.[18]

Those who have actually experienced daily fellowship with Christ
know that it surpasses all worldly activities.[19]

There are so many professing Christians who are walking hand in hand
with the world that you cannot tell the difference
between the Christian and the unbeliever. This should never be.[20]

We are never to do anything of which we are
not perfectly clear and certain.
If you have a doubt about that particular thing that is bothering you,
as to whether it is worldly or not, the best policy is "don't do it."[21]

The Christian should stand out like a sparkling
diamond against a rough background.
He should be more wholesome than anyone else.
He should be poised, cultured, courteous, gracious,
but firm in the things that he does and does not do.
He should laugh and be radiant,
but he should refuse to allow the world to pull him down to its level.[22]

Do not expect me to fall in with the evil customs and ways of the world.
I am in Rome, but I will not do as Rome does.
I am an alien, a stranger, and a foreigner. My citizenship is in heaven.[23]

It is only the consecrated, Spirit-filled Christian
who can have victory over the world, the flesh, and the devil.
It is the Holy Spirit who will do the fighting for you.[24]

When the Christian brings the standards of Jesus Christ to bear
upon life in a material and secular world, it is often resented.
Because the moral and spiritual demands of Jesus Christ are so high,
they often set the Christian "apart."[25]

Worldliness is actually a spirit, an atmosphere,
an influence permeating the whole of life and human society,
and it needs to be guarded against constantly and strenuously.[26]

In the world in which we live, we give most attention to
satisfying the appetites of the body and practically none to the soul . . .
We become fat physically and materially,
while spiritually we are lean, weak, and anemic.[27]

Too many people today want a brotherly world
in which they can remain unbrotherly;
a decent world in which they can live indecently.
Too many individuals want economic security
without spiritual security.[28]

Our world needs to be touched by Christians who are
Spirit-filled, Spirit-led, and Spirit-empowered.[29]

The entire world is in turmoil.
We are living in a time of enormous conflict
and cultural transformation.
We have been stunned by shockwaves of change in nation after nation,
all around the globe.[30]

Too many people want to have one foot in the world and
one foot in the kingdom of God, and it is like straddling a fence.
You are not happy either way. Declare yourself for Christ.[31]

Worldliness doesn't fall like an avalanche upon
a person and sweep him or her away.
It is the steady drip, drip, drip of the water that wears away the stone.
The world is exerting a steady pressure on us every day.
Most of us would go down under it, if it weren't for the Holy Spirit
who lives inside us, and holds us up, and keeps us.[32]

The Bible teaches that we are to live in this world,
but we are not to partake of the evils of the world.
We are to be separated from the world of evil.
When I face something in the world, I ask:
"Does it violate any principle of Scripture?
Does it take the keen edge off my Christian life?
Can I ask God's blessing on it?
Will it be a stumbling block to others?
Would I like to be there, or reading that, or be watching that,
if Christ should return at that time?"[33]

In the struggle for righteousness, there is nothing more helpful than
being passionately in tune with Christ through His Spirit and being
passionately committed to doing His will. It has been said that
in order to tune in to God's voice, we must tune out this world's noise.[34]

We live in a hostile world that constantly
seeks to pull us away from God.[35]

How do we counter the trend of worldliness?
We must saturate our minds, hearts, and souls with God's Word.
The Bible says, "Train yourself to be godly" (1 Timothy 4:7).[36]

While we're looking up to see the rainbow—God's promises—we're ignoring floodwaters rising. While we're looking down to see how close we can get to the edge of the world without being trapped by Satan, we're taking our eyes off of Christ.[37]

We live in an upside-down world, in which people hate what they should love and love what they should hate.[38]

We're heading for a world showdown, a worldwide confrontation. If we think we can solve our problems without God, then we're living in a fool's paradise.[39]

We have a mandate to speak out against "the sin that so easily entangles" [Hebrews 12:1 NIV]; for though we are not of the world, we are still in it.[40]

The world I once knew as a boy has changed dramatically . . . I don't even recognize the world we live in today.[41]

The world judges the Christian by his life, not by his belief.[42]

There is only one passion that can help us control the many other passions that plague us; that is the passion to know and obey God. When we get out of touch with Christ, we begin touching the things of the world, trying to fill the void that human flesh craves.[43]

———————

The world's sewage system threatens to contaminate
the stream of Christian thought.
Satan will contest every hour you spend in Bible reading or prayer.[44]

———————

Our chaotic, confused world has no greater
need than to hear the Gospel truth.[45]

———————

There are no new sins—only new sinners.
There are no new crimes—only new criminals.
No new evils—only new evildoers.
No new pleasures—only new pleasure seekers.
We must distinguish between wholesome,
God-ordained pleasure and sinful, worldly pleasure.[46]

———————

The world by its advertisements, its conversation, and its philosophy
is engaged in a gigantic brainwashing task . . .
The Christian is beset by secular and worldly propaganda.[47]

———————

The world may argue against a creed,
but it cannot argue against changed lives.[48]

BILLY GRAHAM ON
WORLD EVANGELISM

Go into all the world and preach the good news to all creation.
—MARK 16:15 NIV

Ask God to help you see the world the way He sees it.[1]

One of the great joys of my life has been to travel around the world
and meet thousands of Christians in every country.[2]

We must warn the nations of the world that they must repent
and turn to God while there is yet time.
We must also proclaim that there is forgiveness
and peace in knowing Jesus Christ as Savior and Lord.[3]

I have stood in the places where history was made.
I have seen with my own eyes the part that men and women of faith
have played in these earthshaking events,
and I have heard with my own ears their cries for freedom.[4]

All over the world God is opening doors of opportunity,
making it possible for us to take the Gospel
to millions who have never heard of Christ.[5]

How marvelous it was to stand in a place like the Soviet Union
and talk about the coming kingdom and to tell
them that Communism will not win.
I told them capitalism would not win either;
it's the kingdom of God that is going to win.[6]

I have walked down jungle trails in Africa
where I met fellow Christians;
and immediately we were brothers even though we were separated
by language, race, and culture.[7]

My visits to Hungary over the past twelve years absolutely
fixed my conviction that God's Holy Spirit was releasing a spiritual force
in that part of the world that was bound to challenge the atheistic
philosophy that had dominated nations in that region for decades.[8]

Only God knows when the alarm will sound,
ending the work and ministry of evangelism as we have known it.[9]

I've never seen such a hunger in people for spiritual things . . .
People realize the past is gone, the future is uncertain,
and the present seems to be hopeless.
As a result, many [in Moscow] were open to God.[10]

My visit to Auschwitz will certainly be one of the most
unforgettable events of my life. It is a blot on the whole human race.
It was the invention of minds so depraved and demonic
that they defy any rational explanation.
It reminds us of the terrible potential man
has for violence and inhumanity.[11]

I wept more in Korea than in all the past several years put together.
These experiences changed my life.
I could never be quite the same again . . .
I felt sadder, older.
I felt as though I had gone in a boy and come out a man.[12]

Nations and civilizations rise, flourish for a time, and then decay.
Eventually each comes to an end. This, because of sin,
is the decree of history and the way of life on this planet.[13]

BILLY GRAHAM ON
WORRY

The worry of the world and the deceitfulness of wealth choke the word.

—MATTHEW 13:22 NASB

Worries flee before a spirit of gratitude.[1]

Jesus used the carefree attitude of the birds
to underscore the fact that worrying is unnatural.
I am learning in my own life, day by day,
to keep my mind centered on Christ.[2]

As long as you look only at the situation in the world today,
it will be very hard . . . to overcome your worries because it is true that
there are many problems and the future is unknown to us.
Lift your eyes beyond your circumstances and learn instead to trust God.
Worrying . . . won't change anything.[3]

When worry is present, trust cannot crowd its way in.[4]

Man has always been beset by worry,
and the pressures of modern life have aggravated the problem . . .
Many . . . are filled with a thousand anxieties.
Bring them to Jesus Christ by faith.
He will bring peace to your soul and your mind.[5]

Memorizing the Bible is most important.
"Thinking God's thoughts"
will take the place of worried, anxious concerns.[6]

Only the Holy Spirit can give us peace in the midst of the storms
of restlessness and despair. We should not grieve our Guide
by indulging in worry or paying undue attention to self.[7]

Pray for wisdom to deal with whatever is worrying you.
Pray that God will act to change the
circumstances according to His will.
He doesn't always do what we want Him to—
but He knows what's best for us, and He can be trusted.[8]

Some people spend so much time worrying about what might happen
that they never enjoy what is happening [now] . . .
Today is the tomorrow you worried about yesterday.[9]

BILLY GRAHAM ON
WORSHIP

"I am . . . of those who keep the words of this book. Worship God."

—REVELATION 22:9 NKJV

———◆———

Worship in the truest sense takes place only
when our full attention is on God—on His glory,
power, majesty, love and compassion.[1]

———◆———

Learn to shut out the distractions
that keep you from truly worshiping God.[2]

———◆———

We have come to worship things, status,
fame, popularity, money, security.
Anything that comes between God and ourselves is idolatry.
Jesus demands Lordship over all such things.[3]

———◆———

Many believe that pagan worship is a thing of the past,
but it is ever present—we have just given it a new name: pop culture.[4]

———◆———

The true child of God will have a hunger for worship and God's Word.[5]

We are to till the soil and work the land—not worship it.[6]

God is more concerned about the attitude of our hearts
than the way we express it. Worship isn't supposed to be entertainment.[7]

Our worship must be directed
to the One who holds the world in His hands.[8]

BILLY GRAHAM ON
YOUNG PEOPLE

How can a young person stay pure? By obeying [God's] word.

—PSALM 119:9

———❖———

I don't believe that young people today can live clean,
pure lives without the help of God.
The peer pressure is too great and the
temptations they see in the movies and on television,
and what they hear in their music is too much.
Only Christ can give them the power to say no.[1]

———❖———

Do you know what nearly all the sociologists say today
in their study of young people?
The greatest problem facing young people today is not sex—
it is boredom.[2]

———❖———

Our youth are desperately searching for
purpose and meaning in their lives.
They are searching for fulfillment . . .
I believe that a return to biblical conversion, faith, and conviction
would have a great impact in our day.[3]

Where students talk about being independent and on their own,
you will find them practicing the most rigid conformity in dress,
in speech, in moral attitudes, and in thinking.
Sometimes they follow fashion at the expense of integrity.
They dread to be alone. They do not want to stand out or be different.
They want to conform. After they graduate from college,
many of these young people want nothing more than
a good job with a big firm, and a home somewhere in suburbia.
But they don't find security.[4]

There is a great identity crisis among students today.
Who am I? What is the purpose of life? Where did I come from?
Where am I going?
The Bible has a direct answer to this great big philosophical question
and unless God seals the vacuum among youth today,
then some other ideology will, because young people must have a faith.
They must believe in something to find fulfillment in their lives.[5]

I have found that most young people really want us to spell out a moral
code. They may not accept it or believe it, but they want to hear it,
clearly and without compromise.[6]

In America we have an idolatry called the "adulation of youth."
Apparently distressed by their inability to communicate with
the younger generation, many adults simply imitate it.[7]

———◦•◦———

If we would take the traits that characterized
the Pilgrims and make them our own,
we could regain hope.
We could recover the spiritual and moral strength that we have lost.
We could offer a thrilling challenge to our young people.[8]

———◦•◦———

Millions of young people are shifting from one side to the other.
They are like unguided missiles filled with energy and ambition
and yet somehow not "fitting in."
Peer pressure leads them astray . . . [and] in thousands
of churches they are led astray theologically.[9]

———◦•◦———

All young people sin, and sin produces discord, repellent vibrations
which rifle the concert of life until the strings are gutless and flat.
The kicks soon lead to kickbacks.[10]

———◦•◦———

[Young people,] dress as attractively as you can.
You are an aristocrat, a child of God.[11]

———◦•◦———

In earlier periods of history, adolescence was virtually unknown . . .
Today, the span between childhood and adulthood
may extend over ten years.
Deferred adulthood is synonymous with deferred responsibility.[12]

———◦•◦———

Young people are experts on leisure, water skiing, dancing, rock music,
rapping, TV watching . . . by and large, chores are a thing of the past.[13]

Our magazine shelves are filled with crime and sex pulp-magazines
that are being read and devoured by millions of young people . . .
Scores are seeing each week the trash that Hollywood produces.
Truly our children are "movie mad."[14]

Young people are caught up in whatever appears to be the most bizarre.
They look for truth and settle for folly. False religions and the occult are
clever in reaching seekers who want to experience a rush of any kind.[15]

Don't rebel, but give God the opportunity to change your life
and help you over the problems of youth, for they are many.[16]

Parents do overindulge their children, giving them a profusion of
material things . . . Without the stabilizing effects of earning one's way,
of making decisions, of sweating hard to attain some kind of goal,
young people are grievously handicapped.[17]

Do young people have the moral stamina
to carry through in case of economic depression? . . .
The real tests of the [younger] generations have not yet come,
but they are on their way![18]

Far too many young people coming of age today have no
spiritual or emotional roots. They have been deprived of
values by an agnostic and contemporary culture.[19]

Confrontation is the special business of young people.
They confront their parents, peers, society, law enforcement officers,
and themselves, but primarily they confront God.[20]

What is the most difficult word for young
people to pronounce? It's the word *no.*
When we say no [to what is against God], He will help us to stand by it.
He will give us courage.[21]

I am in favor of hanging the Ten Commandments in every
schoolroom in the country so young people can know the difference
between right and wrong. They don't know the difference and
we're seeing the evidence of that all around us every day.[22]

I come in contact with mixed-up people, young men
and women caught in the anguish of their own unpreparedness,
intellectuals who have been seduced by false science,
and rich men held in the grip of insecurity.
They have no commitment to any goal.
They lack an anchorage for their real self.
And I long to take every one of them by the hand and
lead them into the presence of the One who said,
"Come unto me, all ye that labor and are heavy laden,
and I will give you rest" [Matthew 11:28 KJV].[23]

NOTES

Billy Graham on Abortion

1. Billy Graham, *Answers to Life's Problems* (Waco, TX: Word, 1960), 264.
2. Ibid., 277.
3. *The Billy Graham Christian Worker's Handbook* (Charlotte, NC: BGEA, 1984), 21.
4. Billy Graham, *Storm Warning* (Nashville: Thomas Nelson, 2010), 249.
5. *The Billy Graham Christian Worker's Handbook*, 259.
6. Graham, *Answers to Life's Problems*, 87.
7. Ibid., 266.

Billy Graham on Addiction

1. Billy Graham, *The Journey* (Nashville: W Publishing Group, 2006), 194.
2. Billy Graham, *Day by Day* (Minneapolis, MN: World Wide, 1965), May 19.
3. Billy Graham, *Answers to Life's Problems* (Waco, TX: Word, 1960), 293.
4. Billy Graham, *World Aflame* (New York: Doubleday, 1965), 27.
5. Graham, *Day by Day*, August 2.
6. Graham, *The Journey*, 29.
7. Graham, *World Aflame*, 32.
8. Billy Graham, *The Secret of Happiness* (New York: Doubleday, 1955), 25–26.
9. Billy Graham, *Hope for the Troubled Heart* (Dallas: Word, 1991), 28.
10. Billy Graham, *The Jesus Generation* (Grand Rapids: Zondervan, 1971), 73.
11. Graham, *Answers to Life's Problems*, 70.
12. Billy Graham, *The Holy Spirit* (Nashville: Thomas Nelson, 1978), 109.
13. Billy Graham, *Peace with God* (Waco, TX: Word, 1953), 174.
14. Graham, *World Aflame*, 32.
15. Ibid., 35.
16. Ibid., 33.
17. Graham, *Answers to Life's Problems*, 293.
18. Graham, *Day by Day*, August 28.
19. Graham, *Answers to Life's Problems*, 293.
20. Graham, *The Jesus Generation*, 66.
21. Ibid., 67.
22. Ibid., 99.
23. *The Billy Graham Christian Worker's Handbook* (Charlotte, NC: BGEA, 1984), 42.
24. Graham, *Answers to Life's Problems*, 160.
25. Graham, *The Journey*, 194.
26. *Billy Graham London Crusade* (Minneapolis, MN: World Wide, 1966), 12.
27. Billy Graham, *Billy Graham Talks to Teen-agers* (Wheaton: Miracle Books, 1958), 29.
28. Billy Graham, *Storm Warning* (Nashville: Thomas Nelson, 2010), 174.
29. *The Billy Graham Christian Worker's Handbook*, 42.

Billy Graham on Age

1. Billy Graham, *The Journey* (Nashville: W Publishing Group, 2006), 294.
2. Ibid., 293.
3. Ibid., 295.
4. Ibid., 294.
5. Ibid., 293.
6. Ibid., 295.
7. Billy Graham, *Answers to Life's Problems* (Waco, TX: Word, 1960), 225.
8. Graham, *The Journey*, 299.

Billy Graham on America

1. Billy Graham, *World Aflame* (New York: Doubleday, 1965), 198.
2. Billy Graham, *Peace with God* (Waco, TX: Word, 1953), 22.
3. Billy Graham, *Hope for the Troubled Heart* (Dallas: Word, 1991), 170.
4. Billy Graham, *Day by Day* (Minneapolis, MN: World Wide, 1965), June 23.
5. Russ Busby, *Billy Graham: God's Ambassador* (San Diego: Tehabi Books, 1999), 260.
6. Graham, *World Aflame*, 198.
7. Billy Graham, *The Holy Spirit* (Nashville: Thomas Nelson, 1978), 252.
8. Graham, *Peace with God*, 9.
9. *Breakfast with Billy Graham: 100 Daily Readings* (Ann Arbor, MI: Servant, 1996), 106.
10. Billy Graham, *Storm Warning* (Dallas: Word, 1992), 40.
11. Graham, *Day by Day*, May 9.
12. Ibid., May 27.
13. Graham, *World Aflame*, 36–37.
14. Billy Graham, *Calling Youth to Christ* (Grand Rapids: Zondervan, 1947), 14.
15. Graham, *World Aflame*, 198.
16. Billy Graham, *The Secret of Happiness* (New York: Doubleday, 1955), 92.
17. *Breakfast with Billy Graham*, 106.
18. Ibid., 108.
19. Graham, *Answers to Life's Problems*, 26.
20. Billy Graham, *Storm Warning* (Nashville: Thomas Nelson, 2010), 173.
21. Ibid., 177.
22. Billy Graham, *The Journey* (Nashville: W Publishing Group, 2006), 58.
23. Billy Graham, *Storm Warning* (Nashville: Thomas Nelson, 2010), 176.
24. Ibid., 183.
25. Ibid., 12.
26. Ibid.
27. Ibid., 21.
28. Graham, *The Journey*, 170.

Billy Graham on Angels

1. Billy Graham, *Angels* (Waco, TX: Word, 1975), 15.
2. Billy Graham, *Hope for the Troubled Heart* (Dallas: Word, 1991), 142.
3. Graham, *Angels*, xiii.
4. Ibid., xiv.
5. Ibid., 23.
6. Graham, *Hope for the Troubled Heart*, 143.
7. Graham, *Angels*, 23.
8. Ibid., 149.

Billy Graham on Anger

1. Billy Graham, *Wisdom for Each Day* (Nashville: Thomas Nelson, 2008), 160.
2. Billy Graham, *The Journey* (Nashville: W Publishing Group, 2006), 180.
3. Billy Graham, *Answers to Life's Problems* (Waco, TX: Word, 1960), 37.
4. Graham, *The Journey*, 213.
5. Ibid., 180.
6. Graham, *Answers to Life's Problems*, 191.
7. Graham, *The Journey*, 20.
8. Ibid., 178.
9. Ibid., 179–80.
10. Ibid., 180.
11. Ibid.
12. Ibid., 181.
13. *The Billy Graham Christian Worker's Handbook* (Charlotte, NC: BGEA, 1984), 45.
14. Graham, *The Journey*, 178.
15. Ibid., 179.
16. Ibid., 178–79.
17. Billy Graham, *Storm Warning* (Nashville: Thomas Nelson, 2010), 117.

Billy Graham on Anxiety

1. Billy Graham, *Day by Day* (Minneapolis, MN: World Wide, 1965), April 22.
2. Ibid.
3. Billy Graham, *The Secret of Happiness* (New York: Doubleday, 1955), 52.
4. Billy Graham, *The Journey* (Nashville: W Publishing Group, 2006), 181.
5. Ibid., 184.
6. Graham, *Day by Day*, September 24.
7. Graham, *The Journey*, 184.
8. Graham, *The Secret of Happiness*, 120–21.

Billy Graham on the Bible

1. Billy Graham, *The Journey* (Nashville: W Publishing Group, 2006), 210.
2. Billy Graham, *Day by Day* (Minneapolis, MN: World Wide, 1965), July 11.
3. Billy Graham, *Till Armageddon* (Waco, TX: Word, 1981), 157.
4. Billy Graham, *The Holy Spirit* (Nashville: Thomas Nelson, 1978), 47.
5. Billy Graham, *Wisdom for Each Day* (Nashville: Thomas Nelson, 2008), 42.
6. Graham, *Day by Day*, May 11.
7. *The Billy Graham Library* (Charlotte, NC: BGEA), audio recording.
8. Graham, *Day by Day*, July 1.
9. Billy Graham, *Hope for the Troubled Heart* (Dallas: Word, 1991), 169.
10. Graham, *Day by Day*, May 9.
11. Graham, *The Journey*, 242.
12. Billy Graham, *Peace with God* (Waco, TX: Word, 1953), 206–7.
13. Graham, *The Journey*, 112.
14. Russ Busby, *Billy Graham: God's Ambassador* (San Diego: Tehabi Books, 1999), 25.
15. Graham, *Wisdom for Each Day*, 75.
16. Graham, *The Journey*, 68.
17. Busby, *Billy Graham*, 25.
18. Graham, *The Journey*, 17.
19. Graham, *Wisdom for Each Day*, 300.
20. Busby, *Billy Graham*, 27.

21. Ibid., 202.
22. Graham, *Wisdom for Each Day*, 304.
23. Busby, *Billy Graham*, 221.
24. Ibid., 269.
25. *Decision*, July/August 2006, 16.
26. Graham, *The Holy Spirit*, 36.
27. *Decision*, July/August 2006, 17.
28. Graham, *The Journey*, 116.
29. Billy Graham, *World Aflame* (New York: Doubleday, 1965), xv.
30. Ibid., 69.
31. Ibid., 99.
32. Graham, *Peace with God*, 18.
33. Graham, *Hope for the Troubled Heart*, 14.
34. Graham, *World Aflame*, 108.
35. Billy Graham, *How to Be Born Again* (Waco, TX: Word, 1977), 39.
36. Graham, *Peace with God*, 18.
37. Ibid.
38. Ibid., 20.
39. Graham, *Wisdom for Each Day*, 223.
40. Graham, *Peace with God*, 22.
41. Billy Graham, *Answers to Life's Problems* (Waco, TX: Word, 1960), 274.
42. Ibid., 10.
43. Graham, *Peace with God*, 22.
44. Graham, *Day by Day*, January 9.
45. Graham, *Peace with God*, 26.
46. Graham, *Answers to Life's Problems*, 275.
47. Graham, *How to Be Born Again*, 43.
48. Graham, *Answers to Life's Problems*, 290.
49. Ibid., 274.
50. Ibid., 286.
51. Billy Graham, *Facing Death and the Life After* (Waco, TX: Word, 1987), 227.
52. Graham, *Answers to Life's Problems*, 290–91.
53. Graham, *The Journey*, 17.
54. Graham, *Answers to Life's Problems*, 291.
55. *The Billy Graham Christian Worker's Handbook* (Charlotte, NC: BGEA, 1984), 61.
56. Graham, *The Journey*, 108.
57. Graham, *Answers to Life's Problems*, 292.
58. Ibid.
59. Graham, *The Journey*, 106.
60. Graham, *Answers to Life's Problems*, 292.
61. Ibid., 293–94.
62. Graham, *The Journey*, 17.
63. Graham, *Answers to Life's Problems*, 294.
64. Ibid., 296.
65. Ibid., 298.
66. Graham, *The Holy Spirit*, 42.
67. Graham, *The Journey*, 113.
68. Ibid., 107–8.
69. Billy Graham, *Storm Warning* (Nashville: Thomas Nelson, 2010), 94.
70. *Billy Graham London Crusade* (Minneapolis, MN: World Wide, 1966), 46.
71. Graham, *World Aflame*, 253.
72. Graham, *The Journey*, 105–6.
73. Ibid., 107.

74. Billy Graham, *Alone with the Savior* (Charlotte, NC: BGEA, 2010), 15.
75. Ibid., 17.
76. Ibid., 15.
77. Billy Graham, *The Secret of Happiness* (New York: Doubleday, 1955), 154.
78. Graham, *The Journey*, 108.
79. Graham, *Alone with the Savior*, 18.
80. Graham, *The Journey*, 112.
81. Graham, *Alone with the Savior*, 45.

Billy Graham on the Blood

1. Billy Graham, *Till Armageddon* (Waco, TX: Word, 1981), 76.
2. Billy Graham, *World Aflame* (New York: Doubleday, 1965), 78–79.
3. Ibid.
4. Billy Graham, *Storm Warning* (Nashville: Thomas Nelson, 2010), 159.
5. Billy Graham, *Hope for the Troubled Heart* (Dallas: Word, 1991), 65.
6. Billy Graham, *Day by Day* (Minneapolis, MN: World Wide, 1965), March 29.
7. Billy Graham, *Peace with God* (Waco, TX: Word, 1953), 118.
8. Billy Graham, *Calling Youth to Christ* (Grand Rapids: Zondervan, 1947), 125.
9. Graham, *Peace with God*, 118.
10. Graham, *Till Armageddon*, 72.

Billy Graham on Character

1. Billy Graham, *Facing Death and the Life After* (Waco, TX: Word, 1987), 227.
2. Billy Graham, *Just As I Am* (San Francisco: HarperOne, 1997), 697.
3. Billy Graham, *The Journey* (Nashville: W Publishing Group, 2006), 175.
4. Billy Graham, *The Secret of Happiness* (New York: Doubleday, 1955), 78.
5. Billy Graham, *Till Armageddon* (Waco, TX: Word, 1981), 71.
6. Billy Graham, *Day by Day* (Minneapolis, MN: World Wide, 1965), November 19.
7. Graham, *Till Armageddon*, 61.
8. Graham, *Facing Death and the Life After*, 89.
9. Billy Graham, *Billy Graham Talks to Teen-agers* (Wheaton: Miracle Books, 1958), 29–30.
10. Billy Graham, *Peace with God* (Waco, TX: Word, 1953), 235.

Billy Graham on Children

1. Billy Graham, *Facing Death and the Life After* (Waco, TX: Word, 1987), 81–82.
2. Billy Graham, *The Journey* (Nashville: W Publishing Group, 2006), 268.
3. Billy Graham, *Hope for the Troubled Heart* (Dallas: Word, 1991), 24.
4. Graham, *The Journey*, 272.
5. Ibid., 269.
6. Ibid., 275.
7. *Breakfast with Billy Graham: 100 Daily Readings* (Ann Arbor, MI: Servant, 1996), 111.
8. Graham, *The Journey*, 275.
9. Ibid.
10. *Breakfast with Billy Graham*, 113.
11. Billy Graham, *Day by Day* (Minneapolis, MN: World Wide, 1965), January 27.
12. *Breakfast with Billy Graham*, 113.
13. Graham, *The Journey*, 271–72.
14. *Breakfast with Billy Graham*, 113.
15. Billy Graham, *Hope for the Troubled Heart*, 85.
16. Graham, *Day by Day*, January 8.

17. Graham, *The Journey*, 291.
18. Billy Graham, *Storm Warning* (Nashville: Thomas Nelson, 2010), 179.
19. Graham, *The Journey*, 291.
20. Billy Graham, *Storm Warning* (Nashville: Thomas Nelson, 2010), 178.
21. Graham, *Facing Death and the Life After*, 86.
22. Billy Graham, *The Jesus Generation* (Grand Rapids: Zondervan, 1971), 40.
23. Ibid., 43.
24. *The Billy Graham Christian Worker's Handbook* (Charlotte, NC: BGEA, 1984), 166.
25. Graham, *The Journey*, 276.

Billy Graham on Choice

1. *Breakfast with Billy Graham: 100 Daily Readings* (Ann Arbor, MI: Servant, 1996), 120.
2. Ibid.
3. Billy Graham, *Peace with God* (Waco, TX: Word, 1953), 49.
4. Ibid.
5. Billy Graham, *Day by Day* (Minneapolis, MN: World Wide, 1965), December 11.
6. Ibid., December 13.
7. Billy Graham, *Answers to Life's Problems* (Waco, TX: Word, 1960), 265.
8. Ibid., 301–2.
9. *The Billy Graham Library* (Charlotte, NC: BGEA, n.d.), audio recording.
10. Billy Graham, *The Jesus Generation* (Grand Rapids: Zondervan, 1971), 136–37.
11. Billy Graham, *Till Armageddon* (Waco, TX: Word, 1981), 47.

Billy Graham on Christianity

1. Billy Graham, *The Holy Spirit* (Nashville: Thomas Nelson, 1978), 291.
2. Billy Graham, *Day by Day* (Minneapolis, MN: World Wide, 1965), April 7.
3. Ibid., October 12.
4. Ibid., April 7.
5. Billy Graham, *Hope for the Troubled Heart* (Dallas: Word, 1991), 43.
6. Graham, *Day by Day*, May 26.
7. Graham, *Hope for the Troubled Heart*, 103.
8. Graham, *Day by Day*, April 30.
9. Ibid., July 14.
10. Billy Graham, *Peace with God* (Waco, TX: Word, 1953), 205.
11. Ibid., 251.
12. Graham, *Day by Day*, June 8.
13. Ibid., May 29.
14. Ibid., June 8.
15. Graham, *Peace with God*, 235.
16. Ibid., 237.
17. Graham, *Day by Day*, February 16.
18. Billy Graham, *The Journey* (Nashville: W Publishing Group, 2006), 93.
19. Ibid., 76.
20. Billy Graham, *Till Armageddon* (Waco, TX: Word, 1981), 66.
21. Graham, *Day by Day*, January 8.
22. Graham, *The Journey*, 62.
23. Billy Graham, *Facing Death and the Life After* (Waco, TX: Word, 1987), 95.
24. Ibid., 196.
25. Graham, *Day by Day*, July 28.
26. Billy Graham, *The Secret of Happiness* (New York: Doubleday, 1955), 151–52.
27. Ibid., 152.

28. Billy Graham, *Answers to Life's Problems* (Waco, TX: Word, 1960), 103.
29. Billy Graham, *World Aflame* (New York: Doubleday, 1965), 230.
30. Billy Graham, *The Secret of Happiness* (New York: Doubleday, 1955), 51.
31. Graham, *World Aflame*, 199.
32. Graham, *Day by Day*, May 9.
33. Graham, *The Holy Spirit*, 294.
34. Ibid., 295.
35. Billy Graham, *Wisdom for Each Day* (Nashville: Thomas Nelson, 2008), 25.
36. Graham, *The Secret of Happiness*, 75.
37. Graham, *The Holy Spirit*, 111.
38. Graham, *World Aflame*, 58.
39. Graham, *Till Armageddon*, 98.
40. Graham, *The Secret of Happiness*, 9–10.
41. Graham, *World Aflame*, 110.
42. Ibid., 210.
43. Graham, *The Secret of Happiness*, 123.
44. Graham, *Hope for the Troubled Heart*, 38.
45. Graham, *Day by Day*, February 1.
46. Graham, *Hope for the Troubled Heart*, 36.
47. Graham, *Wisdom for Each Day*, 366.
48. Graham, *Day by Day*, September 16.
49. Ibid., January 8.
50. Ibid., May 14.
51. Graham, *The Holy Spirit*, 148.
52. Graham, *Till Armageddon*, 85.
53. Graham, *Hope for the Troubled Heart*, 36.
54. Graham, *Till Armageddon*, 64.
55. Graham, *Answers to Life's Problems*, 17.
56. Ibid., 270.
57. Billy Graham, *The Jesus Generation* (Grand Rapids: Zondervan, 1971), 152.
58. Graham, *The Journey*, 74.
59. Ibid., 76.
60. Graham, *World Aflame*, 28.
61. Graham, *The Journey*, 179.
62. Billy Graham, *Storm Warning* (Nashville: Thomas Nelson, 2010), 164.
63. Ibid., 187.
64. Ibid., 158.
65. Graham, *World Aflame*, 77.
66. Graham, *Peace with God*, 169.
67. Graham, *The Journey*, 211.
68. Ibid., 135.
69. Billy Graham, *Alone with the Savior* (Charlotte, NC: BGEA, 2010), 24.
70. Ibid., 27.
71. *Decision*, April 2010, 4.
72. Graham, *Alone with the Savior*, 15–16.
73. Graham, *The Holy Spirit*, 28.
74. Graham, *The Journey*, 143.

Billy Graham on Church

1. Billy Graham, *The Holy Spirit* (Nashville: Thomas Nelson, 1978), 295.
2. Billy Graham, *Peace with God* (Waco, TX: Word, 1953), 221.
3. Billy Graham, *Till Armageddon* (Waco, TX: Word, 1981), 29.

4. Ibid., 76.
5. Billy Graham, *World Aflame* (New York: Doubleday, 1965), 184.
6. Russ Busby, *Billy Graham: God's Ambassador* (San Diego: Tehabi Books, 1999), 255.
7. Graham, *Till Armageddon*, 93.
8. Graham, *World Aflame*, 193.
9. Billy Graham, *How to Be Born Again* (Waco, TX: Word, 1977), 58.
10. Graham, *Till Armageddon*, 96.
11. Ibid., 63.
12. Ibid., 85.
13. Graham, *World Aflame*, 181.
14. Graham, *The Holy Spirit*, 202.
15. Billy Graham, *Calling Youth to Christ* (Grand Rapids: Zondervan, 1947), 16.
16. Billy Graham, *Wisdom for Each Day* (Nashville: Thomas Nelson, 2008), 8.
17. Graham, *World Aflame*, 12.
18. Ibid., 181.
19. Graham, *Peace with God*, 229.
20. Billy Graham, *The Secret of Happiness* (New York: Doubleday, 1955), 36.
21. Graham, *World Aflame*, 193.
22. Ibid., 181.
23. Ibid., 220.
24. Graham, *How to Be Born Again*, 62.
25. Billy Graham, *Hope for the Troubled Heart* (Dallas: Word, 1991), 77.
26. Graham, *How to Be Born Again*, 137.
27. Graham, *World Aflame*, 85.
28. Graham, *Till Armageddon*, 99.
29. Billy Graham, *Answers to Life's Problems* (Waco, TX: Word, 1960), 114.
30. Ibid., 116.
31. Ibid., 117.
32. Graham, *Peace with God*, 237.
33. Billy Graham, *The Journey* (Nashville: W Publishing Group, 2006), 125.
34. Billy Graham, *Storm Warning* (Nashville: Thomas Nelson, 2010), 188.
35. Ibid.
36. Ibid., 165.
37. Graham, *Till Armageddon*, 100.
38. Billy Graham, *Storm Warning* (Nashville: Thomas Nelson, 2010), 165.
39. Ibid., 187.
40. Ibid., 163.
41. Ibid., 164.
42. Ibid., 165.
43. Graham, *The Journey*, 133.
44. Billy Graham, *Storm Warning* (Nashville: Thomas Nelson, 2010), 164.
45. Ibid., 110.
46. Ibid., 190.
47. Ibid., 79.
48. Billy Graham, *Alone with the Savior* (Charlotte, NC: BGEA, 2010), 29.
49. Billy Graham, *Storm Warning* (Nashville: Thomas Nelson, 2010), 162–63.
50. Graham, *The Journey*, 59.

Billy Graham on Comfort

1. Billy Graham, *Hope for the Troubled Heart* (Dallas: Word, 1991), 191.
2. Billy Graham, *Facing Death and the Life After* (Waco, TX: Word, 1987), 101.
3. Graham, *Hope for the Troubled Heart*, 104.

4. Billy Graham, *The Secret of Happiness* (New York: Doubleday, 1955), 154.
5. Billy Graham, *Unto the Hills* (Waco, TX: Word, 1986), 225.
6. Billy Graham, *Alone with the Savior* (Charlotte, NC: BGEA, 2010), 38.
7. Graham, *Unto the Hills*, 225.
8. Graham, *The Secret of Happiness*, 95.

Billy Graham on Commitment

1. Billy Graham, *World Aflame* (New York: Doubleday, 1965), 152.
2. Billy Graham, *Peace with God* (Waco, TX: Word, 1953), 80.
3. Billy Graham, *The Secret of Happiness* (New York: Doubleday, 1955), 33.
4. Billy Graham, *The Jesus Generation* (Grand Rapids: Zondervan, 1971), 166.
5. Ibid., 168.
6. Billy Graham, *Alone with the Savior* (Charlotte, NC: BGEA, 2010), 61.
7. Billy Graham, *Wisdom for Each Day* (Nashville: Thomas Nelson, 2008), 35.
8. Billy Graham, *A Biblical Standard for Evangelists* (Minneapolis: World Wide, 1984), 55.
9. Ibid.

Billy Graham on Compromise

1. Billy Graham, *How to Be Born Again* (Waco, TX: Word, 1977), 60.
2. Billy Graham, *Hope for the Troubled Heart* (Dallas: Word, 1991), 43.
3. Billy Graham, *Day by Day* (Minneapolis, MN: World Wide, 1965), March 20.
4. Billy Graham, *Peace with God* (Waco, TX: Word, 1953), 141.
5. Billy Graham, *Till Armageddon* (Waco, TX: Word, 1981), 97.
6. Billy Graham, *World Aflame* (New York: Doubleday, 1965), 223.
7. Graham, *Day by Day*, September 29.
8. Billy Graham, *Storm Warning* (Nashville: Thomas Nelson, 2010), 79.
9. Billy Graham, *Alone with the Savior* (Charlotte, NC: BGEA, 2010), 30.
10. Billy Graham, *Storm Warning* (Nashville: Thomas Nelson, 2010), 86.
11. Ibid., 262–63.
12. Ibid., 79.
13. Billy Graham, *Answers to Life's Problems* (Waco, TX: Word, 1960), 276.

Billy Graham on Conforming

1. Billy Graham, *World Aflame* (New York: Doubleday, 1965), 261.
2. Ibid., xv.
3. Ibid., 38.
4. Billy Graham, *The Jesus Generation* (Grand Rapids: Zondervan, 1971), 73.
5. Billy Graham, *Hope for the Troubled Heart* (Dallas: Word, 1991), 14.
6. Billy Graham, *Answers to Life's Problems* (Waco, TX: Word, 1960), 25.
7. Billy Graham, *Alone with the Savior* (Charlotte, NC: BGEA, 2010), 28.
8. Ibid., 57.
9. Ibid., 31–32.
10. Ibid., 31.
11. Ibid., 55–56.
12. Billy Graham, *Day by Day* (Minneapolis, MN: World Wide, 1965), November 18.

Billy Graham on Conscience

1. Billy Graham, *Facing Death and the Life After* (Waco, TX: Word, 1987), 228.
2. Billy Graham, *Day by Day* (Minneapolis, MN: World Wide, 1965), November 9.

3. Ibid.
4. Billy Graham, *Peace with God* (Waco, TX: Word, 1953), 206.
5. Billy Graham, *How to Be Born Again* (Waco, TX: Word, 1977), 37.
6. Graham, *Day by Day*, November 9.
7. Graham, *Peace with God*, 120.
8. Graham, *Day by Day*, February 26.
9. Ibid., March 26.
10. Graham, *Peace with God*, 14.
11. Ibid., 23.
12. Graham, *Day by Day*, February 6.
13. Billy Graham, *Answers to Life's Problems* (Waco, TX: Word, 1960), 272.
14. *The Billy Graham Christian Worker's Handbook* (Charlotte, NC: BGEA, 1984), 142.
15. Ibid., 290.
16. Billy Graham, *The Holy Spirit* (Nashville: Thomas Nelson, 1978), 279.
17. Billy Graham, *World Aflame* (New York: Doubleday, 1965), 72.
18. Billy Graham, *Alone with the Savior* (Charlotte, NC: BGEA, 2010), 24.
19. *The Billy Graham Christian Worker's Handbook*, 290.
20. Billy Graham, *Till Armageddon* (Waco, TX: Word, 1981), 75.

Billy Graham on Conversion

1. Billy Graham, *World Aflame* (New York: Doubleday, 1965), 149.
2. Ibid., 156.
3. Billy Graham, *Peace with God* (Waco, TX: Word, 1953), 134.
4. Ibid., 136.
5. *Breakfast with Billy Graham: 100 Daily Readings* (Ann Arbor, MI: Servant, 1996), 110.
6. Graham, *Peace with God*, 134.
7. Billy Graham, *The Secret of Happiness* (New York: Doubleday, 1955), 72.
8. Graham, *Peace with God*, 135.

Billy Graham on Convictions

1. Billy Graham, *Peace with God* (Waco, TX: Word, 1953), 252.
2. Billy Graham, *Day by Day* (Minneapolis, MN: World Wide, 1965), April 30.
3. Graham, *Peace with God*, 146.
4. Ibid., 53.
5. Billy Graham, *Wisdom for Each Day* (Nashville: Thomas Nelson, 2008), 195.
6. Billy Graham, *Answers to Life's Problems* (Waco, TX: Word, 1960), 276.
7. Billy Graham, *The Journey* (Nashville: W Publishing Group, 2006), 245.

Billy Graham on Creation

1. Billy Graham, *The Journey* (Nashville: W Publishing Group, 2006), 16.
2. Billy Graham, *World Aflame* (New York: Doubleday, 1965), 51.
3. Billy Graham, *How to Be Born Again* (Waco, TX: Word, 1977), 39–40.
4. Billy Graham, *Day by Day* (Minneapolis, MN: World Wide, 1965), May 11.
5. Ibid., March 21.
6. Russ Busby, *Billy Graham: God's Ambassador* (San Diego: Tehabi Books, 1999), 218.
7. Graham, *World Aflame*, 62.
8. Billy Graham, *Till Armageddon* (Waco, TX: Word, 1981), 48.
9. Billy Graham, *Answers to Life's Problems* (Waco, TX: Word, 1960), 275.
10. Billy Graham, *Storm Warning* (Nashville: Thomas Nelson, 2010), 71.
11. Billy Graham, *Hope for the Troubled Heart* (Dallas: Word, 1991), 91.

Billy Graham on the Cross

1. Billy Graham, *The Secret of Happiness* (New York: Doubleday, 1955), 22.
2. Billy Graham, *Peace with God* (Waco, TX: Word, 1953), 57.
3. Billy Graham, *Day by Day* (Minneapolis, MN: World Wide, 1965), March 30.
4. Graham, *Peace with God*, 62.
5. Ibid., 57.
6. Billy Graham, *Till Armageddon* (Waco, TX: Word, 1981), 94.
7. Billy Graham, *World Aflame* (New York: Doubleday, 1965), 261.
8. Graham, *Peace with God*, 114.
9. Billy Graham, *Wisdom for Each Day* (Nashville: Thomas Nelson, 2008), 105.
10. Ibid.
11. Ibid., 29.
12. Ibid., 30.
13. Graham, *Day by Day*, April 5.
14. Graham, *World Aflame*, xvi.
15. Ibid., 118.
16. Ibid.
17. Graham, *The Secret of Happiness*, 65.
18. Billy Graham, *Hope for the Troubled Heart* (Dallas: Word, 1991), 22.
19. Graham, *Peace with God*, 117.
20. Ibid., 118.
21. Ibid., 244.
22. Billy Graham, *The Journey* (Nashville: W Publishing Group, 2006), 50.
23. Graham, *Till Armageddon*, 68.
24. Billy Graham, *The Jesus Generation* (Grand Rapids: Zondervan, 1971), 168.
25. Billy Graham, *The Holy Spirit* (Nashville: Thomas Nelson, 1978), 289.
26. Graham, *Wisdom for Each Day*, 105.

Billy Graham on Death

1. Billy Graham, *Peace with God* (Waco, TX: Word, 1953), 83.
2. Billy Graham, *Facing Death and the Life After* (Waco, TX: Word, 1987), 85.
3. Billy Graham, *Hope for the Troubled Heart* (Dallas: Word, 1991), 206.
4. Ibid., 209.
5. Graham, *Peace with God*, 83.
6. Ibid., 84.
7. Billy Graham, *Alone with the Savior* (Charlotte, NC: BGEA, 2010), 43.
8. Billy Graham, *The Journey* (Nashville: W Publishing Group, 2006), 220–21.
9. Graham, *Peace with God*, 86.
10. Billy Graham, *Answers to Life's Problems* (Waco, TX: Word, 1960), 236.
11. Graham, *Facing Death and the Life After*, 26.
12. Ibid., 211.
13. Graham, *Hope for the Troubled Heart*, 199.
14. Ibid., 198.
15. Billy Graham, *Till Armageddon* (Waco, TX: Word, 1981), 203.
16. Graham, *Peace with God*, 95.
17. Ibid., 95.
18. Graham, *Till Armageddon*, 197.
19. Graham, *Facing Death and the Life After*, 11.
20. Graham, *Hope for the Troubled Heart*, 207.
21. *The Billy Graham Library* (Charlotte, NC: BGEA, n.d.), audio recording.
22. Graham, *Till Armageddon*, 199.

23. Ibid., 205.
24. Graham, Facing Death and the Life After, 91.
25. Ibid., 106.
26. Graham, *The Journey*, 299.
27. Graham, *Alone with the Savior*, 21–22.
28. Graham, *The Journey*, 299–300.
29. Graham, *Facing Death and the Life After*, 267.
30. *Decision*, April 2010.
31. Graham, *Till Armageddon*, 213.
32. Graham, *Alone with the Savior*, 45.
33. Russ Busby, *Billy Graham: God's Ambassador*, end sheet (San Diego: Tehabi Books, 1999).

Billy Graham on Deception

1. Billy Graham, *World Aflame* (New York: Doubleday, 1965), 84.
2. Billy Graham, *Storm Warning* (Dallas: Word, 1992), 176.
3. Graham, *World Aflame*, 84.
4. Billy Graham, *Till Armageddon* (Waco, TX: Word, 1981), 67.
5. Graham, *World Aflame*, 85.
6. Billy Graham, *How to Be Born Again* (Waco, TX: Word, 1977), 58.
7. Billy Graham, *The Holy Spirit* (Nashville: Thomas Nelson, 1978), 196.
8. Billy Graham, *Storm Warning* (Nashville: Thomas Nelson, 2010), 146.
9. Graham, *The Holy Spirit*, 197.

Billy Graham on Decision

1. Russ Busby, *Billy Graham: God's Ambassador* (San Diego: Tehabi Books, 1999), 25.
2. Ibid., 33.
3. Ibid., 29.
4. Billy Graham, *Wisdom for Each Day* (Nashville: Thomas Nelson, 2008), 201.
5. Billy Graham, *The Journey* (Nashville: W Publishing Group, 2006), 238.
6. *Breakfast with Billy Graham: 100 Daily Readings* (Ann Arbor, MI: Servant, 1996), 120.
7. Billy Graham, *Day by Day* (Minneapolis, MN: World Wide, 1965), January 30.
8. Billy Graham, *The Holy Spirit* (Nashville: Thomas Nelson, 1978), 182.
9. Graham, *The Journey*, 199.
10. Billy Graham, *Till Armageddon* (Waco, TX: Word, 1981), 23.
11. Billy Graham, *Storm Warning* (Nashville: Thomas Nelson, 2010), 154–55.
12. Graham, *Till Armageddon*, 50.
13. Graham, *The Journey*, 245.
14. Billy Graham, *Answers to Life's Problems* (Waco, TX: Word, 1960), 236.

Billy Graham on the Devil/Satan

1. Billy Graham, *Peace with God* (Waco, TX: Word, 1953), 65.
2. Russ Busby, *Billy Graham: God's Ambassador* (San Diego: Tehabi Books, 1999), 27.
3. Billy Graham, *The Journey* (Nashville: W Publishing Group, 2006), 188.
4. Ibid., 207.
5. Ibid., 103.
6. Billy Graham, *Wisdom for Each Day* (Nashville: Thomas Nelson, 2008), 284.
7. Ibid., 309.
8. Ibid., 313.
9. Ibid., 196.
10. Ibid., 61.

11. Ibid.
12. Graham, *The Journey* (Nashville: W Publishing Group, 2006), 189.
13. Graham, *Peace with God* (Waco, TX: Word, 1953), 69.
14. Graham, *Wisdom for Each Day* (Nashville: Thomas Nelson, 2008), 307.
15. Billy Graham, *The Secret of Happiness* (New York: Doubleday, 1955), 83.
16. Billy Graham, *The Holy Spirit* (Nashville: Thomas Nelson, 1978), 267.
17. Ibid., 285.
18. Graham, *Peace with God*, 191–92.
19. Billy Graham, *Answers to Life's Problems* (Waco, TX: Word, 1960), 295.
20. *Decision*, July/August 2010, 5.
21. Graham, *Peace with God*, 259.
22. Ibid., 191.
23. Ibid., 12.
24. Billy Graham, *Till Armageddon* (Waco, TX: Word, 1981), 60.
25. Graham, *The Journey*, 188.
26. Billy Graham, *Storm Warning* (Nashville: Thomas Nelson, 2010), 162.
27. Ibid., 187.
28. Ibid., 175.
29. Billy Graham, *Billy Graham Talks to Teen-agers* (Wheaton: Miracle Books, 1958), 51.
30. Billy Graham, *The Jesus Generation* (Grand Rapids: Zondervan, 1971), 69.
31. Busby, *Billy Graham*, 270.
32. Billy Graham, *World Aflame* (New York: Doubleday, 1965), 114–15.
33. Billy Graham, *Hope for the Troubled Heart* (Dallas: Word, 1991), 50.
34. Ibid., 53.
35. Ibid., 165.
36. Billy Graham, *Storm Warning* (Nashville: Thomas Nelson, 2010), 189.
37. Ibid., 202.
38. Graham, *Peace with God*, 63.
39. *Decision*, April 2010, 4.
40. Ibid.
41. Graham, *The Journey*, 297.
42. Graham, *Hope for the Troubled Heart*, 49.
43. Graham, *The Journey*, 108.
44. Graham, *The Jesus Generation*, 163.
45. Graham, *The Journey*, 301.
46. Graham, *Wisdom for Each Day*, 180.
47. Billy Graham, *Alone with the Savior* (Charlotte, NC: BGEA, 2010), 35–36.

Billy Graham on Disappointment

1. Billy Graham, *The Journey* (Nashville: W Publishing Group, 2006), 200.
2. Ibid., 204.
3. Billy Graham, *Wisdom for Each Day* (Nashville: Thomas Nelson, 2008), 370.
4. Billy Graham, *Day by Day* (Minneapolis, MN: World Wide, 1965), August 21.
5. Graham, *The Journey*, 204.
6. Ibid., 203.
7. Billy Graham, *The Holy Spirit* (Nashville: Thomas Nelson, 1978), 281.
8. Graham, *Day by Day*, March 27.
9. Billy Graham, *Facing Death and the Life After* (Waco, TX: Word, 1987), 254.
10. Graham, *The Journey*, 201.
11. Graham, *The Holy Spirit*, 280.
12. Graham, *The Journey*, 202.
13. Ibid., 203.

Billy Graham on Discipleship and Discipline

1. Billy Graham, *The Journey* (Nashville: W Publishing Group, 2006), 89.
2. Billy Graham, *Hope for the Troubled Heart* (Dallas: Word, 1991), 36.
3. Billy Graham, *The Secret of Happiness* (New York: Doubleday, 1955), 135.
4. Graham, *Hope for the Troubled Heart*, 37.
5. Ibid., 40.
6. Ibid., 38.
7. *The Billy Graham Christian Worker's Handbook* (Charlotte, NC: BGEA, 1984), 90.
8. Ibid., 217.
9. Graham, *The Journey*, 89.
10. Billy Graham, *A Biblical Standard for Evangelists* (Minneapolis: World Wide, 1984), 53.
11. Ibid., 62.

Billy Graham on Encouragement

1. Billy Graham, *Hope for the Troubled Heart* (Dallas: Word, 1991), 188.
2. Ibid.
3. Billy Graham, *Wisdom for Each Day* (Nashville: Thomas Nelson, 2008), 324.
4. Billy Graham, *Answers to Life's Problems* (Waco, TX: Word, 1960), 226.
5. Billy Graham, *The Holy Spirit* (Nashville: Thomas Nelson, 1978), 10.
6. Billy Graham, *The Journey* (Nashville: W Publishing Group, 2006), 130.
7. Ibid., 191.
8. Graham, *The Holy Spirit*, 291.

Billy Graham on End Times

1. Billy Graham, *The Holy Spirit* (Nashville: Thomas Nelson, 1978), 28.
2. Billy Graham, *Approaching Hoofbeats* (Waco, TX: Word, 1983), 19.
3. Ibid., 26.
4. Billy Graham, *Day by Day* (Minneapolis, MN: World Wide, 1965), May 9.
5. Graham, *Approaching Hoofbeats*, 11.
6. Billy Graham, *Hope for the Troubled Heart* (Dallas: Word, 1991), 177.
7. Billy Graham, *Wisdom for Each Day* (Nashville: Thomas Nelson, 2008), 17.
8. *Breakfast with Billy Graham: 100 Daily Readings* (Ann Arbor, MI: Servant, 1996), 119.
9. *The Billy Graham Library* (Charlotte, NC: BGEA, n.d.), audio recording.
10. Billy Graham, *World Aflame* (New York: Doubleday, 1965), 1–2.
11. Ibid., 200–201.
12. Ibid., 203.
13. Billy Graham, *Till Armageddon* (Waco, TX: Word, 1981), 59.
14. Billy Graham, *Alone with the Savior* (Charlotte, NC: BGEA, 2010), 4.
15. Billy Graham, *The Jesus Generation* (Grand Rapids: Zondervan, 1971), 177.
16. Billy Graham, *Answers to Life's Problems* (Waco, TX: Word, 1960), 302.
17. Graham, *The Jesus Generation*, 187.
18. Billy Graham, *Storm Warning* (Nashville: Thomas Nelson, 2010), 75.
19. Ibid., 65.
20. Graham, *The Jesus Generation*, 188.
21. Graham, *Alone with the Savior*, 5.
22. Billy Graham, press conference in Poland, 16 October 1978, audio recording.

Billy Graham on Eternity

1. Billy Graham, *Hope for the Troubled Heart* (Dallas: Word, 1991), 203.

2. *Breakfast with Billy Graham: 100 Daily Readings* (Ann Arbor, MI: Servant, 1996), 118.
3. Billy Graham, *Calling Youth to Christ* (Grand Rapids: Zondervan, 1947), 127.
4. Billy Graham, *Facing Death and the Life After* (Waco, TX: Word, 1987), 221.
5. Ibid., 191.
6. Billy Graham, *The Holy Spirit* (Nashville: Thomas Nelson, 1978), 111.
7. Graham, *Facing Death and the Life After*, 204.
8. Billy Graham, *The Journey* (Nashville: W Publishing Group, 2006), 299.
9. Graham, *Facing Death and the Life After*, 267.
10. Billy Graham, *A Biblical Standard for Evangelists* (Minneapolis: World Wide, 1984), 45.
11. Ibid., 58.

Billy Graham on Evangelism

1. *The Billy Graham Library* (Charlotte, NC: BGEA), audio recording.
2. Russ Busby, *Billy Graham: God's Ambassador* (San Diego: Tehabi Books, 1999), 197.
3. Billy Graham, *Facing Death and the Life After* (Waco, TX: Word, 1987), 245.
4. Busby, *Billy Graham*, 257.
5. Billy Graham, *The Holy Spirit* (Nashville: Thomas Nelson, 1978), 182.
6. Ibid.
7. Ibid., 183.
8. Billy Graham, *Just As I Am* (San Francisco: HarperOne, 1997), 696.
9. Graham, *The Holy Spirit*, 183.
10. Billy Graham, *A Biblical Standard for Evangelists* (Minneapolis, MN: World Wide, 1984), 32.
11. Graham, *The Holy Spirit*, 292.
12. *Decision*, May 2010.
13. Busby, *Billy Graham*, 25.
14. Graham, *Just As I Am*, 642.
15. Graham, *A Biblical Standard for Evangelists*, 109–10.

Billy Graham on Evil

1. Billy Graham, *The Journey* (Nashville: W Publishing Group, 2006), 197.
2. Ibid., 196.
3. Ibid., 212.
4. Ibid., 213.
5. Ibid., 212.
6. Billy Graham, *Till Armageddon* (Waco, TX: Word, 1981), 65.
7. Billy Graham, *Alone with the Savior* (Charlotte, NC: BGEA, 2010), 29.
8. Graham, *Till Armageddon*, 51.
9. Billy Graham, *Peace with God* (Waco, TX: Word, 1953), 51.
10. Billy Graham, *The Holy Spirit* (Nashville: Thomas Nelson, 1978), 163–64.
11. Billy Graham, *Day by Day* (Minneapolis, MN: World Wide, 1965), April 9.

Billy Graham on Faith

1. Billy Graham, *Peace with God* (Waco, TX: Word, 1953), 160.
2. Billy Graham, *How to Be Born Again* (Waco, TX: Word, 1977), 162.
3. Billy Graham, *Hope for the Troubled Heart* (Dallas: Word, 1991), 37.
4. Billy Graham, *Wisdom for Each Day* (Nashville: Thomas Nelson, 2008), 362.
5. Billy Graham, *Day by Day* (Minneapolis, MN: World Wide, 1965), October 25.
6. Billy Graham, *The Journey* (Nashville: W Publishing Group, 2006), 105.
7. Graham, *Day by Day*, November 10.
8. Graham, *Peace with God*, 164.

9. Graham, *Hope for the Troubled Heart*, 103.
10. Graham, *Peace with God*, 160.
11. Graham, *Wisdom for Each Day*, 158.
12. Graham, *The Journey*, 230.
13. Graham, *Day by Day*, July 29.
14. Graham, *The Journey*, 182.
15. Ibid., 182–83.
16. Ibid., 182.
17. Ibid., 105.
18. Ibid., 187.
19. Billy Graham, *Alone with the Savior* (Charlotte, NC: BGEA, 2010), 21.
20. Ibid., 25.
21. Billy Graham, *Answers to Life's Problems* (Waco, TX: Word, 1960), 287.
22. Billy Graham, *My Daily Prayer Journal* (Minneapolis, MN: Grason, 2007), 143.

Billy Graham on Family

1. Billy Graham, *Hope for the Troubled Heart* (Dallas: Word, 1991), 8.
2. Billy Graham, *The Journey* (Nashville: W Publishing Group, 2006), 269.
3. Billy Graham, *Till Armageddon* (Waco, TX: Word, 1981), 186.
4. Graham, *Hope for the Troubled Heart*, 175.
5. Graham, *The Journey*, 127.
6. Billy Graham, *Day by Day* (Minneapolis, MN: World Wide, 1965), May 14.
7. Graham, *Hope for the Troubled Heart*, 174–75.
8. Ibid., 9.
9. Graham, *Till Armageddon*, 84.
10. Graham, *The Journey*, 124.
11. Graham, *Till Armageddon*, 179.
12. *The Billy Graham Christian Worker's Handbook* (Charlotte, NC: BGEA, 1984), 163.
13. Graham, *The Journey*, 251.
14. Billy Graham, *Storm Warning* (Nashville: Thomas Nelson, 2010), 177.
15. Graham, *The Journey*, 58.
16. Billy Graham, *Alone with the Savior* (Charlotte, NC: BGEA, 2010), 7–8.
17. Graham, *Hope for the Troubled Heart*, 176.

Billy Graham on Followers

1. Billy Graham, *Day by Day* (Minneapolis, MN: World Wide, 1965), September 1.
2. *Breakfast with Billy Graham: 100 Daily Readings* (Ann Arbor, MI: Servant, 1996), 110.
3. Billy Graham, *Wisdom for Each Day* (Nashville: Thomas Nelson, 2008), 42.
4. Billy Graham, *The Secret of Happiness* (New York: Doubleday, 1955), 140.
5. Billy Graham, *Storm Warning* (Dallas: Word, 1992), 36.
6. Billy Graham, *Hope for the Troubled Heart* (Dallas: Word, 1991), 40.
7. Billy Graham, *Till Armageddon* (Waco, TX: Word, 1981), 98.
8. Billy Graham, *Storm Warning* (Nashville: Thomas Nelson, 2010), 162.
9. Ibid., 187.
10. Graham, *Hope for the Troubled Heart*, 164–65.
11. Graham, *The Secret of Happiness*, 135.
12. Graham, *Hope for the Troubled Heart*, 40.
13. Graham, *Till Armageddon*, 165.
14. Billy Graham, *Answers to Life's Problems* (Waco, TX: Word, 1960), 288.
15. *The Billy Graham Library* (Charlotte, NC: BGEA), audio recording.

Billy Graham on Forgiveness

1. *The Billy Graham Christian Worker's Handbook* (Charlotte, NC: BGEA, 1984), 129.
2. Billy Graham, *Answers to Life's Problems* (Waco, TX: Word, 1960), 40.
3. *The Billy Graham Christian Worker's Handbook*, 129.
4. Billy Graham, *The Jesus Generation* (Grand Rapids: Zondervan, 1971), 69.
5. Billy Graham, *The Journey* (Nashville: W Publishing Group, 2006), 163.
6. *The Billy Graham Christian Worker's Handbook*, 129.
7. Graham, *Answers to Life's Problems*, 129.
8. *The Billy Graham Christian Worker's Handbook*, 130.
9. Ibid., 129.
10. Billy Graham, *A Biblical Standard for Evangelists* (Minneapolis: World Wide, 1984), 15–16.
11. Ibid., 52.

Billy Graham on Glorifying God

1. Billy Graham, *The Holy Spirit* (Nashville: Thomas Nelson, 1978), 128.
2. Ibid., 129.
3. Billy Graham, *Storm Warning* (Nashville: Thomas Nelson, 2010), 117.
4. Billy Graham, *Storm Warning* (Dallas: Word, 1992), 127.
5. Billy Graham, *Till Armageddon* (Waco, TX: Word, 1981), 200.
6. Billy Graham, *My Daily Prayer Journal* (Minneapolis, MN: Grason, 2007), 8.
7. Billy Graham, *Day by Day* (Minneapolis, MN: World Wide, 1965), May 28.
8. Billy Graham, *Just As I Am* (San Francisco: HarperOne, 1997), 723.
9. Billy Graham, *Alone with the Savior* (Charlotte, NC: BGEA, 2010), 55.
10. Graham, *The Holy Spirit*, 130.

Billy Graham on God

1. Billy Graham, *World Aflame* (New York: Doubleday, 1965), 89.
2. Billy Graham, *Day by Day* (Minneapolis, MN: World Wide, 1965), January 14.
3. Graham, *World Aflame*, 98.
4. Graham, *Day by Day* (Minneapolis, MN: World Wide, 1965), August 16.
5. Ibid., September 21.
6. Ibid., November 8.
7. Ibid., May 25.
8. Billy Graham, *Peace with God* (Waco, TX: Word, 1953), 30.
9. Billy Graham, *Hope for the Troubled Heart* (Dallas: Word, 1991), 96.
10. Billy Graham, *Day by Day* (Minneapolis, MN: World Wide, 1965), May 30.
11. Graham, *Peace with God*, 31.
12. Graham, *Day by Day*, March 13.
13. Graham, *Peace with God*, 34.
14. Graham, *Hope for the Troubled Heart*, 167.
15. Graham, *Day by Day*, February 24.
16. Graham, *Peace with God*, 169.
17. Ibid., 36.
18. Graham, *Day by Day*, May 13.
19. Graham, *Peace with God*, 30.
20. Billy Graham, *Wisdom for Each Day* (Nashville: Thomas Nelson, 2008), 364.
21. Graham, *Day by Day*, April 25.
22. Graham, *World Aflame*, 101.
23. Billy Graham, *The Secret of Happiness* (New York: Doubleday, 1955), 154.
24. Graham, *Peace with God*, 37.

25. Billy Graham, *Till Armageddon* (Waco, TX: Word, 1981), 23.
26. Graham, *World Aflame*, 68.
27. Graham, *Wisdom for Each Day*, 136.
28. Graham, *Peace with God*, 31.
29. Ibid., 38.
30. Russ Busby, *Billy Graham: God's Ambassador* (San Diego: Tehabi Books, 1999), 24.
31. Graham, *Day by Day*, June 26.
32. Graham, *Till Armageddon*, 155.
33. Billy Graham, *Storm Warning* (Nashville: Thomas Nelson, 2010), 151.
34. Ibid., 207.
35. Billy Graham, *Answers to Life's Problems* (Waco, TX: Word, 1960), 304.
36. Billy Graham, *The Journey* (Nashville: W Publishing Group, 2006), 13.
37. Ibid., 56–62.
38. Ibid., 101.
39. *Billy Graham London Crusade* (Minneapolis, MN: World Wide, 1966), 46.
40. Graham, *The Journey*, 102.
41. Graham, *Answers to Life's Problems*, 305.
42. Billy Graham, *Storm Warning* (Nashville: Thomas Nelson, 2010), 3.

Billy Graham on God's Will

1. Billy Graham, *The Journey* (Nashville: W Publishing Group, 2006), 78–79.
2. Billy Graham, *Day by Day* (Minneapolis, MN: World Wide, 1965), June 12.
3. Graham, *The Journey*, 242.
4. Ibid., 245.
5. Billy Graham, *The Secret of Happiness* (New York: Doubleday, 1955), 64.
6. Billy Graham, *Till Armageddon* (Waco, TX: Word, 1981), 24.
7. Graham, *The Journey*, 240.
8. Ibid., 122.
9. Ibid., 242.
10. Ibid., 241.
11. Billy Graham, *A Biblical Standard for Evangelists* (Minneapolis: World Wide, 1984), 128.

Billy Graham on the Gospel

1. Billy Graham, *World Aflame* (New York: Doubleday, 1965), 76.
2. Billy Graham, *The Secret of Happiness* (New York: Doubleday, 1955), 90.
3. Billy Graham, *Peace with God* (Waco, TX: Word, 1953), 236.
4. Ibid., 181.
5. Russ Busby, *Billy Graham: God's Ambassador* (San Diego: Tehabi Books, 1999), 18.
6. Billy Graham, *Day by Day* (Minneapolis, MN: World Wide, 1965), September 26.
7. Graham, *World Aflame*, 180.
8. Graham, *The Secret of Happiness*, 95.
9. *The Billy Graham Library* (Charlotte, NC: BGEA), audio recording.
10. Billy Graham, *Answers to Life's Problems* (Waco, TX: Word, 1960), 120.
11. Billy Graham, *Approaching Hoofbeats* (Waco, TX: Word, 1983), 25.
12. Billy Graham, *Storm Warning* (Nashville: Thomas Nelson, 2010), 81.
13. *Billy Graham London Crusade* (Minneapolis, MN: World Wide, 1966), 13–14.

Billy Graham on Grace

1. Billy Graham, *World Aflame* (New York: Doubleday, 1965), 263.
2. Billy Graham, *Day by Day* (Minneapolis, MN: World Wide, 1965), July 23.

3. Ibid., November 1.
4. Ibid., March 23.
5. Billy Graham, *Unto the Hills* (Waco, TX: Word, 1986), 289.
6. Ibid., 289.
7. Graham, *Day by Day*, August 11.
8. Billy Graham, *Storm Warning* (Nashville: Thomas Nelson, 2010), 214.
9. Ibid., 156.
10. Billy Graham, *Just As I Am* (San Francisco: HarperOne, 1997), 730.

Billy Graham on Greed

1. Billy Graham, *The Journey* (Nashville: W Publishing Group, 2006), 172.
2. Billy Graham, *Day by Day* (Minneapolis, MN: World Wide, 1965), August 4.
3. Graham, *The Journey*, 172.
4. Ibid., 174.
5. Billy Graham, *Peace with God* (Waco, TX: Word, 1953), 246.
6. Ibid., 245.
7. Graham, *Day by Day*, October 4.
8. Billy Graham, *Storm Warning* (Dallas: Word, 1992), 19.
9. Billy Graham, *Answers to Life's Problems* (Waco, TX: Word, 1960), 270.
10. Ibid., 269–70.
11. Ibid., 270.

Billy Graham on Grief

1. Billy Graham, *Storm Warning* (Nashville: Thomas Nelson, 2010), 77.
2. Billy Graham, *Facing Death and the Life After* (Waco, TX: Word, 1987), 159.
3. Ibid., 163.
4. Ibid.
5. Billy Graham, *The Journey* (Nashville: W Publishing Group, 2006), 223.
6. Ibid., 221.
7. Billy Graham, *Hope for the Troubled Heart* (Dallas: Word, 1991), 117.
8. Ibid., 116.

Billy Graham on Happiness

1. Billy Graham, *The Secret of Happiness* (New York: Doubleday, 1955), 15.
2. Ibid., 23.
3. Billy Graham, *Facing Death and the Life After* (Waco, TX: Word, 1987), 164.
4. Billy Graham, *Day by Day* (Minneapolis, MN: World Wide, 1965), March 7.
5. Billy Graham, *Peace with God* (Waco, TX: Word, 1953), 50.
6. Graham, *The Secret of Happiness*, 101.
7. Graham, *Day by Day*, April 4.
8. Ibid., September 12.
9. Billy Graham, *The Journey* (Nashville: W Publishing Group, 2006), 29–30.

Billy Graham on the Heart

1. Billy Graham, *Wisdom for Each Day* (Nashville: Thomas Nelson, 2008), 44.
2. Ibid.
3. Billy Graham, *The Secret of Happiness* (New York: Doubleday, 1955), 62.
4. Graham, *Wisdom for Each Day*, 44.
5. Billy Graham, *Till Armageddon* (Waco, TX: Word, 1981), 74–75.

6. Billy Graham, *Unto the Hills* (Waco, TX: Word, 1986), 151.
7 Billy Graham, *Day by Day* (Minneapolis, MN: World Wide, 1965), August 30.
8. Ibid., March 5.
9. Ibid., March 1.
10. Ibid., August 24.
11. Billy Graham, *How to Be Born Again* (Waco, TX: Word, 1977), 57.

Billy Graham on Heaven

1. Billy Graham, *The Journey* (Nashville: W Publishing Group, 2006), 308.
2. Billy Graham, *Hope for the Troubled Heart* (Dallas: Word, 1991), 220.
3. Ibid., 219.
4. Ibid., 206.
5. Graham, *The Journey*, 302.
6. Ibid., 26.
7. Billy Graham, press conference in Asheville, NC, 21 March 1977, audio recording.
8. Billy Graham, *Facing Death and the Life After* (Waco, TX: Word, 1987), 216.
9. Ibid., 235.
10. Ibid., 244.
11. Ibid., 251.
12. Ibid., 267.
13. Graham, *The Journey*, 309.
14. Billy Graham, *World Aflame* (New York: Doubleday, 1965), 257.
15. Graham, *Hope for the Troubled Heart*, 207.
16. Billy Graham, *Till Armageddon* (Waco, TX: Word, 1981), 210.
17. Graham, *Facing Death and the Life After*, 238.
18. Ibid., 226.
19. Ibid., 238.
20. Ibid., 232.
21. Graham, *Till Armageddon*, 209.
22. Graham, *World Aflame*, 239.
23. *The Billy Graham Library* (Charlotte, NC: BGEA), audio recording.

Billy Graham on Hell

1. Billy Graham, *Calling Youth to Christ* (Grand Rapids: Zondervan, 1947), 114.
2. Billy Graham, *World Aflame* (New York: Doubleday, 1965), 75.
3. Billy Graham, *Peace with God* (Waco, TX: Word, 1953), 56.
4. Ibid., 96.
5. Billy Graham, *The Journey* (Nashville: W Publishing Group, 2006), 307.
6. Graham, *Peace with God*, 89–90.
7. Graham, *Calling Youth to Christ*, 125.
8. Billy Graham, *Facing Death and the Life After* (Waco, TX: Word, 1987), 220.
9. Ibid., 219.
10. Ibid., 217.
11. Ibid., 219.
12. Graham, *The Journey* (Nashville: W Publishing Group, 2006), 307.

Billy Graham on Holiness

1. Billy Graham, *The Holy Spirit* (Nashville: Thomas Nelson, 1978), 81.
2. Ibid., 288.
3. Billy Graham, *Till Armageddon* (Waco, TX: Word, 1981), 41.

4. Billy Graham, *Answers to Life's Problems* (Waco, TX: Word, 1960), 269.
5. Billy Graham, *The Journey* (Nashville: W Publishing Group, 2006), 21.
6. Graham, *The Holy Spirit*, 288.
7. Graham, *The Journey*, 22.
8. Billy Graham, *The Secret of Happiness* (New York: Doubleday, 1955), 31.
9. Billy Graham, *Storm Warning* (Nashville: Thomas Nelson, 2010), 155.

Billy Graham on the Holy Spirit

1. Billy Graham, *The Holy Spirit* (Nashville: Thomas Nelson, 1978), 5.
2. Billy Graham, *Wisdom for Each Day* (Nashville: Thomas Nelson, 2008), 174.
3. Billy Graham, *Day by Day* (Minneapolis, MN: World Wide, 1965), September 27.
4. Graham, *The Holy Spirit*, 294.
5. Billy Graham, *The Journey* (Nashville: W Publishing Group, 2006), 135.
6. Graham, *The Holy Spirit*, 11.
7. Ibid., 25.
8. Ibid., 27.
9. Billy Graham, *How to Be Born Again* (Waco, TX: Word, 1977), 173.
10. Graham, *The Holy Spirit*, 92–93.
11. Ibid., 101.
12. Ibid., 292.
13. Ibid., 33.
14. Ibid., 269.
15. Ibid., 99.
16. Graham, *The Journey*, 19.
17. Ibid., 60.
18. Ibid., 138.
19. Ibid.

Billy Graham on Home

1. Billy Graham, *Day by Day* (Minneapolis, MN: World Wide, 1965), May 27.
2. Russ Busby, *Billy Graham: God's Ambassador* (San Diego: Tehabi Books, 1999), 237.
3. Billy Graham, *Peace with God* (Waco, TX: Word, 1953), 20.
4. Ibid., 239.
5. Ibid.
6. *Breakfast with Billy Graham: 100 Daily Readings* (Ann Arbor, MI: Servant, 1996), 71.
7. Graham, *Day by Day*, July 1.
8. Ibid., July 25.
9. Billy Graham, *The Holy Spirit* (Nashville: Thomas Nelson, 1978), 290.
10. Billy Graham, *World Aflame* (New York: Doubleday, 1965), 39–40.
11. Billy Graham, *Till Armageddon* (Waco, TX: Word, 1981), 197.
12. Graham, *Day by Day*, May 14.
13. Ibid., December 1.
14. Ibid., May 14.
15. *The Billy Graham Christian Worker's Handbook* (Charlotte, NC: BGEA, 1984), 31.
16. Ibid., 198.
17. Billy Graham, *Facing Death and the Life After* (Waco, TX: Word, 1987), 245.
18. Ibid., 224.
19. Graham, *Till Armageddon*, 208.
20. *Decision*, April 2010, 5.
21. Billy Graham, *Storm Warning* (Nashville: Thomas Nelson, 2010), 168.
22. Billy Graham, *The Journey* (Nashville: W Publishing Group, 2006), 11.

Billy Graham on Hope

1. Billy Graham, *Hope for the Troubled Heart* (Dallas: Word, 1991), ix.
2. Russ Busby, *Billy Graham: God's Ambassador* (San Diego: Tehabi Books, 1999), 181.
3. Billy Graham, *Answers to Life's Problems* (Waco, TX: Word, 1960), 236.
4. Billy Graham, *The Journey* (Nashville: W Publishing Group, 2006), 182–83.
5. Ibid., 306.
6. Billy Graham, *Day by Day* (Minneapolis, MN: World Wide, 1965), December 26.
7. Graham, *The Journey*, 219.
8. Billy Graham, *The Jesus Generation* (Grand Rapids: Zondervan, 1971), 177.
9. Billy Graham, *A Biblical Standard for Evangelists* (Minneapolis: World Wide, 1984), 17.
10. Ibid., 129.

Billy Graham on Human Nature

1. Billy Graham, *The Holy Spirit* (Nashville: Thomas Nelson, 1978), 92.
2. Billy Graham, *World Aflame* (New York: Doubleday, 1965), 168–69.
3. Russ Busby, *Billy Graham: God's Ambassador* (San Diego: Tehabi Books, 1999), 27.
4. Billy Graham, *Day by Day* (Minneapolis, MN: World Wide, 1965), September 2.
5. Ibid., April 9.
6. Ibid., March 9.
7. Billy Graham, *Till Armageddon* (Waco, TX: Word, 1981), 18.
8. Graham, *Day by Day*, April 8.
9. Busby, *Billy Graham*, 219.
10. Graham, *The Holy Spirit*, 102.
11. Graham, *World Aflame*, 61.
12. Graham, *Till Armageddon*, 65.
13. Ibid., 67.
14. Graham, *World Aflame*, 177.

Billy Graham on Imagination, Entertainment, and Fun

1. Billy Graham, *The Secret of Happiness* (New York: Doubleday, 1955), 108.
2. Billy Graham, *Till Armageddon* (Waco, TX: Word, 1981), 97.
3. Billy Graham, *Day by Day* (Minneapolis, MN: World Wide, 1965), July 9.
4. Billy Graham, *World Aflame* (New York: Doubleday, 1965), 218.
5. *Breakfast with Billy Graham: 100 Daily Readings* (Ann Arbor, MI: Servant, 1996), 79.
6. Graham, *Till Armageddon*, 218.
7. Billy Graham, *The Journey* (Nashville: W Publishing Group, 2006), 231.
8. Billy Graham, *Facing Death and the Life After* (Waco, TX: Word, 1987), 253.

Billy Graham on Influence

1. Billy Graham, *Peace with God* (Waco, TX: Word, 1953), 273.
2. Billy Graham, *Till Armageddon* (Waco, TX: Word, 1981), 183.
3. Billy Graham, *Day by Day* (Minneapolis, MN: World Wide, 1965), January 27.
4. Russ Busby, *Billy Graham: God's Ambassador* (San Diego: Tehabi Books, 1999), 270.
5. Billy Graham, *Storm Warning* (Nashville: Thomas Nelson, 2010), 116–17.
6. Graham, *Till Armageddon*, 188.
7. Billy Graham, *The Holy Spirit* (Nashville: Thomas Nelson, 1978), 27.

Billy Graham on Integrity

1. Billy Graham, *The Journey* (Nashville: W Publishing Group, 2006), 189.
2. Billy Graham, *Day by Day* (Minneapolis, MN: World Wide, 1965), November 17.
3. Russ Busby, *Billy Graham: God's Ambassador* (San Diego: Tehabi Books, 1999), 209.
4. Graham, *Day by Day*, October 14.
5. Billy Graham, *The Secret of Happiness* (New York: Doubleday, 1955), 137.
6. Busby, *Billy Graham*, 209.
7. Graham, *The Journey*, 189.
8. Billy Graham, *Till Armageddon* (Waco, TX: Word, 1981), 179.
9. Busby, *Billy Graham*, 209.
10. Billy Graham, *A Biblical Standard for Evangelists* (Minneapolis: World Wide, 1984), 73.
11. Ibid., 90.

Billy Graham on Jesus

1. Billy Graham, *Wisdom for Each Day* (Nashville: Thomas Nelson, 2008), 59.
2. Billy Graham, *World Aflame* (New York: Doubleday, 1965), 148.
3. Billy Graham, *Hope for the Troubled Heart* (Dallas: Word, 1991), 63.
4. Graham, *Wisdom for Each Day*, 252.
5. Ibid., 349.
6. Billy Graham, *Peace with God* (Waco, TX: Word, 1953), 112.
7. Ibid., 111.
8. Billy Graham, *Till Armageddon* (Waco, TX: Word, 1981), 70.
9. Billy Graham, *Facing Death and the Life After* (Waco, TX: Word, 1987), 248.
10. Ibid., 265.
11. Billy Graham, *The Jesus Generation* (Grand Rapids: Zondervan, 1971), 155.
12. Billy Graham, *Storm Warning* (Nashville: Thomas Nelson, 2010), 121.
13. Ibid., 229.
14. Russ Busby, *Billy Graham: God's Ambassador* (San Diego: Tehabi Books, 1999), 271.

Billy Graham on Joy

1. Billy Graham, *Till Armageddon* (Waco, TX: Word, 1981), 142.
2. *Breakfast with Billy Graham: 100 Daily Readings* (Ann Arbor, MI: Servant, 1996), 100.
3. Billy Graham, *Hope for the Troubled Heart* (Dallas: Word, 1991), 107.
4. Ibid., 109.
5. Ibid.
6. Ibid., 136.
7. Billy Graham, *The Secret of Happiness* (New York: Doubleday, 1955), 138–39.
8. Billy Graham, *World Aflame* (New York: Doubleday, 1965), 64.
9. *Breakfast with Billy Graham*, 100.
10. Billy Graham, *Billy Graham Talks to Teen-agers* (Wheaton: Miracle Books, 1958), 11.

Billy Graham on Judgment

1. Billy Graham, *Facing Death and the Life After* (Waco, TX: Word, 1987), 264.
2. *Decision*, May 2010, 4.
3. Billy Graham, *Till Armageddon* (Waco, TX: Word, 1981), 85.
4. *Decision*, May 2010, 4.
5. Billy Graham, *The Journey* (Nashville: W Publishing Group, 2006), 187.
6. *Breakfast with Billy Graham: 100 Daily Readings* (Ann Arbor, MI: Servant, 1996), 107.
7. Graham, *Till Armageddon*, 176.

8. Billy Graham, *Storm Warning* (Nashville: Thomas Nelson, 2010), 152–53.
9. Ibid., 210.
10. Graham, *Facing Death and the Life After*, 264.
11. Billy Graham, *A Biblical Standard for Evangelists* (Minneapolis: World Wide, 1984), 44.
12. Ibid., 45.

Billy Graham on Knowledge

1. Billy Graham, *World Aflame* (New York: Doubleday, 1965), 190.
2. Ibid., 13.
3. Ibid., 27.
4. Ibid., 46.
5. Billy Graham, *The Secret of Happiness* (New York: Doubleday, 1955), 93.
6. Billy Graham, *How to Be Born Again* (Waco, TX: Word, 1977), 18.
7. Billy Graham, *Wisdom for Each Day* (Nashville: Thomas Nelson, 2008), 14.
8. Billy Graham, *Peace with God* (Waco, TX: Word, 1953), 30.
9. Ibid., 5.

Billy Graham on Life

1. Billy Graham, *The Journey* (Nashville: W Publishing Group, 2006), 3, 4, 9.
2. Russ Busby, *Billy Graham: God's Ambassador* (San Diego: Tehabi Books, 1999), 181.
3. Billy Graham, *World Aflame* (New York: Doubleday, 1965), 33.
4. Billy Graham, *Hope for the Troubled Heart* (Dallas: Word, 1991), 35.
5. Graham, *World Aflame*, 176.
6. Billy Graham, *Day by Day* (Minneapolis, MN: World Wide, 1965), July 26.
7. Graham, *The Journey*, 311.
8. Graham, *Day by Day*, June 28.
9. Graham, *Hope for the Troubled Heart*, 200.
10. *The Billy Graham Library* (Charlotte, NC: BGEA), audio recording.
11. Billy Graham, *The Secret of Happiness* (New York: Doubleday, 1955), 140.
12. Graham, *World Aflame*, 191.
13. Billy Graham, *Wisdom for Each Day* (Nashville: Thomas Nelson, 2008), 229.
14. Ibid., 71.
15. Billy Graham, *Answers to Life's Problems* (Waco, TX: Word, 1960), 9–10.
16. Graham, *Wisdom for Each Day*, 347.
17. Ibid., 268.
18. Ibid., 279.
19. Graham, *The Journey*, 192.
20. Graham, *Wisdom for Each Day*, 167.
21. Ibid., 271.
22. Billy Graham, *The Holy Spirit* (Nashville: Thomas Nelson, 1978), 127.
23. Graham, *Wisdom for Each Day*, 215.
24. Graham, *The Secret of Happiness*, 46.
25. Busby, *Billy Graham*, 271.
26. Graham, *World Aflame*, xvi–xvii.
27. Billy Graham, *Just As I Am* (San Francisco: HarperOne, 1997), xiii.
28. Billy Graham, *Till Armageddon* (Waco, TX: Word, 1981), 24.
29. Graham, *Wisdom for Each Day*, 88.
30. Graham, *Till Armageddon*, 163.
31. Ibid., 135.
32. Ibid., 166.
33. Ibid., 181.

34. Ibid., 198.
35. Ibid.
36. Graham, *Answers to Life's Problems*, 276.
37. Ibid., 286.
38. Billy Graham, *Facing Death and the Life After* (Waco, TX: Word, 1987), 124.
39. *The Billy Graham Christian Worker's Handbook* (Charlotte, NC: BGEA, 1984), 216.
40. Billy Graham, *Storm Warning* (Nashville: Thomas Nelson, 2010), 245.
41. Billy Graham, *The Jesus Generation* (Grand Rapids: Zondervan, 1971), 34.
42. Ibid., 117.
43. Graham, *The Journey*, viii.
44. Ibid., 7.
45. Ibid., viii.
46. Ibid., 4.
47. Ibid., 53.
48. Ibid., 54.
49. Ibid., 81.
50. Ibid., 82.
51. Ibid., 94.
52. Ibid., 167.
53. Ibid., 161.
54. Ibid.
55. Ibid., 168.
56. Ibid., 291.
57. Graham, *The Jesus Generation*, 167.
58. Graham, *The Journey*, 201.
59. Graham, *World Aflame*, 74.
60. Graham, *The Journey*, 51.
61. *Billy Graham London Crusade* (Minneapolis, MN: World Wide, 1966), 46.
62. Graham, *The Journey*, 189.
63. Billy Graham, *Billy Graham Talks to Teen-agers* (Wheaton: Miracle Books, 1958), 31.
64. Billy Graham, *Storm Warning* (Nashville: Thomas Nelson, 2010), 61.

Billy Graham on Living the Christian Life

1. Billy Graham, *The Holy Spirit* (Nashville: Thomas Nelson, 1978), 268.
2. Billy Graham, *Wisdom for Each Day* (Nashville: Thomas Nelson, 2008), 207.
3. Billy Graham, *Hope for the Troubled Heart* (Dallas: Word, 1991), 120.
4. Graham, *Wisdom for Each Day*, 255.
5. Ibid., 10.
6. Graham, *The Holy Spirit*, 104.
7. Ibid., 268.
8. Ibid., 142.
9. Ibid., 158.
10. Ibid., 114.
11. Ibid., 115.
12. Ibid., 42.
13. Billy Graham, *Till Armageddon* (Waco, TX: Word, 1981), 98.
14. Billy Graham, *The Secret of Happiness* (New York: Doubleday, 1955), 147.
15. Billy Graham, *Peace with God* (Waco, TX: Word, 1953), 217.
16. Billy Graham, *Answers to Life's Problems* (Waco, TX: Word, 1960), 268–69.
17. Graham, *Wisdom for Each Day*, 80.
18. Graham, *The Holy Spirit*, 103.
19. Graham, *Hope for the Troubled Heart*, 183.

20. Graham, *Peace with God*, 190, 193, 196.
21. Billy Graham, *World Aflame* (New York: Doubleday, 1965), 197.
22. Graham, *The Secret of Happiness*, 28.
23. Graham, *The Holy Spirit*, 284.

Billy Graham on Loneliness

1. Billy Graham, *Day by Day* (Minneapolis, MN: World Wide, 1965), February 29.
2. Billy Graham, *Alone with the Savior* (Charlotte, NC: BGEA, 2010), 11–12.
3. *The Billy Graham Christian Worker's Handbook* (Charlotte, NC: BGEA, 1984), 191.
4. Ibid., 189.
5. Ibid., 191.
6. Ibid., 189.
7. Billy Graham, *The Journey* (Nashville: W Publishing Group, 2006), 27.
8. Billy Graham, *Facing Death and the Life After* (Waco, TX: Word, 1987), 151.
9. Graham, *Alone with the Savior*, 9.
10. *The Billy Graham Christian Worker's Handbook*, 191.

Billy Graham on Love

1. Russ Busby, *Billy Graham: God's Ambassador* (San Diego: Tehabi Books, 1999), 129.
2. Billy Graham, *The Journey* (Nashville: W Publishing Group, 2006), 208.
3. Billy Graham, *Hope for the Troubled Heart* (Dallas: Word, 1991), 95.
4. Busby, *Billy Graham*, 114.
5. Billy Graham, *World Aflame* (New York: Doubleday, 1965), 96.
6. Billy Graham, *Peace with God* (Waco, TX: Word, 1953), 39.
7. Graham, *World Aflame*, 236.
8. Ibid.
9. Billy Graham, *Day by Day* (Minneapolis, MN: World Wide, 1965), March 24.
10. Graham, *Hope for the Troubled Heart*, 21.
11. Ibid., 22.
12. Ibid., 23.
13. Ibid., 25.
14. Ibid., 26.
15. Billy Graham, *Till Armageddon* (Waco, TX: Word, 1981), 46.
16. Billy Graham, *The Secret of Happiness* (New York: Doubleday, 1955), 34.
17. Billy Graham, *The Jesus Generation* (Grand Rapids: Zondervan, 1971), 63.
18. Graham, *The Journey*, 214.
19. Billy Graham, *Storm Warning* (Nashville: Thomas Nelson, 2010), 164.
20. Graham, *The Journey*, 208.
21. *The Billy Graham Christian Worker's Handbook* (Charlotte, NC: BGEA, 1984), 193.
22. Billy Graham, *Storm Warning* (Nashville: Thomas Nelson, 2010), 112.
23. Graham, *The Journey*, 188.
24. Ibid.
25. Ibid., 255.

Billy Graham on Lust

1. Billy Graham, *The Journey* (Nashville: W Publishing Group, 2006), 250.
2. Billy Graham, *World Aflame* (New York: Doubleday, 1965), 21.
3. Ibid., 20.
4. Ibid., 21.
5. Billy Graham, *Day by Day* (Minneapolis, MN: World Wide, 1965), November 29.

6. Billy Graham, *The Jesus Generation* (Grand Rapids: Zondervan, 1971), 75.

7. Ibid., 169.

8. *The Billy Graham Christian Worker's Handbook* (Charlotte, NC: BGEA, 1984), 171.

9. Ibid., 172.

10. Graham, *World Aflame*, 19.

11. Ibid., 172.

12. Graham, *World Aflame*, 20.

13. Billy Graham, *Alone with the Savior* (Charlotte, NC: BGEA, 2010), 60.

Billy Graham on Marriage

1. Billy Graham, *Answers to Life's Problems* (Waco, TX: Word, 1960), 38.

2. Billy Graham, *Peace with God* (Waco, TX: Word, 1953), 241.

3. *The Billy Graham Christian Worker's Handbook* (Charlotte, NC: BGEA, 1984), 197.

4. Billy Graham, *The Journey* (Nashville: W Publishing Group, 2006), 247.

5. Billy Graham, *Day by Day* (Minneapolis, MN: World Wide, 1965), October 28.

6. Ibid., May 27.

7. Graham, *The Journey*, 257.

8. Graham, *Day by Day*, July 25.

9. Ibid., June 20.

10. Graham, *The Journey*, 259.

11. Ibid., 265.

12. Billy Graham, *Wisdom for Each Day* (Nashville: Thomas Nelson, 2008), 305.

13. Russ Busby, *Billy Graham: God's Ambassador* (San Diego: Tehabi Books, 1999), 232.

14. Ibid.

15. Ibid.

16. Ibid.

17. Billy Graham, *Hope for the Troubled Heart* (Dallas: Word, 1991), 75.

18. Ibid., 187.

19. Graham, *Answers to Life's Problems*, 13.

20. Ibid., 15.

21. Ibid., 26.

22. Ibid., 30.

23. Ibid., 31.

24. Ibid., 35.

25. Ibid., 37.

26. Ibid., 39.

27. Ibid., 264–65.

28. *The Billy Graham Christian Worker's Handbook*, 197.

29. Graham, *The Journey*, 248.

30. Ibid., 253.

31. Ibid.

32. Ibid., 255.

33. Ibid., 254.

34. Billy Graham, *Billy Graham Talks to Teen-agers* (Wheaton: Miracle Books, 1958), 22.

Billy Graham on Money

1. Billy Graham, *Day by Day* (Minneapolis, MN: World Wide, 1965), August 4.

2. Ibid., February 7.

3. Ibid., June 25.

4. Billy Graham, *Peace with God* (Waco, TX: Word, 1953), 82.

5. Graham, *Day by Day*, June 25.

6. Ibid.

7. Graham, *Peace with God*, 244.

8. Russ Busby, *Billy Graham: God's Ambassador* (San Diego: Tehabi Books, 1999), 267.

9. Billy Graham, *World Aflame* (New York: Doubleday, 1965), 11.

10. Billy Graham, *Hope for the Troubled Heart* (Dallas: Word, 1991), 7.

11. Graham, *Day by Day*, June 3.

12. Graham, *Hope for the Troubled Heart*, 35.

13. Graham, *Day by Day*, August 18.

14. Graham, *Peace with God*, 235.

15. Graham, *Hope for the Troubled Heart*, 11.

16. Graham, *Peace with God*, 245–46.

17. Billy Graham, *Answers to Life's Problems* (Waco, TX: Word, 1960), 120.

18. Billy Graham, *Storm Warning* (Nashville: Thomas Nelson, 2010), 157.

19. Billy Graham, *The Holy Spirit* (Nashville: Thomas Nelson, 1978), 292.

20. Billy Graham, *Storm Warning* (Nashville: Thomas Nelson, 2010), 234.

21. Billy Graham, press conference in Minneapolis, MN, September 1977, audio recording.

22. Billy Graham, *Till Armageddon* (Waco, TX: Word, 1981), 146.

Billy Graham on Morals

1. Billy Graham, *World Aflame* (New York: Doubleday, 1965), 18.

2. Billy Graham, *Till Armageddon* (Waco, TX: Word, 1981), 62.

3. Billy Graham, *The Secret of Happiness* (New York: Doubleday, 1955), 48.

4. Billy Graham, *Storm Warning* (Dallas: Word, 1992), 23.

5. Graham, *World Aflame*, 142.

6. Billy Graham, *Wisdom for Each Day* (Nashville: Thomas Nelson, 2008), 311.

7. Graham, *The Secret of Happiness*, 106–7.

8. Billy Graham, *The Jesus Generation* (Grand Rapids: Zondervan, 1971), 92.

9. *The Billy Graham Christian Worker's Handbook* (Charlotte, NC: BGEA, 1984), 221.

10. Billy Graham, *Storm Warning* (Nashville: Thomas Nelson, 2010), 113.

11. *The Billy Graham Christian Worker's Handbook*, 259.

12. Graham, *World Aflame*, 39.

13. Billy Graham, *Answers to Life's Problems* (Waco, TX: Word, 1960), 287.

Billy Graham on Parents

1. Russ Busby, *Billy Graham: God's Ambassador* (San Diego: Tehabi Books, 1999), 238.

2. Billy Graham, *The Journey* (Nashville: W Publishing Group, 2006), 293.

3. Billy Graham, *Day by Day* (Minneapolis, MN: World Wide, 1965), January 8.

4. Ibid., November 19.

5. Graham, *The Journey*, 293.

6. Billy Graham, *Facing Death and the Life After* (Waco, TX: Word, 1987), 180.

7. Ibid.

8. Billy Graham, *Hope for the Troubled Heart* (Dallas: Word, 1991), 24.

9. Billy Graham, *Storm Warning* (Nashville: Thomas Nelson, 2010), 179.

10. Graham, *Day by Day*, May 8.

11. Ibid.

12. *Breakfast with Billy Graham: 100 Daily Readings* (Ann Arbor, MI: Servant, 1996), 72.

13. Graham, *The Journey*, 267.

14. Graham, *Hope for the Troubled Heart*, 200.

15. Ibid., 186.

Billy Graham on Patience

1. *The Billy Graham Christian Worker's Handbook* (Charlotte, NC: BGEA, 1984), 221.
2. Billy Graham, *The Holy Spirit* (Nashville: Thomas Nelson, 1978), 258.
3. Ibid., 259.
4. Billy Graham, *Answers to Life's Problems* (Waco, TX: Word, 1960), 90.
5. Graham, *The Holy Spirit*, 259.
6. Ibid.
7. *The Billy Graham Christian Worker's Handbook*, 221.
8. Graham, *The Holy Spirit*, 259.
9. Ibid.

Billy Graham on Peace

1. Billy Graham, *Peace with God* (Waco, TX: Word, 1953), 107.
2. Russ Busby, *Billy Graham: God's Ambassador* (San Diego: Tehabi Books, 1999), 137.
3. Ibid., 221.
4. *Breakfast with Billy Graham: 100 Daily Readings* (Ann Arbor, MI: Servant, 1996), 116.
5. Billy Graham, *Hope for the Troubled Heart* (Dallas: Word, 1991), 43.
6. Billy Graham, *The Holy Spirit* (Nashville: Thomas Nelson, 1978), 255.
7. Billy Graham, *World Aflame* (New York: Doubleday, 1965), 56.
8. Billy Graham, *Till Armageddon* (Waco, TX: Word, 1981), 18.
9. Graham, *Peace with God*, 271.
10. Billy Graham, *The Secret of Happiness* (New York: Doubleday, 1955), 116.
11. Ibid., 131.
12. Graham, *Peace with God*, 269.
13. Graham, *The Secret of Happiness*, 130.
14. Graham, *Peace with God*, 273.
15. Ibid., 275.
16. Billy Graham, *Day by Day* (Minneapolis, MN: World Wide, 1965), July 6.
17. Billy Graham, *Storm Warning* (Dallas: Word, 1992), 19.
18. Graham, *Peace with God*, 273.
19. Billy Graham, *The Journey* (Nashville: W Publishing Group, 2006), 182.
20. Graham, *Day by Day*, January 13.
21. Ibid., December 31.

Billy Graham on People

1. Billy Graham, *Wisdom for Each Day* (Nashville: Thomas Nelson, 2008), 200.
2. Billy Graham, *Day by Day* (Minneapolis, MN: World Wide, 1965), January 20.
3. Ibid., May 28.
4. Billy Graham, *The Journey* (Nashville: W Publishing Group, 2006), 209.
5. Graham, *Day by Day*, September 18.
6. Billy Graham, *Calling Youth to Christ* (Grand Rapids: Zondervan, 1947), 14.
7. Graham, *Day by Day*, May 26.
8. Billy Graham, *World Aflame* (New York: Doubleday, 1965), 123.
9. Billy Graham, *Peace with God* (Waco, TX: Word, 1953), 191.
10. Billy Graham, *Hope for the Troubled Heart* (Dallas: Word, 1991), 14.
11. Graham, *Day by Day*, January 12.
12. Graham, *The Journey*, 285–86.
13. Billy Graham, *The Holy Spirit* (Nashville: Thomas Nelson, 1978), 202.
14. Graham, *The Journey*, 130.
15. Ibid., 205–6.

16. Ibid., 711.
17. Ibid., 200.
18. Billy Graham, *Till Armageddon* (Waco, TX: Word, 1981), 70–71.
19. Billy Graham, *The Jesus Generation* (Grand Rapids: Zondervan, 1971), 126.
20. Billy Graham, *Answers to Life's Problems* (Waco, TX: Word, 1960), 84–85.
21. *Breakfast with Billy Graham: 100 Daily Readings* (Ann Arbor, MI: Servant, 1996), 103.
22. Graham, *The Jesus Generation*, 184.
23. Billy Graham, *How to Be Born Again* (Waco, TX: Word, 1977), 10.
24. *The Billy Graham Library* (Charlotte, NC: BGEA), audio recording.

Billy Graham on Persecution

1. Billy Graham, *The Secret of Happiness* (New York: Doubleday, 1955), 144.
2. Billy Graham, *World Aflame* (New York: Doubleday, 1965), 206.
3. Graham, *The Secret of Happiness*, 142.
4. Billy Graham, *Hope for the Troubled Heart* (Dallas: Word, 1991), 42–43.
5. Ibid., 119.
6. Billy Graham, *Facing Death and the Life After* (Waco, TX: Word, 1987), 262.
7. Graham, *Hope for the Troubled Heart*, 41.
8. Billy Graham, *Till Armageddon* (Waco, TX: Word, 1981), 29.
9. Billy Graham, *Storm Warning* (Nashville: Thomas Nelson, 2010), 115.
10. Graham, *Till Armageddon*, 103.
11. *Decision*, July/August 2010, 2.
12. Graham, *Till Armageddon*, 110.

Billy Graham on Pleasure

1. Billy Graham, *The Secret of Happiness* (New York: Doubleday, 1955), 3.
2. Billy Graham, *World Aflame* (New York: Doubleday, 1965), 253.
3. Graham, *The Secret of Happiness*, 68.
4. Billy Graham, *Storm Warning* (Dallas: Word, 1992), 110.
5. Graham, *World Aflame*, 218.
6. Billy Graham, *Day by Day* (Minneapolis, MN: World Wide, 1965), August 20.
7. Billy Graham, *Till Armageddon* (Waco, TX: Word, 1981), 62.
8. Graham, *The Secret of Happiness*, 3.

Billy Graham on Prayer

1. Billy Graham, *Till Armageddon* (Waco, TX: Word, 1981), 153.
2. Russ Busby, *Billy Graham: God's Ambassador* (San Diego: Tehabi Books, 1999), 245.
3. Billy Graham, *Day by Day* (Minneapolis, MN: World Wide, 1965), October 25.
4. Graham, *Till Armageddon*, 153.
5. Ibid., 152–53.
6. Billy Graham, *The Journey* (Nashville: W Publishing Group, 2006), 285.
7. Ibid.
8. Billy Graham, *Hope for the Troubled Heart* (Dallas: Word, 1991), 171.
9. Ibid., 170.
10. Graham, *The Journey*, 212.
11. Billy Graham, *Hope for the Troubled Heart* (Dallas: Word, 1991), 147.
12. Ibid., 149.
13. Ibid., 151.
14. Ibid., 159.
15. Ibid., 152.

16. Ibid., 154.
17. Ibid., 149.
18. Ibid.
19. Ibid.
20. Ibid., 148.
21. Ibid.
22. Ibid., 147.
23. Busby, *Billy Graham*, 247.
24. Graham, *Hope for the Troubled Heart*, 137.
25. *Breakfast with Billy Graham: 100 Daily Readings* (Ann Arbor, MI: Servant, 1996), 87.
26. Billy Graham, *Wisdom for Each Day* (Nashville: Thomas Nelson, 2008), 30.
27. Ibid., 260.
28. Ibid., 128.
29. Ibid., 135.
30. Ibid.
31. Billy Graham, *My Daily Prayer Journal* (Minneapolis, MN: Grason, 2007), 48.
32. Billy Graham, *Wisdom for Each Day* (Nashville: Thomas Nelson, 2008), 124.
33. Billy Graham, *Calling Youth to Christ* (Grand Rapids: Zondervan, 1947), 36.
34. Billy Graham, *The Holy Spirit* (Nashville: Thomas Nelson, 1978), 146.
35. Graham, *My Daily Prayer Journal*, 48.
36. Billy Graham, *The Secret of Happiness* (New York: Doubleday, 1955), 155.
37. Graham, *Hope for the Troubled Heart*, 92.
38. Ibid.
39. Graham, *Wisdom for Each Day*, 159.
40. Billy Graham, *Peace with God* (Waco, TX: Word, 1953), 193.
41. Graham, *Day by Day*, January 8.
42. Ibid., June 30.
43. Ibid.
44. Ibid.
45. Ibid., January 29.
46. Billy Graham, *Unto the Hills* (Waco, TX: Word, 1986), 6.
47. Graham, *Hope for the Troubled Heart*, 157.
48. Billy Graham, *Answers to Life's Problems* (Waco, TX: Word, 1960), 168.
49. *Decision*, July/August 1999, 2.
50. Graham, *Till Armageddon*, 89.
51. Ibid., 155.
52. Graham, *Answers to Life's Problems*, 291.
53. Graham, *My Daily Prayer Journal*, 6.
54. Ibid., 7.
55. Ibid.
56. Ibid.
57. Ibid., 9.
58. Ibid., 11.
59. Ibid.
60. Ibid., 12.
61. Ibid., 33.
62. Ibid., 39.
63. Ibid., 55.
64. Ibid., 57.
65. Ibid., 59.
66. Ibid., 69.
67. Ibid., 85.
68. Graham, *The Journey*, 121.

69. Ibid.
70 Ibid., 120.
71. Ibid., 123.
72. Ibid., 122.
73. Ibid., 123.
74. Graham, *My Daily Prayer Journal*, 117.
75. Graham, *The Journey*, 117.
76. Graham, *My Daily Prayer Journal*, 125.
77. Ibid., 129.
78. Graham, *The Journey*, 118.
79. Billy Graham, *Storm Warning* (Nashville: Thomas Nelson, 2010), 170.
80. Graham, *The Journey*, 116.
81. Graham, *My Daily Prayer Journal*, 135.
82. Billy Graham, *Storm Warning* (Nashville: Thomas Nelson, 2010), 163.
83. Billy Graham, "Living in Christ," booklet (Charlotte, NC: BGEA, 1980), 1.
84. Graham, *The Journey*, 114.
85. Billy Graham, *Storm Warning* (Nashville: Thomas Nelson, 2010), 209–10.
86. Ibid., 162.
87. Graham, *The Journey*, 115.
88. *The Billy Graham Christian Worker's Handbook* (Charlotte, NC: BGEA, 1984), 49.
89. Graham, *The Journey*, 285.
90. *Breakfast with Billy Graham*, 92.

Billy Graham on Preaching

1. Russ Busby, *Billy Graham: God's Ambassador* (San Diego: Tehabi Books, 1999), 35.
2. Ibid., 23.
3. Ibid., 111.
4. Billy Graham, *World Aflame* (New York: Doubleday, 1965), 114.
5. Billy Graham, *Day by Day* (Minneapolis, MN: World Wide, 1965), May 30.
6. Busby, *Billy Graham*, 55.
7. Ibid., 255.
8. Ibid., 11.
9. Ibid., 100.
10. Ibid., 138.
11. Ibid., 257.
12. Ibid., 22.
13. Billy Graham, *Hope for the Troubled Heart* (Dallas: Word, 1991), 39.
14. Billy Graham, *Storm Warning* (Nashville: Thomas Nelson, 2010), 190.
15. Billy Graham, *The Holy Spirit* (Nashville: Thomas Nelson, 1978), 46–47.
16. Billy Graham, *Facing Death and the Life After* (Waco, TX: Word, 1987), 254.
17. Graham, *The Holy Spirit*, 46.
18. Ibid.
19. Billy Graham, *Answers to Life's Problems* (Waco, TX: Word, 1960), 278.

Billy Graham on Pride

1. Billy Graham, *World Aflame* (New York: Doubleday, 1965), 47.
2. Billy Graham, *The Holy Spirit* (Nashville: Thomas Nelson, 1978), 274.
3. Billy Graham, *Peace with God* (Waco, TX: Word, 1953), 172.
4. Graham, *World Aflame*, 47.
5. Ibid., 54.
6. Billy Graham, *The Secret of Happiness* (New York: Doubleday, 1955), 155.

7. Billy Graham, *The Journey* (Nashville: W Publishing Group, 2006), 170.

8. Ibid., 171.

Billy Graham on Race

1. *Breakfast with Billy Graham: 100 Daily Readings* (Ann Arbor, MI: Servant, 1996), 105.

2. Billy Graham, *Peace with God* (Waco, TX: Word, 1953), 261.

3. Billy Graham, *World Aflame* (New York: Doubleday, 1965), 7.

4. Graham, *Peace with God*, 93.

5. Graham, *World Aflame*, 7–8.

6. Ibid., 184–85.

7. Billy Graham, *Till Armageddon* (Waco, TX: Word, 1981), 148.

8. Billy Graham, *Day by Day* (Minneapolis, MN: World Wide, 1965), September 14.

9. Billy Graham, *Angels* (Waco, TX: Word, 1975), 123–24.

10. Graham, *World Aflame*, 22.

11. Graham, *Peace with God*, 244.

12. Graham, *World Aflame*, 241–42.

13. Graham, *Day by Day*, May 21.

14. Billy Graham, *Hope for the Troubled Heart* (Dallas: Word, 1991), 27.

Billy Graham on Religion

1. Russ Busby, *Billy Graham: God's Ambassador* (San Diego: Tehabi Books, 1999), 216.

2. Billy Graham, *World Aflame* (New York: Doubleday, 1965), 86.

3. Graham, *World Aflame*, 104.

4. Billy Graham, *Day by Day* (Minneapolis, MN: World Wide, 1965), April 7.

5. Ibid., September 19.

6. Ibid., December 30.

7. Ibid., August 9.

8. Billy Graham, *Wisdom for Each Day* (Nashville: Thomas Nelson, 2008), 164.

9. Graham, *World Aflame*, 45.

10. Graham, *Day by Day*, August 23.

11. Graham, *Wisdom for Each Day*, 164.

12. Graham, *World Aflame*, xvi.

13. Graham, *Day by Day*, March 23.

14. Ibid., February 22.

15. Busby, *Billy Graham*, 27.

16. Graham, *World Aflame*, 53–54.

17. Billy Graham, *How to Be Born Again* (Waco, TX: Word, 1977), 53.

18. Ibid., 57.

19. Billy Graham, *Hope for the Troubled Heart* (Dallas: Word, 1991), 13.

20. Graham, *How to Be Born Again*, 29.

21. Ibid., 31–32.

22. Ibid., 64.

23. Ibid.

24. Graham, *Hope for the Troubled Heart*, 49.

25. Graham, *World Aflame*, 82.

26. Ibid., 86.

27. Ibid.

28. Graham, *How to Be Born Again*, 50.

29. Ibid.

30. Ibid.

31. Billy Graham, *Till Armageddon* (Waco, TX: Word, 1981), 97.

32. Graham, *World Aflame*, 83.

33. Graham, *Hope for the Troubled Heart*, 139.

34. Graham, *How to Be Born Again*, 22.

35. Graham, *Till Armageddon*, 58.

36. Billy Graham, *Storm Warning* (Nashville: Thomas Nelson, 2010), 152.

37. Graham, *World Aflame*, 42.

38. Billy Graham, *Storm Warning* (Nashville: Thomas Nelson, 2010), 152.

39. Billy Graham, *Answers to Life's Problems* (Waco, TX: Word, 1960), 303.

40. Graham, *World Aflame*, 104.

41. Billy Graham, *The Holy Spirit* (Nashville: Thomas Nelson, 1978), 196.

Billy Graham on Repentance

1. Billy Graham, *Peace with God* (Waco, TX: Word, 1953), 141.

2. Ibid., 143.

3. Billy Graham, *Wisdom for Each Day* (Nashville: Thomas Nelson, 2008), 230.

4. Billy Graham, *The Secret of Happiness* (New York: Doubleday, 1955), 33.

5. Ibid., 32.

6. Billy Graham, *The Holy Spirit* (Nashville: Thomas Nelson, 1978), 141.

7. Russ Busby, *Billy Graham: God's Ambassador* (San Diego: Tehabi Books, 1999), 257.

8. Billy Graham, *The Holy Spirit*, 142.

9. Ibid., 294.

10. Billy Graham, *Storm Warning* (Nashville: Thomas Nelson, 2010), 209.

11. Ibid., 203.

12. Ibid., 208.

13. *Decision*, July/August, 2010, 5.

14. Graham, *The Holy Spirit* (Nashville: Thomas Nelson, 1978), 217.

Billy Graham on the Resurrection

1. Billy Graham, *Day by Day* (Minneapolis, MN: World Wide, 1965), July 15.

2. Billy Graham, *Till Armageddon* (Waco, TX: Word, 1981), 9.

3. Ibid., 50.

4. Ibid., 200.

5. Billy Graham, *Answers to Life's Problems* (Waco, TX: Word, 1960), 300.

6. Billy Graham, *Facing Death and the Life After* (Waco, TX: Word, 1987), 240.

7. Ibid., 249.

8. *The Billy Graham Christian Worker's Handbook* (Charlotte, NC: BGEA, 1984), 78.

9. Billy Graham, *The Journey* (Nashville: W Publishing Group, 2006), 50.

10. Billy Graham, *World Aflame* (New York: Doubleday, 1965), 125.

11. Ibid., 126.

Billy Graham on Right and Wrong

1. Billy Graham, *Answers to Life's Problems* (Waco, TX: Word, 1960), 263.

2. Billy Graham, *The Holy Spirit* (Nashville: Thomas Nelson, 1978), 269.

3. Billy Graham, *Till Armageddon* (Waco, TX: Word, 1981), 63.

4. Billy Graham, *Day by Day* (Minneapolis, MN: World Wide, 1965), July 14.

5. Billy Graham, *Storm Warning* (Dallas: Word, 1992), 22.

6. Billy Graham, *Wisdom for Each Day* (Nashville: Thomas Nelson, 2008), 126.

7. Billy Graham, *The Secret of Happiness* (New York: Doubleday, 1955), 71.

8. Billy Graham, *How to Be Born Again* (Waco, TX: Word, 1977), 63.

9. Billy Graham, *The Journey* (Nashville: W Publishing Group, 2006), 44.

10. Graham, *Till Armageddon*, 60.
11. Graham, *Answers to Life's Problems*, 263.
12. Ibid., 97.

Billy Graham on Salvation

1. Billy Graham, *Day by Day* (Minneapolis, MN: World Wide, 1965), May 30.
2. Billy Graham, *World Aflame* (New York: Doubleday, 1965), 108.
3. Billy Graham, *Peace with God* (Waco, TX: Word, 1953), 167–68.
4. Graham, *Day by Day*, May 30.
5. Billy Graham, *Just As I Am* (San Francisco: HarperOne, 1997), 724.
6. Graham, *World Aflame*, 138.
7. Ibid., 80–81.
8. Ibid., 253.
9. Billy Graham, *Till Armageddon* (Waco, TX: Word, 1981), 73.
10. Billy Graham, *The Journey* (Nashville: W Publishing Group, 2006), 67.
11. Graham, *World Aflame*, 241.
12. Graham, *The Journey*, 73.
13. Ibid., 64.
14. Billy Graham, *Alone with the Savior* (Charlotte, NC: BGEA, 2010), 18.
15. *Billy Graham London Crusade* (Minneapolis, MN: World Wide, 1966), 46.
16. Graham, *The Journey*, 73.
17. Billy Graham, *A Biblical Standard for Evangelists* (Minneapolis: World Wide, 1984), 49.

Billy Graham on Service

1. Billy Graham, *The Secret of Happiness* (New York: Doubleday, 1955), 76–77.
2. Russ Busby, *Billy Graham: God's Ambassador* (San Diego: Tehabi Books, 1999), 15.
3. Ibid., 25.
4. Billy Graham, *Wisdom for Each Day* (Nashville: Thomas Nelson, 2008), 336.
5. Ibid., 316.
6. Ibid., 208.
7. Busby, *Billy Graham: God's Ambassador*, 30.
8. Billy Graham, *World Aflame* (New York: Doubleday, 1965), 179.
9. Billy Graham, *Hope for the Troubled Heart* (Dallas: Word, 1991), 40.
10. Billy Graham, *The Journey* (Nashville: W Publishing Group, 2006), 286.
11. Billy Graham, *The Holy Spirit* (Nashville: Thomas Nelson, 1978), 202.
12. Billy Graham, *Facing Death and the Life After* (Waco, TX: Word, 1987), 99–100.
13. *The Billy Graham Christian Worker's Handbook* (Charlotte, NC: BGEA, 1984), 49.
14. Billy Graham, *Billy Graham Talks to Teen-agers* (Wheaton: Miracle Books, 1958), 59.

Billy Graham on Sin

1. Billy Graham, *The Holy Spirit* (Nashville: Thomas Nelson, 1978), 136.
2. Billy Graham, *Peace with God* (Waco, TX: Word, 1953), 78.
3. Billy Graham, *Wisdom for Each Day* (Nashville: Thomas Nelson, 2008), 333.
4. Graham, *The Holy Spirit*, 25.
5. Graham, *Peace with God*, 103.
6. Graham, *Wisdom for Each Day*, 64.
7. Ibid., 171.
8. Graham, *The Holy Spirit*, 111.
9. Graham, *Peace with God*, 52.
10. Ibid., 53.

11. Billy Graham, *Calling Youth to Christ* (Grand Rapids. Zondervan, 1947), 125.
12. Graham, *Peace with God*, 197–98.
13. Billy Graham, *The Journey* (Nashville: W Publishing Group, 2006), 42.
14. Ibid., 41.
15. Graham, *Peace with God*, 56.
16. Graham, *Wisdom for Each Day*, 318.
17. Graham, *Calling Youth to Christ*, 100.
18. Billy Graham, *World Aflame* (New York: Doubleday, 1965), 118.
19. Graham, *Wisdom for Each Day*, 80.
20. Russ Busby, *Billy Graham: God's Ambassador* (San Diego: Tehabi Books, 1999), 27.
21. Graham, *Wisdom for Each Day*, 143.
22. Ibid., 81.
23. Ibid., 136.
24. Billy Graham, *The Holy Spirit* (Nashville: Thomas Nelson, 1978), 110.
25. Busby, *Billy Graham*, 27.
26. Graham, *World Aflame*, 67.
27. Billy Graham, *The Secret of Happiness* (New York: Doubleday, 1955), 68.
28. Graham, *World Aflame*, 166.
29. Billy Graham, *Hope for the Troubled Heart* (Dallas: Word, 1991), 55.
30. Graham, *The Holy Spirit*, 54.
31. Graham, *World Aflame*, 72.
32. Graham, *The Holy Spirit*, 140.
33. Graham, *World Aflame*, 24.
34. Ibid., 166.
35. Graham, *Hope for the Troubled Heart*, 75.
36. Ibid., 74.
37. Ibid., 55.
38. Billy Graham, *Facing Death and the Life After* (Waco, TX: Word, 1987), 253.
39. Graham, *Wisdom for Each Day*, 290.
40. Graham, *World Aflame*, 151.
41. Graham, *The Journey*, 36.
42. Billy Graham, *Till Armageddon* (Waco, TX: Word, 1981), 60–61.
43. Billy Graham, *Answers to Life's Problems* (Waco, TX: Word, 1960), 34.
44. *The Billy Graham Christian Worker's Handbook* (Charlotte, NC: BGEA, 1984), 287.
45. Graham, *The Journey*, 230.
46. Graham, *The Holy Spirit*, 138.
47. Billy Graham, *Storm Warning* (Nashville: Thomas Nelson, 2010), 160.
48. Graham, *The Journey*, 301.
49. Graham, *World Aflame*, 22.
50. Graham, *Till Armageddon*, 57.
51. Billy Graham, *Angels* (Waco, TX: Word, 1975), 141.
52. Billy Graham, *Alone with the Savior* (Charlotte, NC: BGEA, 2010), 22.
53. Graham, *Peace with God*, 268.
54. Billy Graham, *Day by Day* (Minneapolis, MN: World Wide, 1965), January 8.

Billy Graham on Society

1. Billy Graham, *Day by Day* (Minneapolis, MN: World Wide, 1965), September 19.
2. Ibid., October 12.
3. Ibid., March 9.
4. Ibid., July 21.
5. Ibid.
6. Ibid., April 22.

7. Billy Graham, *Storm Warning* (Nashville: Thomas Nelson, 2010), 176.

8. Billy Graham, *Till Armageddon* (Waco, TX: Word, 1981), 60.

9. Billy Graham, *Storm Warning* (Nashville: Thomas Nelson, 2010), 170.

10. Ibid., 23.

Billy Graham on the Soul

1. Billy Graham, *The Journey* (Nashville: W Publishing Group, 2006), 25.

2. Billy Graham, *Day by Day* (Minneapolis, MN: World Wide, 1965), March 7.

3. Graham, *The Journey*, 29.

4. Billy Graham, *Wisdom for Each Day* (Nashville: Thomas Nelson, 2008), 174.

5. Billy Graham, *World Aflame* (New York: Doubleday, 1965), 41.

6. Graham, *Wisdom for Each Day*, 315.

7. Graham, *Day by Day*, July 9.

8. Ibid., June 26.

9. Ibid., December 15.

10. Graham, *Wisdom for Each Day*, 26.

11. Billy Graham, *The Secret of Happiness* (New York: Doubleday, 1955), 18.

12. Ibid., 94.

13. Ibid., 19.

14. Ibid., 22.

15. Billy Graham, *Peace with God* (Waco, TX: Word, 1953), 90.

16. Billy Graham, *Storm Warning* (Nashville: Thomas Nelson, 2010), 253.

17. Graham, *Peace with God*, 89.

18. Billy Graham, *Storm Warning* (Nashville: Thomas Nelson, 2010), 240.

19. Billy Graham, *Till Armageddon* (Waco, TX: Word, 1981), 173.

20. Graham, *The Secret of Happiness*, 19.

21. Billy Graham, *My Daily Prayer Journal* (Minneapolis, MN: Grason, 2007), 153.

22. Billy Graham, *Facing Death and the Life After* (Waco, TX: Word, 1987), 219.

23. *The Billy Graham Christian Worker's Handbook* (Charlotte, NC: BGEA, 1984), 90.

24. Billy Graham, *Alone with the Savior* (Charlotte, NC: BGEA, 2010), 19.

25. Graham, *The Journey*, 25.

26. *Decision*, April 2010, 5.

Billy Graham on Speech

1. Billy Graham, *The Secret of Happiness* (New York: Doubleday, 1955), 52.

2. Billy Graham, *Facing Death and the Life After* (Waco, TX: Word, 1987), 166.

3. Graham, *The Secret of Happiness*, 75.

4. *The Billy Graham Library* (Charlotte, NC: BGEA), audio recording.

5. Graham, *The Secret of Happiness*, 109.

6. Billy Graham, *Day by Day* (Minneapolis, MN: World Wide, 1965), March 11.

7. Graham, *The Secret of Happiness*, 111.

8. Billy Graham, *World Aflame* (New York: Doubleday, 1965), 36.

9. *Breakfast with Billy Graham: 100 Daily Readings* (Ann Arbor, MI: Servant, 1996), 90.

10. Graham, *Day by Day*, February 19.

11. Billy Graham, *Wisdom for Each Day* (Nashville: Thomas Nelson, 2008), 363.

12. Graham, *Day by Day*, February 19.

13. Billy Graham, *Till Armageddon* (Waco, TX: Word, 1981), 27.

14. Billy Graham, *The Jesus Generation* (Grand Rapids: Zondervan, 1971), 169.

15. Billy Graham, *The Journey* (Nashville: W Publishing Group, 2006), 212.

Billy Graham on Strength

1. Billy Graham, *Hope for the Troubled Heart* (Dallas: Word, 1991), 104.
2. Ibid., 116.
3. Ibid., 96.
4. Billy Graham, *Unto the Hills* (Waco, TX: Word, 1986), 93.
5. Billy Graham, *Till Armageddon* (Waco, TX: Word, 1981), 24.
6. Ibid., 161–62.
7. Billy Graham, *The Jesus Generation* (Grand Rapids: Zondervan, 1971), 117.
8. Billy Graham, *A Biblical Standard for Evangelists* (Minneapolis: World Wide, 1984), 84.
9. Ibid., 86.

Billy Graham on Success

1. Billy Graham, *The Secret of Happiness* (New York: Doubleday, 1955), 20.
2. Billy Graham, *Wisdom for Each Day* (Nashville: Thomas Nelson, 2008), 330.
3. Graham, *The Secret of Happiness*, 27.
4. Billy Graham, *Till Armageddon* (Waco, TX: Word, 1981), 62.
5. Billy Graham, *Hope for the Troubled Heart* (Dallas: Word, 1991), 188.
6. Ibid., 124.
7. Billy Graham, *Storm Warning* (Dallas: Word, 1992), 40.
8. Graham, *Hope for the Troubled Heart*, 39.
9. Ibid., 36.
10. Billy Graham, *Answers to Life's Problems* (Waco, TX: Word, 1960), 105.
11. Billy Graham, *World Aflame* (New York: Doubleday, 1965), 26.
12. *The Billy Graham Christian Worker's Handbook* (Charlotte, NC: BGEA, 1984), 88.
13. Billy Graham Training Center at The Cove, gallery posting.

Billy Graham on Suffering

1. Billy Graham, *Hope for the Troubled Heart* (Dallas: Word, 1991), 30.
2. Billy Graham, *The Secret of Happiness* (New York: Doubleday, 1955), 134.
3. Billy Graham, *Day by Day* (Minneapolis, MN: World Wide, 1965), March 16.
4. Billy Graham, *The Journey* (Nashville: W Publishing Group, 2006), 219.
5. Ibid., 218.
6. Graham, *Hope for the Troubled Heart*, 193.
7. Billy Graham, *The Holy Spirit* (Nashville: Thomas Nelson, 1978), 49.
8. Billy Graham, *Till Armageddon* (Waco, TX: Word, 1981), 191.
9. Graham, *Hope for the Troubled Heart*, 12–13.
10. Ibid., 14–15.
11. Ibid., 22.
12. Graham, *Till Armageddon*, 110–11.
13. Graham, *Hope for the Troubled Heart*, 63.
14. Ibid., 71.
15. Billy Graham, *Storm Warning* (Nashville: Thomas Nelson, 2010), 229.
16. Graham, *Hope for the Troubled Heart*, 84.
17. Graham, *Till Armageddon*, 110.
18. Graham, *Hope for the Troubled Heart*, 53.
19. Graham, *Till Armageddon*, 9.
20. Ibid., 105.
21. Graham, *Hope for the Troubled Heart*, 44–45.
22. Graham, *Till Armageddon*, 24.
23. Ibid., 25.

24. Billy Graham, *Facing Death and the Life After* (Waco, TX: Word, 1987), 220.
25. Graham, *Till Armageddon*, 26.
26. Ibid., 27.
27. Ibid., 92.
28. Graham, *Facing Death and the Life After*, 101.
29. Billy Graham, *Alone with the Savior* (Charlotte, NC: BGEA, 2010), 40.

Billy Graham on Surrender

1. Billy Graham, *World Aflame* (New York: Doubleday, 1965), 152.
2. Billy Graham, *The Holy Spirit* (Nashville: Thomas Nelson, 1978), 143.
3. Billy Graham, *Peace with God* (Waco, TX: Word, 1953), 148.
4. Ibid., 181.
5. Ibid., 149.
6. Billy Graham, *The Jesus Generation* (Grand Rapids: Zondervan, 1971), 168.
7. Graham, *The Holy Spirit*, 146.

Billy Graham on Temptation

1. Billy Graham, *The Journey* (Nashville: W Publishing Group, 2006), 162.
2. Ibid.
3. Billy Graham, *Day by Day* (Minneapolis, MN: World Wide, 1965), September 23.
4. Billy Graham, *Peace with God* (Waco, TX: Word, 1953), 216.
5. Billy Graham, *Till Armageddon* (Waco, TX: Word, 1981), 97.
6. Billy Graham, *The Jesus Generation* (Grand Rapids: Zondervan, 1971), 158.
7. Graham, *The Journey*, 289.
8. Ibid., 185.
9. Graham, *Day by Day*, February 20.
10. Graham, *The Journey*, 162.
11. Graham, *Day by Day*, February 20.
12. Billy Graham, *Storm Warning* (Nashville: Thomas Nelson, 2010), 85–86.
13. *Decision*, July/August 2010, 5.
14. Graham, *Day by Day*, February 20.
15. Graham, *The Jesus Generation*, 164.
16. Graham, *The Journey*, 105.
17. *The Billy Graham Christian Worker's Handbook* (Charlotte, NC: BGEA, 1984), 274.
18. Graham, *The Journey*, 157.
19. Ibid., 193.

Billy Graham on Testimony

1. Billy Graham, *The Journey* (Nashville: W Publishing Group, 2006), 16.
2. Billy Graham, *Peace with God* (Waco, TX: Word, 1953), 192.
3. Billy Graham, *Till Armageddon* (Waco, TX: Word, 1981), 101.
4. Billy Graham, *How to Be Born Again* (Waco, TX: Word, 1977), 164.
5. Billy Graham, *World Aflame* (New York: Doubleday, 1965), 253.
6. Billy Graham, *Storm Warning* (Nashville: Thomas Nelson, 2010), 159.

Billy Graham on Thankfulness

1. Billy Graham, *Wisdom for Each Day* (Nashville: Thomas Nelson, 2008), 335.
2. *Breakfast with Billy Graham: 100 Daily Readings* (Ann Arbor, MI: Servant, 1996), 98.
3. Billy Graham, *Day by Day* (Minneapolis, MN: World Wide, 1965), November 23.

4. Ibid.
5. Billy Graham, *The Journey* (Nashville: W Publishing Group, 2006), 119.
6. Billy Graham, *Storm Warning* (Nashville: Thomas Nelson, 2010), 110.
7. Billy Graham, *Answers to Life's Problems* (Waco, TX: Word, 1960), 224.

Billy Graham on Time

1. Billy Graham, *Alone with the Savior* (Charlotte, NC: BGEA, 2010), 59.
2. Billy Graham, *Day by Day* (Minneapolis, MN: World Wide, 1965), May 11.
3. Billy Graham, *The Journey* (Nashville: W Publishing Group, 2006), 233.
4. Ibid.
5. Billy Graham, *Answers to Life's Problems* (Waco, TX: Word, 1960), 247.
6. Graham, *The Journey*, 233.
7. Ibid., 308.
8. Billy Graham, *Hope for the Troubled Heart* (Dallas: Word, 1991), 201.
9. Graham, *The Journey*, 231.
10. Billy Graham, *World Aflame* (New York: Doubleday, 1965), 74.
11. Graham, *Answers to Life's Problems*, 286.
12. Graham, *The Journey*, 102.
13. Graham, *Answers to Life's Problems*, 225.
14. *Decision*, May 2010, 5.
15. Graham, *Alone with the Savior*, 50.
16. Billy Graham, *The Holy Spirit* (Nashville: Thomas Nelson, 1978), 287.

Billy Graham on Truth

1. Billy Graham, *Peace with God* (Waco, TX: Word, 1953), 24.
2. Billy Graham, *Calling Youth to Christ* (Grand Rapids: Zondervan, 1947), 114.
3. Billy Graham, *Wisdom for Each Day* (Nashville: Thomas Nelson, 2008), 157.
4. Billy Graham, *World Aflame* (New York: Doubleday, 1965), 73.
5. Billy Graham, *How to Be Born Again* (Waco, TX: Word, 1977), 58.
6. Graham, *Wisdom for Each Day*, 141.
7. Graham, *World Aflame*, 55.
8. Billy Graham, *Day by Day* (Minneapolis, MN: World Wide, 1965), September 23.
9. Billy Graham, *Till Armageddon* (Waco, TX: Word, 1981), 193.
10. Billy Graham, *Answers to Life's Problems* (Waco, TX: Word, 1960), 287.
11. Billy Graham, *The Journey* (Nashville: W Publishing Group, 2006), 190.

Billy Graham on War

1. Billy Graham, *Till Armageddon* (Waco, TX: Word, 1981), 148.
2. Billy Graham, *World Aflame* (New York: Doubleday, 1965), 224.
3. Ibid., 197.
4. Billy Graham, *Hope for the Troubled Heart* (Dallas: Word, 1991), 51.
5. Billy Graham, *Storm Warning* (Nashville: Thomas Nelson, 2010), 206.
6. Ibid., 216.
7. *The Billy Graham Christian Worker's Handbook* (Charlotte, NC: BGEA, 1984), 289.
8. Ibid., 291.

Billy Graham on Witnessing

1. Billy Graham, *Wisdom for Each Day* (Nashville: Thomas Nelson, 2008), 77.
2. Ibid., 168.

3. Billy Graham, *Day by Day* (Minneapolis, MN: World Wide, 1965), April 12.
4. Billy Graham, *Peace with God* (Waco, TX: Word, 1953), 212.
5. Billy Graham, *Till Armageddon* (Waco, TX: Word, 1981), 180.
6. *The Billy Graham Christian Worker's Handbook* (Charlotte, NC: BGEA, 1984), 297.
7. Billy Graham, *The Journey* (Nashville: W Publishing Group, 2006), 142.
8. Billy Graham, *Answers to Life's Problems* (Waco, TX: Word, 1960), 225.
9. Billy Graham, *The Holy Spirit* (Nashville: Thomas Nelson, 1978), 286.
10. Graham, *The Journey*, 207.
11. Graham, *Answers to Life's Problems*, 103–4.
12. Billy Graham, *Billy Graham Talks to Teen-agers* (Wheaton: Miracle Books, 1958), 56.

Billy Graham on the Word of God

1. Billy Graham, *Wisdom for Each Day* (Nashville: Thomas Nelson, 2008), 139.
2. Billy Graham, *The Holy Spirit* (Nashville: Thomas Nelson, 1978), 58.
3. Graham, *Wisdom for Each Day*, 75.
4. Billy Graham, *Day by Day* (Minneapolis, MN: World Wide, 1965), June 16.
5. Ibid., May 13.
6. Billy Graham, *Peace with God* (Waco, TX: Word, 1953), 205.
7. Russ Busby, *Billy Graham: God's Ambassador* (San Diego: Tehabi Books, 1999), 157.
8. Billy Graham, *The Journey* (Nashville: W Publishing Group, 2006), 104.
9. Billy Graham, *The Secret of Happiness* (New York: Doubleday, 1955), 153.
10. Graham, *Wisdom for Each Day*, 276.
11. Ibid., 139.
12. Ibid., 159.
13. Graham, *The Holy Spirit* (Nashville: Thomas Nelson, 1978), 48.
14. *Decision*, July/August 2006, 17.
15. *Breakfast with Billy Graham: 100 Daily Readings* (Ann Arbor, MI: Servant, 1996), 66.
16. Graham, *The Holy Spirit*, 44.
17. Billy Graham, *How to Be Born Again* (Waco, TX: Word, 1977), 45.
18. Graham, *The Journey*, 210.
19. Billy Graham, *Hope for the Troubled Heart* (Dallas: Word, 1991), 216.
20. *The Billy Graham Library* (Charlotte, NC: BGEA), audio recording.
21. Graham, *Hope for the Troubled Heart*, 157–58.
22. Billy Graham, *Till Armageddon* (Waco, TX: Word, 1981), 174.
23. Billy Graham, *Answers to Life's Problems* (Waco, TX: Word, 1960), 274.
24. Ibid., 274–75.
25. Ibid., 292.
26. Billy Graham, *Storm Warning* (Nashville: Thomas Nelson, 2010), 235.
27. Ibid., 253.
28. Graham, *Answers to Life's Problems*, 296.
29. Billy Graham, *Alone with the Savior* (Charlotte, NC: BGEA, 2010), 20.
30. Billy Graham, *Storm Warning* (Nashville: Thomas Nelson, 2010), 234–35.
31. Billy Graham, *Storm Warning* (Dallas: Word, 1992), 7.
32. Billy Graham, *Storm Warning* (Nashville: Thomas Nelson, 2010), 162.

Billy Graham on Work

1. Billy Graham, *Day by Day* (Minneapolis, MN: World Wide, 1965), September 4.
2. Billy Graham, *World Aflame* (New York: Doubleday, 1965), 33.
3. Billy Graham, *Facing Death and the Life After* (Waco, TX: Word, 1987), 265.
4. Billy Graham, *The Journey* (Nashville: W Publishing Group, 2006), 293–94.
5. Graham, *Day by Day*, September 3.

6. Billy Graham, *Till Armageddon* (Waco, TX: Word, 1981), 211.
7. Billy Graham, *Answers to Life's Problems* (Waco, TX: Word, 1960), 96.
8. Ibid.
9. Ibid., 98.
10. Ibid., 99.
11. Billy Graham, *The Holy Spirit* (Nashville: Thomas Nelson, 1978), 285–86.
12. Graham, *The Journey*, 64–65.
13. Ibid., 236.
14. Graham, *The Holy Spirit*, 28.
15. Graham, *World Aflame*, 240.

Billy Graham on the World

1. Billy Graham, *Day by Day* (Minneapolis, MN: World Wide, 1965), December 20.
2. *The Billy Graham Christian Worker's Handbook* (Charlotte, NC: BGEA, 1984), 291.
3. Graham, *Day by Day*, September 10.
4. Billy Graham, *The Journey* (Nashville: W Publishing Group, 2006), 159.
5. Billy Graham, *Till Armageddon* (Waco, TX: Word, 1981), 97.
6. *Breakfast with Billy Graham: 100 Daily Readings* (Ann Arbor, MI: Servant, 1996), 79.
7. Ibid., 83.
8. Billy Graham, *Calling Youth to Christ* (Grand Rapids: Zondervan, 1947), 89.
9. Graham, *The Journey*, 161.
10. *Breakfast with Billy Graham*, 83.
11. Russ Busby, *Billy Graham: God's Ambassador* (San Diego: Tehabi Books, 1999), 148.
12. Graham, *Calling Youth to Christ*, 64.
13. Graham, *The Journey*, 280–81.
14. Billy Graham, *Hope for the Troubled Heart* (Dallas: Word, 1991), 121.
15. Ibid., 39–40.
16. Graham, *Till Armageddon*, 97.
17. Ibid.
18. Billy Graham, *Wisdom for Each Day* (Nashville: Thomas Nelson, 2008), 227.
19. Billy Graham, *Peace with God* (Waco, TX: Word, 1953), 232.
20. Ibid., 196.
21. Ibid.
22. Ibid.
23. Billy Graham, *World Aflame* (New York: Doubleday, 1965), 261.
24. Graham, *Peace with God*, 200.
25. Graham, *Till Armageddon*, 108–9.
26. Graham, *Day by Day*, March 8.
27. Ibid., September 15.
28. Billy Graham, *The Holy Spirit* (Nashville: Thomas Nelson, 1978), 290.
29. Ibid., 286.
30. Billy Graham, *Storm Warning* (Dallas: Word, 1992), 18.
31. *The Billy Graham Christian Worker's Handbook* (Charlotte, NC: BGEA, 1984), 55.
32. Ibid., 301.
33. Ibid., 300–301.
34. Billy Graham, *Storm Warning* (Nashville: Thomas Nelson, 2010), 114.
35. Graham, *The Journey*, 156.
36. Billy Graham, *Storm Warning* (Nashville: Thomas Nelson, 2010), 180.
37. Ibid., 90.
38. Graham, *The Journey*, 159.
39. *Billy Graham London Crusade* (Minneapolis, MN: World Wide, 1966), 12.
40. Billy Graham, *Storm Warning* (Dallas: Word, 1992), 31.

41. Billy Graham, *Storm Warning* (Nashville: Thomas Nelson, 2010), 1.

42. Graham, *World Aflame*, 188.

43. Billy Graham, *Storm Warning* (Nashville: Thomas Nelson, 2010), 111.

44. Billy Graham, *Alone with the Savior* (Charlotte, NC: BGEA, 2010), 58.

45. Billy Graham, *Storm Warning* (Nashville: Thomas Nelson, 2010), 73.

46. *Decision*, June 2010, 2, 4.

47. Graham, *Alone with the Savior*, 57.

48. Graham, *World Aflame*, 188.

Billy Graham on World Evangelism

1. Billy Graham, *The Journey* (Nashville: W Publishing Group, 2006), 281.

2. Billy Graham, *World Aflame* (New York: Doubleday, 1965), 174–75.

3. Billy Graham, *Storm Warning* (Dallas: Word, 1992), 185.

4. Russ Busby, *Billy Graham: God's Ambassador* (San Diego: Tehabi Books, 1999), 148.

5. Billy Graham, *Wisdom for Each Day* (Nashville: Thomas Nelson, 2008), 342.

6. Busby, *Billy Graham*, 144.

7. Graham, *World Aflame*, 174.

8. Busby, *Billy Graham*, 147.

9. Graham, *Storm Warning* (Nashville: Thomas Nelson, 2010), 204.

10. Busby, *Billy Graham*, 149; referring to Moscow Crusade 1992.

11. Ibid., 220.

12. Ibid., 223.

13. *Breakfast with Billy Graham: 100 Daily Readings* (Ann Arbor, MI: Servant, 1996), 118.

Billy Graham on Worry

1. Billy Graham, *Wisdom for Each Day* (Nashville: Thomas Nelson, 2008), 204.

2. Billy Graham, *Day by Day* (Minneapolis, MN: World Wide, 1965), August 17.

3. Billy Graham, *Answers to Life's Problems* (Waco, TX: Word, 1960), 224.

4. Billy Graham, *Unto the Hills* (Waco, TX: Word, 1986), 151.

5. Graham, *Day by Day*, December 5.

6. *The Billy Graham Christian Worker's Handbook* (Charlotte, NC: BGEA, 1984), 49.

7. Billy Graham, *The Holy Spirit* (Nashville: Thomas Nelson, 1978), 255.

8. Billy Graham, *The Journey* (Nashville: W Publishing Group, 2006), 184.

9. Billy Graham, *Hope for the Troubled Heart* (Dallas: Word, 1991), 43.

Billy Graham on Worship

1. Billy Graham, *Wisdom for Each Day* (Nashville: Thomas Nelson, 2008), 16.

2. Ibid.

3. Billy Graham, *Peace with God* (Waco, TX: Word, 1953), 148–49.

4. Billy Graham, *Storm Warning* (Nashville: Thomas Nelson, 2010), 114.

5. Billy Graham, *Answers to Life's Problems* (Waco, TX: Word, 1960), 121.

6. Billy Graham, *Storm Warning* (Nashville: Thomas Nelson, 2010), 245.

7. Billy Graham, *The Journey* (Nashville: W Publishing Group, 2006), 129.

8. Billy Graham, *Storm Warning* (Nashville: Thomas Nelson, 2010), 245.

Billy Graham on Young People

1. Billy Graham, *Wisdom for Each Day* (Nashville: Thomas Nelson, 2008), 188.

2. Billy Graham, *Day by Day* (Minneapolis, MN: World Wide, 1965), October 11.

3. *Breakfast with Billy Graham: 100 Daily Readings* (Ann Arbor, MI: Servant, 1996), 103.

4. Graham, *Day by Day*, November 16.
5. Russ Busby, *Billy Graham: God's Ambassador* (San Diego: Tehabi Books, 1999), 206.
6. Billy Graham, *Calling Youth to Christ* (Grand Rapids: Zondervan, 1947), dust cover.
7. Billy Graham, *World Aflame* (New York: Doubleday, 1965), 45.
8. *Breakfast with Billy Graham*, 108.
9. Billy Graham, *Till Armageddon* (Waco, TX: Word, 1981), 62.
10. Billy Graham, *The Jesus Generation* (Grand Rapids: Zondervan, 1971), 64.
11. Graham, *Calling Youth to Christ*, 90.
12. Graham, *The Jesus Generation*, 95.
13. Ibid., 97.
14. Graham, *Calling Youth to Christ*, 16.
15. Billy Graham, *Storm Warning* (Nashville: Thomas Nelson, 2010), 146–47.
16. Billy Graham, *Answers to Life's Problems* (Waco, TX: Word, 1960), 295.
17. Graham, *The Jesus Generation*, 98.
18. Ibid., 103.
19. Billy Graham, *Storm Warning* (Nashville: Thomas Nelson, 2010), 77.
20. Graham, *The Jesus Generation*, 119.
21. *Decision*, July/August 2010, 2.
22. Busby, *Billy Graham*, 243.
23. Graham, *The Jesus Generation*, 70.

ABOUT THE AUTHORS

BILLY GRAHAM, THE WORLD-RENOWNED AUTHOR, PREACHER, and evangelist, has delivered the gospel message to more people face-to-face than anyone in history and has ministered on every continent of the world in more than 185 countries. Millions have read his inspirational classics, including *Angels, The Secret of Happiness, Peace with God, The Holy Spirit, Hope for the Troubled Heart,* and *How to Be Born Again.*

FRANKLIN GRAHAM IS PRESIDENT AND CEO OF SAMARITAN'S Purse, a Christian relief and evangelism organization. He is also president and CEO of the Billy Graham Evangelistic Association. Franklin is the fourth of Billy and Ruth Bell Graham's five children. He is the author of the best-selling autobiography *Rebel with a Cause, All for Jesus, Living Beyond the Limits, The Name,* and the children's book *Miracle in a Shoebox.* An avid outdoorsman and pilot, Franklin and his wife, Jane, make their home in North Carolina and have four children, Will, Roy, Edward, and Cissie; and seven grandchildren.

DONNA LEE TONEY, A COLLEAGUE OF FRANKLIN GRAHAM for thirty years, has been involved in the ministries of Samaritan's Purse and the Billy Graham Evangelistic Association and in literary collaboration since 1982, most recently on the re-release of *Storm Warning* with Billy Graham.